FACE THE FIRE

~ Book 5 ~
Moore Family Saga

Michele Sims

Other Titles by Michele Sims

MOORE FAMILY SAGA

Seed on Fire (Book 1)
Playing with Fire (Book 2)
The Fire God Tour (Book 3)
A Moore Affair (Book 4)

I dedicate this book to God, the source of all good things,
to my mother, the late Vermell G. Simmons
and to all challenged by defining moments in life.
You, too, can Face the Fire.

Chapter 1

Miles 'Ari" Moore, CEO of AriMusic, understood that in the City of Angels, it was business before pleasure. "Work hard, play harder," that was his motto. He and his wife Bella were out on the town looking forward to having some fun.

"I didn't realize how much I needed this night." Bella leaned across the driver's seat and placed a kiss on her husband's cheek. Waiting for the stoplight to change, he interlaced their fingers and raised her hand to his lips, caressing it with warm kisses.

"You deserve some time to relax. It's been a while since it was just the two of us." Miles's chest warmed as he gazed into her soft brown eyes. "Hard to believe that last year we were a young, recently married couple, and now we're the parents of two beautiful babies."

"A true labor of love." Her smile lit up the night. Their infants, Ashe and Ariana, turned six weeks old yesterday.

"Tonight, it's all about you, babe." Slowing down at the

intersection, he made a left turn, heading toward downtown LA. "How was your dinner?"

"Fantastic." She reached for the radio to turn down the volume. "How did you get a reservation? I heard that place was booked for months."

"It was, but I know people." He winked, then reached over to touch her thigh. "Nothing but the best for you." Gently stroking her smooth skin, he took in a deep breath and smiled as his body heated with desire.

"Are you sure you want to go to The Club?" His fingers inched beneath her skirt, causing her to look down. "Just checking things out."

Nodding, she placed her hand on top of his. "All the parts are present and accounted for. My doctor gave me the green light." She winked. "I'm ready for action."

"All types of action?" He wagged his eyebrows. "Our sex drought while you were on bedrest and after having the twins was brutal."

"The drought is definitely over." She smiled. "I'll reward your patience later, but for now, Mama wants some time on the dance floor." Turning away, she glanced at the traffic through the passenger-side mirror.

"Keep your eyes on the road. It's busy out here tonight. We have a lot to celebrate, and I want to get there in one piece." She shimmied her shoulders.

"While on our club crawl, we can check out Lil' Pharaoh's show."

Pharaoh Little, 'Lil Pharaoh', was one of the first artist signed to their record company, AriMusic. A music phenom, he had come to Miles's attention as a young teen. Unlike other record companies, Miles had given Pharaoh's mother, Elizabeth Little, his personal reassurance that he would protect him from predators and vultures that often found their way into the circles of young stars.

"We were able to book him at one of the premiere clubs downtown at the last minute." Miles gripped the steering wheel. "I want to see how he handles a different crowd, and I could use your help marketing him. He has been more than I bargained for." He sighed. "Lately, it's one problem after another. I'm also not amused that he's crushing on you." With a quick glance at the rearview and side mirror, he moved into the fast lane.

"He's young and still trying to find his way in this business." She shrugged. "You realize Pharaoh is a natural flirt who plays around with everyone."

"I hope you're right about him. His acting-out is beginning to concern me." He took in a deep breath. "After we check out the clubs, we can get back to honoring you, my gorgeous wife, who has blessed me with two of the most amazing babies on the planet."

Placing a hand above his on the stick shift, she rubbed her thumb across his knuckles.

"I'm biased, but I agree." She looked ahead at the traffic. "We'll find out how amazing they are after their next check-up. It's clear that both of them have your medical condition, but they're still investigating the effect of the condition on their development." Out of the corner of his eye, he noted her lips tightening and shoulders slumping against the leather seat.

If you think it's hard hearing about it, try living with it. Miles peered at the rearview mirror.

Miles had an extended stay as a child at the National Institute of Health in Maryland to investigate a high fever that placed him in a coma. The medical team and research consultants discovered that as a result of a genetic condition, he was able to create fireballs, withstand high heat without burning his skin, and tolerate higher than normal smoke inhalation without damage to his lungs.

"Don't worry." His mouth felt like dried cotton as he squared his shoulders with an air of confidence. "We'll handle it together."

"I'm not worried, and sorry for airing my thoughts." Resting her head on his shoulders, she rubbed his chest. "You've gone to great lengths to make this a pleasurable night. We haven't done a club crawl in over a year. It should be fun."

Traffic slowed to a stop. The six lanes, clogged with cars, resembled a mall parking lot. Minutes ticked by before they started moving again. Miles looked around as fire truck sirens blared, but he didn't see any coming toward him. Accelerating to beat the light changing red as they came off the freeway, he abruptly put on the brakes to avoid hitting the car that stopped in front of him.

"Miles!" Bella lurched forward, but she was pushed backward by the quick reflex of his arm extended across her torso.

Clenching his jaw, he calmed the adrenaline surge coursing through his body. "What is this clown doing in front of me?"

With a tightened grip on the steering wheel, he swiveled his head, looking around to get out the way of any emergency vehicles that may be heading their way. The harsh sounds of sirens were getting louder.

"Sounds like a two-alarm fire." He peered at the sky, which was blanketed by thick black smoke.

"Why do you think that?" Repositioning herself, she leaned forward for a better view.

"Listen." He paused. "The alarms sound different."

Turning on a side street, out of the flow of traffic, he activated the custom emergency radio scanner and GPS.

"It sounds like multiple alarms." Bella inclined her ear toward the window.

"Exactly. This fire is too much for one firehouse's resources to handle, so when other groups are called in, the alarm count increases – a two-alarm or multiple-alarm fire. We can try to detour around the traffic or wait it out."

"Detour." They looked at each other, answering in unison.

"The Santa Ana winds are high tonight, and the smoke is getting worse. I hope it doesn't fan a wildfire." He kept his eyes on the road while Bella pulled out her phone and texted a message.

"I hope they're able to get the fire under control quickly." Bella bit her lip, toying with a strand of her long brown hair. "The babies are still asleep." She smiled. "Our sitter returned my message promptly. She said they were having a peaceful night."

"She came highly recommended." Miles patted her hand. Puckering his lips, he blew her a kiss. "I knew that was the only way I would get you out of the house."

Bella knitted her brow. Returning her attention to her phone, she scrolled through the posts on social media popping up at a frenzied pace.

Her jaw slackened as minutes went by. "I don't believe this."

"What are you looking at?" Her silence concerned him. "Is there something going on at the house?"

She shook her head, not breaking her gaze on the screen. *This isn't going as I planned*. He frowned. "What then?"

Before she could answer, his phone attached to Bluetooth

began ringing.

"Hello," he answered quickly. His tone was sharp.

"Miles, we've got a problem." A tense voice, placed on speaker, filled the car. It was Bradley Marshall, the head of Security and Safety for AriMusic. Bradley was also affiliated with The Network, an international clandestine organization of former military men, captains of industry, and government officials. A group largely unknown except to a select few on the planet. They had a long reach and access to intelligence most countries would kill – yes, kill – to have. Miles had come to their attention as a result of his genetic condition. His father, Kaiden Moore, and his uncle Vincent Moore, had also been affiliated with The Network before he was born.

"I know you and Bella are downtown." He sounded short of breath, as if he was running. "I'm at the estate and leaving right now." They heard the sound of a car's engine starting.

"What the hell is going on?" Miles pulled out of traffic and on to a side street. He parked at the curb.

"It's Pharaoh...again." Bradley paused and Bella covered her ears as the high-pitched sound of wheels screeching was annoying. "I just got a call from a contact at the police station. They're on their way after receiving a report of a riot from an unruly crowd at The Club. It seems an alert on social media summoned Lil Pharaoh's fans to come to The Club before he arrived. When they weren't allowed in the venue, fights broke out. Someone set a fire in the parking lot and embers from that fire travelled to businesses nearby. Several fires are now blazing out of control."

"Has he lost his mind?" Miles fumed as Bella showed him the thread of messages from his followers, responding that they were on their way. "The club can hold maybe five hundred people?"

6

"Exactly," Bradley agreed. "It was already filled to capacity, according to my sources, before Pharaoh's crew sent out the message. Several squad cars were summoned after they got calls about drugs, underage drinking, noise nuisance, and then the fight. They arrested several people, including a few members of the crew as they tried to leave. Pharaoh was scheduled to arrive, but he must have gotten wind of all the trouble. He's in lockdown in one of the company's apartments he's been using downtown. The police officers are waiting for a search warrant before forcing an entry. I spoke to Pharaoh. He confirmed he was partying before his set tonight. There are drugs and guns at the place, but they belonged to his friends."

"Yeah, right. Did anyone get hurt?" Miles's chest was tight and his mouth dry. "This is a PR nightmare." Bella closed her eyes briefly and nodded.

"The preliminary report was that no one was hurt other than a few scratches. The police want to talk to Pharaoh, but he's refusing to come out. He was scared, Miles. I think he realized he was in over his head. I have one of our lawyers on the way there, and I'm also heading there now. I just wanted you to know what's going on so you can decide how you want to spin this in the morning."

"We have a couple of holdings downtown. Is it the one in the Old Bank District?"

"Yes, but I don't think you need to get involved."

"Our business is a family business and I need to be there," he asserted, and Bella agreed. Grateful she understood his decision, he squeezed her knee. "Bradley, I need to see for myself what trouble Pharaoh has gotten himself into."

"Okay. I'll meet you there."

Chapter 2

When Miles and Bella arrived, the apartment was surrounded by patrol cars, sirens, and flashing blue lights bouncing off the cars and buildings. It was a scene of controlled chaos.

Looking out the window at the situation playing out before him, he still hadn't decided what to do. He hoped his adrenaline, instincts for decisive action, and the criminal lawyers he kept on retainer would help guide him in his decisions.

"Let's wait for Bradley," Bella suggested. Miles turned off the engine and parked the car.

He had his hand on the handle. "I'll call Bradley on my way to the door."

"If you're going, I'm going with you," she insisted.

Miles shook his head. He wasn't aware Bradley was approaching from the rear of the vehicle until he pulled open the door and got into the back seat.

"Hi," Bradley said as he leaned forward. "A few of my

friends on the force are here. They're willing to let you into the house if you consent to a pat-down and pocket-search before and after leaving. You have to agree not to take anything in or out of the place. I'll try to buy you some time before they come in with the search warrant. I've been on the phone with Pharaoh, and he wants to talk to you. He's calm, and he's not a danger to you or himself. Are you okay with the terms, or do you want to wait here and talk to him on the phone? I'm comfortable handling this with advice from our lawyers. It's your call."

He turned to Bella while Miles contemplated his options. "One of our drivers will take you home."

"That's a good idea. Bella, I'll feel better if one of us is home with the children."

"I'll go home if you promise to keep in touch." She placed a hand on his arm.

"Of course." He placed a hand on top of hers before turning his attention to Bradley.

"I want to see him." Miles opened the door and started taking off his coat and emptying his pockets of everything but his phone. "Tell the police I'll comply with the terms. I'm going in."

Bradley ran ahead of him to let them know he was willing to be searched. After a brief frisk, they allowed him to keep his phone.

Miles knocked on the door. "Pharaoh. It's Miles. I'm coming in alone," he yelled.

He heard the cylinders in the lock of the door turn before Pharaoh yelled back, "Fine."

Miles entered and closed the door behind him. Pharaoh stood in the center of the room with his mouth drawn, tired from the ordeal. The apartment had been trashed by the partygoers. Alcohol bottles and food containers littered the floors of every surface of the main room.

"I don't know what happened, Miles. Things got out of control." Pharaoh looked at him with his hands planted on both sides of his head. "I didn't know most of the people. They just kept coming in. I was getting laid in the bedroom when I opened the door and saw the mob. I never made it to The Club."

Miles walked around, looking at the mess with his hands on his hips.

"Is it true that guns and drugs are still in here? Because if that's true, we've got trouble."

Pharaoh nodded and opened a drawer in the TV console, which still contained the drugs and several guns. Miles looked inside the drawer and closed his eyes tightly, as if willing its contents to disappear.

"These aren't mine, Miles."

"So who do they belong to?"

Pharaoh said nothing, but maintained eye contact.

Miles lunged at Pharaoh and grabbed him by his shirt, nostrils flaring. "I warned you, Pharaoh. I warned you, and now you're acting like you can't answer a few questions?" Realizing he was making things worse, he loosened his grip on Pharaoh's shirt. His phone began ringing in his pocket. As he stepped away, Pharaoh tightened his fists at his side. They both knew things were spiraling out of control.

Miles looked at Bella's smiling face on the phone display before answering. "I'm okay, baby," he told her. "I'm here with Pharaoh... Yes, he's unharmed." He looked at Pharaoh and handed him the phone. "She wants to talk to you."

Pharaoh accepted Miles's phone and placed it to his ear. "This is Pharaoh. I'm listening... Yeah, yeah, I hear you...

Bella, I know you care about me. Okay, bye." He handed the phone back to Miles.

Miles put the phone back to his ear, but Pharaoh had ended the call. "What did she say to you?"

"She told me to do my part to put aside our differences, and that you're here to help me."

Miles paced as he thought about how to handle the situation. "I need you to lock yourself in the bathroom. Don't come out until I tell you to."

"What? Why?"

"Listen, you either do as I say, or I can walk out the door right now."

Pharaoh turned and headed to the bathroom without saying another word. Miles waited to hear the click of the lock on the bathroom door before proceeding.

"Having a genetic abnormality can come in handy in times like these," he murmured.

First, he looked at the electric fireplace, went to turn it on, and sighed with relief when it was still in working condition. He turned the knob to increase the intensity of the flames. Knowing that the fireplace had to be extra hot to disintegrate the drugs without leaving a characteristic smell, he wrapped the drugs in layers of napkins and created a fireball to incinerate them quickly enough to avoid a smell.

Incinerating the guns would be more difficult, but after the results of his last medical assessment, he'd discovered he could create fireballs as hot as several hundred degrees Fahrenheit – but he needed the fireplace to act as a receptacle, since he couldn't handle an object that hot without damaging his skin. He took the guns – 9mm Lugers like the one Bella had – out of the drawer and started the combustion in his hands before tossing them into the fireplace. He threw additional fireballs into the blaze to accelerate the process.

The guns were melting quickly when Bradley texted him that the authorities were on their way with a search warrant. He was running out of time.

Miles let out a breath, hoping that the contents of the fireplace had burned beyond recognition.

Once all evidence of the drugs and guns were reduced to ashes in the flames, he turned off the fireplace. He hadn't anticipated that the room would fill with black and gray smoke.

"Oh well." He waved the fumes from his face. Inspecting the ashes with the small metal shovel on the side, he confirmed that there was no remaining evidence of contraband before closing the fireplace door. Pushing the trash on the dark leather couch onto the floor, he took a seat before calling Pharaoh out of the bathroom.

"What the hell happened in here?" He coughed, covering his mouth and nose with his elbow.

"Have a seat," Miles told him, just as the authorities arrived with the search warrant.

"It sure is hot in here," the officers commented and coughed. "Why is it so smoky? Is something burning?" He looked at the smoke coming out of the fireplace.

Miles shrugged. He remained silent and seated on the couch.

"Have someone from the fire investigative division come in here. There's something strange going on." The chief officer alerted his assistant as they combed through the gray ash from the fireplace. After it cooled, they deposited the ashes into evidence bags before they left. After hours of searching and finding nothing, they took Pharaoh into custody for further questioning.

Once the police departed, Miles walked downstairs and

spoke to Bradley.

"I'm going to ride with Pharaoh to the police station," Bradley told him. We have a team of lawyers who will meet us there. You're tired, so one of my men will drive you home."

"Thanks." He patted Bradley on the back and went to the car waiting for him to return home to the comfort of his bed and wife.

On the drive up into the hills, Miles gazed out of the window at the dark sky. The streets were quiet and desolate, except for the night's dreary mist, which mirrored his mood. He had the ominous feeling that Lil' Pharaoh's days as an artist with AriMusic were numbered.

Miles opened the door to their home. Looking toward the study, he noticed a warm light coming from the room. Sticking his head in the doorway, he saw Bella lower her laptop and place her hands on the desk, leaning over and exposing the mounds of her breast. She wore a sheer black negligee with matching kitten slippers and a smile.

"What are you still doing up?" He raised an eyebrow. "Surely, you're not still working."

She came from behind the desk and beckoned him with her index finger. "I was waiting for you." She licked her lips. "We have some unfinished business."

"Is that so, Mrs. Moore?" He locked the door behind him. His heart raced as lust provided the fuel to restore the energy lost in dealing with Pharaoh. His body warmed with a passion for Bella. It had been months since they'd made love. The two of them had always been good together. She hadn't forgotten her promise for a night of fun. He outstretched his arms and smiled, welcoming the surprise. He witnessed her eyes widening and her pupils dilating with anticipation as she placed her arms around his neck and breathed in his scent.

In one smooth motion, he lifted her and placed her on top of the desk, positioning himself between her legs spread wide as he kissed her along her neck. As she leaned back and steadied herself on the desk, he untied the satin ribbon on her sheer covering, exposing her lacy black bra. His chest heaved as he saw her skin flushed with the heat of passion even as he exposed it to the cool air.

Taking his time to breathe in her aroma, he nuzzled his nose between her breasts before pulling the cups of her bra to the side and gently taking in a mouthful of her right and then her left breast. He lifted her up again and gathered the skimpy fabric in his hands before tearing away her thong and tossing it to the floor.

"Oh, my beautiful Bella." He pushed the covering over her shoulders. As it fell on the desk, he made a hasty glance at the window in front of them to ensure the blinds were drawn. It was hours before dawn, but he didn't want the groundskeepers or members of security to interrupt their private act.

He kissed her lips. Electric shocks tingled down his spine. Removing the pins which held her hair in a bun, he bit his lip as her hair fell in a cascade to her shoulders. She turned her head, exposing the skin on her neck, heating up from his breath as he placed kisses all the way to her shoulders. He massaged her breasts in a circular motion and then with his hands low around her hips, grinded against her as he whispered words of love in her ear. Of all of love's languages, words of affirmation were their favorite, with acts of service coming in a close second. Lowering his head, he kissed the light stretch marks on her abdomen reverently, to honor the womb that once held his beautiful babies.

Loosening his pants, he let it and his underwear fall in a puddle around his ankles.

"Bella, I love you. I'll always love you, adore you. You're my queen," he declared as he pushed into her heated channel, wet with longing.

"Baby, that feels so good," she moaned her pleasure.

Holding her firmly by the hips, he pushed back and forth inside her at just the right angle, causing her to pant with desire. Her breath quickened and became shallow as her face contorted while she called out his name. "Miles, oh Miles—" Those words short-circuited his brain, sending him over the edge. Muffling her moans with his mouth planted firmly over hers, he let out a deep satisfying breath and threw his head back as the walls of her core pulsed tightly around him.

His hungry tongue darted in and out of her mouth as he reached his climax. Their dampened bodies moved across the smooth surface of the desk, sweat dripping from his forehead onto her belly. She smiled at him, as he watched her come down from the high of an orgasm. He continued to embrace her while their breaths settled back to a normal rate.

"Do you know how much I love you, Miles?"

"Yes, I think I do," he said, making no effort to move outside of the warmth of her body. "I could stay inside of you forever."

"I missed this about us." She smiled at him.

"This evening didn't go as planned, but it couldn't have ended any better." He kissed her lips. Moving away from her, his skin damp with sweat, he pulled up his pants before going over to grab the small blanket thrown over a chair. He picked her up, wrapped in the soft fabric.

"Let's rest," he told her as she placed her arms around his neck. "Afterward, I have plans for you." Leaning against his chest, she was eager to hear about his plans.

Just as he made it to the door of the study, the phone rang.

"What now?' he huffed.

Chapter 3

Miles answered the phone. It was Bradley.

"How are things going at the station?" Miles placed the call on speaker so Bella, who remained at his side, could listen.

"Pharaoh said he's no snitch," he responded. "He's refusing to divulge the name of the *friend* who left the drugs and guns at the place. I think they're going to release him soon."

"Good." He yawned. "Anything else? I'm going to get some rest. We can talk about this later."

"Just wanted to update you," Bradley said. "Later."

He hung up the phone and placed his arms around Bella's shoulders.

"I'm wasted." He covered another yawn with his hand. His lids were heavy as they stumbled up the stairs.

"Time for bed, big boy." She patted his chest.

"Right. Bedtime." They made it to their bedroom and closed the door.

Pharaoh never apologized to Miles for his behavior or expressed gratitude for the time and money AriMusic spent to have all the vandalization and public nuisance charges dropped, not to mention the damage control needed to spin the incident in the media. When he joined AriMusic, many saw him as the one who would eventually eclipse Miles's fame as a recording artist. As soon as he introduced Pharaoh to Bella, the Chief Marketing Officer for the company and her team, it was clear that with his handsome good looks, charisma that played well to the camera, and authenticity, he had the makings of a megastar. His sensual manner, smooth, cocoa-brown skin, soft and expressive brown eyes, and more swagger than he knew how to control were also a plus for the young artist.

Initially, he was like a sponge, soaking up the knowledge and advice Miles provided, but their relationship had grown tense over the years. Two days after his most recent fiasco, he made his way to Bella's office.

"I'm sorry that I caused problems for you." He took a seat and slumped in the chair. "It's not like I planned what happened."

She took off her glasses and powered down her screen. "Who in their right mind would plan something like that?" She glared at him and placed her hands on the desk.

"Listen, I didn't come to argue with you," he said as he straightened his posture. "I just want to say I'm sorry."

She tilted her head. "Did you discuss this with Miles? I think he's in his office. He didn't mention that you talked to him about it."

"We don't vibe like we used to, Bella." He rubbed his forehead. "I thought you could say something to him for me. I don't want to make things worse."

"You've known Miles since you were a child. What do you mean that the two of you don't *vibe*?" She crossed her arms. "Tell me, what is that all about?"

"That. Is the problem, Bella." He pointed his finger and pursed his lips. "He still treats me like I'm a kid. Like I don't have a mind of my own. As long as I do what he says, we cool. The minute I don't, he's down my throat. I don't want problems with him, that's all."

"You're going to have to find a way to straighten this out." She knitted her brow. "He's the CEO of this company and your boss."

"Thanks, Bella," he said as he rose from his seat. "I thought you would be willing to help."

"Pharaoh," she called out to him. He continued to walk away, refusing to look back.

"Good morning." Bella looked up at Miles entering her office later that morning.

"I was preparing to come to your office." She smoothed her black pencil skirt. Her matching jacket was spread across the back of her chair.

Dressed in her power suit, she was professionally attired as the Chief Marketing Officer of their growing enterprise. It was at times a challenge, but they worked hard to maintain the lines of business and marital partners, each with an equal say in important matters.

Bella often came in the office later than he did. Miles had shared how much he loved having quiet time before the chaos of the day started. She, on the other hand, enjoyed her early morning hours with the twins.

"What held you up?" He looked at his Rolex watch. "I was expecting you an hour ago."

"Pharaoh came in to speak to me." She sat in the chair in front of her desk, opposite where he sat. "Did he talk to you?"

"No he didn't." He frowned and crossed his legs at the ankle. "We need to come up with an exit plan. It's time for him to go."

Clutching the arms of her chair, she leaned forward.

"You seem surprised," he said as he stared at her.

"I thought we were going to discuss Pharaoh's future plans with AriMusic." She placed a hand under her chin and sat back. "It appears you've made a decision without talking to me first."

"What's there to talk about? I've asked him many times to clean up his act and he has refused." He loosened his tie and frowned. "He has cost the company a lot of cash paying hush money, lawyer fees, and now payment to The Club for a breach of contract. Did you forget that he didn't show for his performance?" His voice grew louder. The temperature in the room rose prompting the air conditioner to kick in. "To be honest, Bella, I'm surprised that there is even a question in your mind if he should stay." Sweat gathered on his brow and his chest heaved. He narrowed his eyes and turned away from her.

"Miles," she said, leaning over to touch his hand. "I'm just wondering why you're in such a hurry to toss him to the curb. You've known him since he was a kid." She smiled, attempting to lighten his mood. "You've watched him grow up." She paused and let her words sink in. "Two days ago, we were family."

"Family?" His laugh was deep, almost like a grunt. "What kind of family member causes this kind of trouble?"

She side-eyed him and slapped the arm of her chair laughing.

"What the hell is so funny?"

"Have you forgotten how much trouble you caused your family when you were younger?" She smoothed back a strand of hair that had brushed her cheek. "Your mother and your cousin NeNe told me that you were kicked out of school for fighting and starting fires. Their money covered a multitude of your sins, Miles Moore." She sat up. "You frequently disobeyed your parents, yet they didn't turn their backs on you." Her heartbeat quickened as she stared at him, brown eyes to brown eyes. She knew her man. The familiar tick in his squared jaw had returned.

"Did I hit a nerve?" She raised her chin.

"You hit something," he said. His face darkened. "I thought this would be quick, but you turned it into a revisiting of my past. I was a kid when those things happened. Get it through your head." He rose and touched the side of her cheek with his index finger. "Pharaoh is a grown man. He's not my brother or my son. I see him for who he is."

"Miles, believe it or not, I see him too." She blew out a breath. "Let's talk about this calmly. I don't want to throw out the good with the bad. That's all I'm saying. I know AriMusic is your baby. You created this company. But didn't we want to do something different in the music industry? Music is the expression of the souls of black folks. Didn't we want Ari-Music to be a place where we saved some souls?"

"This is the City of Angels, a land of fallen angels." He

stood over her. "Bad things happen here every day."

"Please sit down." She motioned to his seat.

"I think I'd better leave." He turned, but looked back. "I don't want us to say something we'll both regret."

Chapter 4

D ays after the fire, the situation between him and Bella had progressed to agreeing to disagree about Pharaoh's future with the company. Stretching his tired limbs, he sighed. As if he didn't have enough to think about... there was something else.

Waiting on his desk was a packet containing information on yet another lawsuit he feared could be tried in the court of public opinion. He couldn't face this current situation alone. Fuming, he'd called his management team together to avert a crisis that could turn into another PR nightmare. Miles didn't need – nor would he allow – anything to distract him from promoting the new artists who had just signed with the Vesta division of his company, AriMusic.

Parker Middleton, his business manager, was the first person he'd called. Darien Grayson, his personal assistant, had contacted Bradley.

Miles maintained his grim look as he quietly flipped through a mound of papers while his team avoided eye contact with one another. Only Parker had some idea of what was troubling their boss, but it didn't stop him from fidgeting with the buttons on his shirt or pulling at the lapel of his jacket.

"My lawyers felt it was important to send these papers by courier this morning to review as soon as possible," Miles informed them, not looking up from the stack of papers with the heading *Gleason, Johnson, and Manning* on the cover page. He rubbed his hands through his hair and tensed his jaw. "It appears Kelly Productions Studio has joined Daryl Nyland's company in a suit against us for unfair business practices after a number of their artists left to sign with us." He pushed the papers away in disgust, as if the words were emitting a noxious smell. An uncomfortable silence chilled the room.

Parker fidgeted in his chair but eventually broke the silence, punctuated only by the sound of the central air kicking on.

Miles slid the stack toward him with such force that Parker had to use both hands to stop the papers from sliding off the table. He flipped through them quickly until he came across the information he needed, and pointed his index finger to its location.

"According to these dates, some of the artists were no longer under contract when they signed with us. I'm concerned that the real issue is to tie the company up in litigation and financially ruin you."

Miles was about to respond when Mr. Curtis, his estate manager, entered the room and whispered something in his ear.

"Was she on her computer?"

"Yes, Mr. Moore, she was on the computer. She asked me to bring her some tea, but shortly after I arrived in her office, she stormed out of the room."

"Did you see what was on her screen?"

"Sir, I'm not in the habit of spying on the two of you. I didn't see what she was reading." Mr. Curtis's back stiffened and his lips drew taut, as if he were being to put to a test he was destined to fail.

Miles bolted from his seat, heading for the door. Bella was home at their estate adjoining the property.

"I need to check on Bella. I hope this lie hasn't been posted. Let's get back together later after I've had a chance to talk to her. I need all of you to stay close to your phones. That's all for now."

Miles found Bella in their bedroom, pacing back and forth from their bed to her dresser.

"Baby, please don't be angry. I'll fix this. I promise I will."

"You can't fix this," she said, choking on her words. "And I don't know how to fix this either. I'm not sure what to do."

He placed his hands on her back gently, but she stiffened under his touch before moving away from him and falling on the bed. Hugging her pillow, she turned her back to him.

"I understand the realities of life, but why is it that the people you care about also hurt you the most?"

He moved closer to her to rub her back and sighed with a heavy heart. "Bella, I understand why you might believe that the allegations are true, but I told you a while back that you shouldn't believe everything you read about me."

Leaning against her back, he kissed her shoulder. "You've changed me. I no longer believe in success by any means necessary. I'm a better man because of you. There's no way I would resort to predatory practices and leave us in financial ruin."

The tension loosened in her jaw as she turned slowly to face him for the first time.

"What are you talking about? This isn't about you. I'm frustrated that the fire at The Club is still making headlines on some of the smaller media sites. It's not like Pharaoh is the only bad boy in town. Why did you think this was about you and me?"

He slid closer to her and took her into his arms. She looked up at him, waiting for him to speak.

"I received a legal notice for another lawsuit against us." He sighed, then smiled as she placed a hand on his arm in support. "I thought it might have been released to the press. It also crossed my mind that maybe, yet another story about me and my former *sexcapades* before we got married had been printed in the *trash tabloids*."

"I don't pay attention to that mess. It's more important that your actions surrounding the fire don't cause suspicions to gather." Furrowing her brow, she rose and paced the room. "You said the fire investigator was definitely curious that you weren't affected by the heat and smoke in the apartment. For the sake of the children, we can't answer any questions about your condition."

"We're on the same page, babe." He stood, placing his hands on his waist. "They deserve the chance at a happy, *normal* childhood. I was taken to doctors and spent months in hospitals because my parents didn't know what was wrong with me. We have an advantage they didn't have. I'm not willing to let anyone invade their privacy. I'm the public figure, not them."

"I've searched most of the reputable sites, and other than the fact that you were on the scene, there's little mention or details of the incident." Placing a hand on her face, she covered the dark circles under her eyes as she pondered how to handle the situation.

"We have to protect our babies." Her eyes moistened.

"It's under control." He stepped in front of her, stopping her from creating a path in the carpet. "I have our personal security and media teams along with members of The Network doing whatever is necessary to bury the story so deep in the news cycle, most won't notice it. Fires occur all the time in California. The report of what happened that night will disappear, you'll see."

"I hope you're right." She leaned her head against his chest. "I'm confident we'll get through this together."

"Then why are you so sad?" Turning her chin, he gazed into her eyes.

"You're good at reading my moods," she said with a slight smile. "You're right. What's out of my hands shouldn't occupy my mind."

"I agree, babe." He kissed her forehead. Bella had given him his most cherished gifts – her love, and the blessings of their children. That fact endeared her to him – and would for the rest of his life. He would protect them at all costs.

Except for the rare babysitter, Bella tried for six weeks to care of the babies, with Miles helping out when he could. Both were exhausted, and Miles encouraged her to allow someone to come in to assist them full-time. Lecia, Miles's mother, had arranged to have a distant cousin, Carmen Diaz from North Carolina, come to help as a surprise, but Bella really liked how the nanny from the agency handled the babies.

"Let's keep them both," Miles had insisted, as he didn't want to cause problems in the family or hurt his cousin's feelings. She had cared for him for a brief time when he was a toddler. It didn't hurt that they had the added bonus of more time to enjoy making love while their babies slept, before he had to return to the studio for an afternoon of work.

Two weeks had passed with the nannies, and everything was going well. They walked to the studio, located on the adjoining property, and used the time together to talk without interruption from the babies. "Aren't you glad we have the extra help and you have more time for yourself?" Miles asked.

"Yes, it's good having family in the house, and I can't complain about getting some sleep at night."

The two arrived at the studio locked in each other's arms. It had been their home before they turned it into a working studio and offices for AriMusic. Parker and NeNe Moore, Miles's cousin and lawyer, greeted them in the great room as they entered.

Miles and Bella stood next to each other, waiting for either Parker or NeNe to tell them what was going on. NeNe's unannounced visits often meant something was brewing.

Instead of immediately sharing her concerns, NeNe reached out to hug them before heading for the bar. "Hey, you two. I need a drink before we discuss this situation. Come and join me." She urged them all to follow her to the study.

"Please, make yourself at home, cousin." Miles chuckled.

"I always do." She smiled as she poured glasses for Miles and Parker. Bella held up her hand to decline a drink, since she was still breastfeeding the twins. She looked on as NeNe leaned back to take a swallow before addressing them. "I don't agree with going public with this matter." She motioned her hand in the air in a grand gesture as she spoke.

Parker jumped in. "Miles, I called NeNe because I was concerned about you, man. I didn't like that you're being made to choose between fighting another time-consuming case or settling for terms amounting to no less than extortion. I couldn't stand by and let all that happen."

NeNe went on, "I've already responded to their communications that the artists you recently signed are in breach of their contracts. I know my cousin. It didn't even cross my mind that he wouldn't fight it. So, here is where we are with this situation. I demanded a full review of the contracts, and guess what?" Miles shrugged. "These companies are the main ones with unfair business practices. The artists are within their rights to sign with another company after the agreed upon terms of the contract have ended. They don't have to accept predatory practices or remain with organizations that will not compensate them for their talents."

"But isn't it up to the artists to review their contracts before they sign?" Bella interjected.

"That's not relevant at this point. I used it as leverage. No one wants to support companies that are unfair to their employees. It doesn't play well in the press and the financial damage can be astronomical." She looked into Miles' eyes. "So, dear cousin, *could* you ever be guilty of the same thing?"

Miles gave her a side-eyed glance. "I never knowingly take advantage of someone trying to make it in this cut-throat industry. I thought you said you trusted me?"

"I trust you, but it's always best to verify it. That we weren't guilty of something similar. Though it would've been an easy case to defend even if it went to court. I consider this matter settled, then. We'll never discuss it again. How are those sweet little babies of yours?"

Chapter 5

Love unleashed a fury
Love caused a fury
Acquitted by jury
Defeated a conspiracy
of those who envy
that we love ourselves
respect ourselves
cherish ourselves

I chose her
I didn't want you
Flamed a fury
of a woman scorned
love me, need me
hatin' the day that I was born

You misunderstood my attention
Thought it was my affection

FACE THE FIRE

The paternity test showed no sign
That your beautiful baby boy was mine

M iles had originally written the song for himself two years ago, based on the life experiences of a friend. But in light of the fact that he was now a married man, he didn't want to fan any flames of suspicion NeNe would have to put out. In his own past, women had come forward accusing him of fathering their children, but none of the claims were substantiated.

He decided to let Lil' Pharaoh record the song, with urgings from Bella. For several weeks, he avoided conflict with others. He was AriMusic's most cooperative recording artist. When things were good with Pharaoh, they were very good.

He laid down solid tracks on the first recording, but by the time they were ready for the final recording, Lil' Pharaoh was on fire. Everyone felt the heat of his passion, including Miles. He had the right balance of the edgy anger that accompanied being wrongly accused, but he could also maintain sensual tones during the verses about the woman he loved, while the female artists of Vesta Music sang the background vocals.

After a relatively short night of recording, Miles smiled at Lil' Pharaoh and gave him a thumbs up. He knew the song would be a hit, but he had bigger plans for his young protégés – he wanted all of them to appear on the compilation he was working on. Miles planned to be featured on some of the tracks, but his main goal was to make an album that showcased all their blossoming talents, before giving them solo projects.

Despite his musical gifts, Lil' Pharaoh still had the oppositional behavior of a teen toward authority figures. He was known to act out in dramatic fashion, due to unresolved grief over the death of his father, who had been a professional musician. Now, Lil' Pharaoh had reservations about appearing on an album with multiple female artists.

"I don't have the same fan base," he explained.

"You need to expand your fan base to include more women," Miles reminded him. *The Pharaoh I know is back.*

"Listen man, I'm not interested in being a romantic crooner."

Bella tracked the song "Love's Fury" on social media, and shared the news with the team assigned to develop Lil' Pharaoh's talent, that his fans were also excited about the planned collaboration between the two artists – Miles's stage persona, the King, aka Ari Moore, and his young prince, Lil' Pharaoh. Ari's edgy vocals were back, and his male fans were elated, but the production team needed to work hard to get Lil' Pharaoh out of Ari's huge shadow.

Miles planned to meet with Lil' Pharaoh again this morning with stats that showed the success of the song "Love's Fury," which featured multiple artists. Relieved that fan demographic studies showed that both male and female fans liked the song, he authorized the release of a large check to Lil' Pharaoh for his vocals.

Despite resuming his habit of partying the night away, Pharaoh surprised Miles by coming to the studio on time without a reminder from his assistant.

"Have a seat, Pharaoh. We need to discuss the plans for your project," Miles told him, extending his hand to the seat next to him.

"I get it, Miles." Lil' Pharaoh disarmed him with his quick acceptance. "I'm okay with being on the compilation album, but in exchange, I want more creative control over my solo project. I want to use some of my own original music, and I want some of my boys backing me up."

Pharaoh was a man of many surprises this morning. Miles had blocked out his schedule for most of the morning to confer with him, but something had clearly happened to change his position. Miles tented his hands over his mouth, contemplating how to address Pharaoh's requests.

"Before we continue, can I ask what changed your mind about the compilation project?"

"I ran into Bella. She was listening to the track – she said she loved it. She was busy with the babies, and she hadn't heard it before. I can tell when people are shittin' me, but she was real, and I liked that. So, what about my requests?"

Miles shook his head. "Pharaoh, I was sincere with you when I told you that you laid down a good track. Did you need more validation?"

"Yeah, but you're a businessman now. Don't be offended, but at your level, the money a song can make is probably more important than the art or quality of the music." Pharaoh gripped his chair and leaned back. "I hope I haven't gone too far with you. I'm just keepin' it real." Pharaoh flashed one of his money-making smiles.

"I'm not offended, but let's agree not to make assumptions about each other. Staying true to the music is still important to me – and remember, some truths are relative."

"I'm not sure what that means, but I learn fast. Life has always been a hard teacher to me."

"That's what we need to discuss. I plan to be one of your teachers. Members of my executive staff have agreed to mentor you on the art and business side of music. You're college-aged, and I want you to consider the sessions we provide to be like an advanced course on the industry. You'll remember that attending the sessions is part of your contract for the next two years. If you successfully complete the requirements and observe the morality clause, we can renegotiate the contract."

"I know what I got to do. I'm here on time, right?"

"Yes, and punctuality is a good sign of your commitment to your career. Now, in regard to your requests, I'm willing to grant you more creative control, but I'll reserve the right of final approval on the project before anything's released. I won't be signing any of your friends to an extended contract, but we can ask NeNe to draw up a condensed contract for contributions to any song they appear on, provided they have the right vocals."

Pharaoh beamed. "I won't disappoint you, Miles. I want to start working on my project as soon as we finish the compilation."

"I'm glad to hear that, but we need to discuss one more thing. I take my role as your mentor seriously, so we need to talk about you limiting the number of people in your inner group to reduce your chance of attracting trouble. I see all the women trying to get your attention. I was once twenty with lots of money and plenty of women. Always carry protection with you and start being discriminating with women. You can't allow yourself to become involved with everybody crossing your path."

Placing one leg over the other, he assumed a more relaxed posture. Pharaoh threw his head back in laughter. "Why are you so serious about having a good time? Don't worry about it."

"I'm not." Closing his eyes, Miles took in a breath. "I need to remind you that there are morality and illegal drug-use clauses. If you bring drugs on any property owned by Ari-Music or do drugs on property owned by AriMusic, your contract will automatically be null and void. Do you under-stand me, Pharaoh? Are there any other questions?"

"Just one… are we done? I have a lot of ideas I want to try out. I'll leave if you don't have more questions."

"We're done, Pharaoh." Miles watched him exit his office. He believed in Pharaoh's talent. But was he in over his head when it came to trying to develop him as an artist? Miles dropped his head on the desk and cradled it in his arms. He was exhausted and it was just the start of the week.

Chapter 6

A couple of weeks later, the plans for the twins' baptisms at the house were going well. They were four months old. The event had been postponed by a month so that Joan Wahlberg, Bella's mother, could attend. She had come in from Texas, and Miles's mother and sisters were due the following day.

"I'm so glad you could be here," Bella told her mother, as they sat around the table enjoying a cup of coffee.

"I'm sorry I couldn't come earlier." Her mother stirred the hot black coffee and took a sip. She was the owner of an international business, Wahlberg Fire Consultants. When Bella was a young girl, Joan was the fire chief in a small Texas town. After the death of Bella's father, John Wahlberg, they moved to California where she started the firm, advising agencies about pyrotechnics and fire safety.

"You were in Europe during the birth of the twins." Bella placed her cup on the table. "I wouldn't be honest if I said that it didn't disappoint me that you hadn't been here for the first three months of the twins' lives." She sighed. "I just thought you would be more involved with your grandchildren."

"Like I was with you?" Bella didn't miss her mother's reminder that she had been there for her. "After your dad's death, it was just the two of us. Now that you're all grown up and married to Miles, I felt it was my time to accomplish my own goals. I thought you would understand. I don't have the resources the Moores have. I can't just dismiss my responsibilities to my folks in Europe at the drop of a hat."

"What about your commitment to family?" Bella's eyes glistened. She turned away, fearing her tears would fall. After taking a breath, she resumed their conversation monitoring the tone of her voice. "We're growing apart and I don't like the distance between us."

Joan buried her lips between her teeth. For Bella, the silence grew uncomfortable and difficult to bear.

"Say something, Mom." She searched her mother's eyes.

"Did the distance bother you when you chose to go with Miles on his yearlong international tour and not come home for any of the holidays?" She blinked back tears. "Did it bother you when you called one hour before midnight to wish me a happy birthday?"

"Mom, I explained…" Bella wiped the tear rolling down her cheek.

"Sweetheart, let's not do this to each other." She placed a hand on top of hers. "I'm here now. I trust that we'll work things out. No matter how long we don't see each other, I'll never stop loving you."

"I don't doubt that, Mom." She took in a deep breath. "How will my children ever grow to love you if they never see you?"

Miles walked into the room and kissed Bella before

hugging Joan. "Everything okay?'

"Fine." They both raised their cups, taking a sip of their coffee.

Miles's father, Kaiden, affectionately known as Cade, and his uncle Vincent – both tall, handsome men – arrived a day early to meet with Miles, Bella, and NeNe, after saying that it was important that they meet in a secure place without interruptions. They agreed to meet at the AriMusic studio complex after Miles gave most of the staff the day off. His office was soundproof. They all assembled mid-morning after enjoying a delicious gourmet brunch and conversation. Cade had called Miles and Bella before his arrival in LA to tell them that his brother wanted to speak to them about their current level of security since the birth of the twins.

"Tell us what this is about. What's the mystery that you all couldn't share with us until today?" NeNe asked them.

The two older men looked at each other before speaking.

"Why don't you take the lead, Cade?" Uncle Vincent suggested, referring to Miles's father by his nickname.

"I know we've been cryptic over the phone, but when we found out that the twins were born with Miles's genetic condition, we felt we had to share additional details with you. It's important you understand the importance of keeping the babies safe – not only because they belong to us and we love them, but because their safety could be a matter of national security."

At this, Bella took Miles's hand. He squeezed hers for support. "Pop, you got our attention. Tell us what this is about."

His speech was clipped. He was irritated that his father was taking his time with his concerns.

His uncle piped up, "You and NeNe already know. Now we need to tell Bella about our grandfather – your great-grandfather, Aaron. We've told you since you were very young that he died a decorated military man in a covert operation. What you don't know is that he was also a member of The Network. You knew we had a loose affiliation, but I've actually worked closely with them for a time now." He paused, letting his admission sink in.

"As you know, The Network is a global syndicate of people from all levels of society that represents the interests of the American people. They may be industry captains, military men, trained mercenaries, or your everyday men and women. They recruited our grandfather because he had the same genetic anomaly he passed to you, Miles. He could produce fire, and he used it to destroy foreign secrets that could have endangered the lives of our people. But they promised our grandmother Mariah that they wouldn't recruit any of her children. They kept that promise until after her death, which was when they recruited me. Your father was briefly involved with The Network, too. I have a sworn promise from them not to recruit you for any covert missions, but the fact that you and your children have the same traits is a game changer."

Bella and NeNe gasped.

Uncle Vincent continued, "They don't plan to recruit your children, but they don't want them to fall into the hands of a terrorist group if their traits are discovered. An agent also passed along information to me that the attempted bombing at your Scotland concert over a year ago may have been a cover – the real intent was to kidnap you, Miles. As a result, we've increased the protection around you and your family.

That's why they showed up at the fire several months ago."

Stone-faced, Miles spoke up. "I have security monitoring my children around the clock. I'm not worried about their safety. My celebrity status already placed them and Bella at risk." He spoke authoritatively.

Bella knew they'd both harbored concerns after the incident in Scotland.

"Son, I respect that you've assembled a great team of professionals, and I suggest you keep them in place as a show of force. But The Network members are excellent when it comes to covert operations. You probably weren't even aware that they've been monitoring you all your life. When I told your mother about your 24/7 coverage long ago, she thought we'd paid for it. Her need for bedrest during the pregnancy with your sisters, along with the knowledge that you would be safe, gave her the courage to give you some breathing room. But she doesn't need to know anything else about The Network. We have a don't ask, don't tell relationship when it comes to the organization," his father said.

Uncle Vincent spoke next. "If NeNe wasn't such a curious child who has always had some difficulty with boundaries, she wouldn't know much about The Network either. Long ago, she intercepted information that was for my eyes only and demanded that I tell her about The Network. Isn't that right, NeNe?"

"Yes, Dad, but I don't know a lot about this shadowy organization. Have they been monitoring me too?"

"Yes. They follow you more than your siblings because you and Miles have been involved in some more *interesting* situations. We're now sharing this with Bella because they're monitoring her whereabouts too. They know Miles would do anything to get her back if something happened to her."

Bella, who had been silent during the discussion, finally spoke. "Do they monitor the conversations we have? Do they intervene in our relationships with others?"

"Generally, no. They realize you have the right to make your own decisions and live your lives as you choose. Their role is to intervene only if the situation becomes dangerous. They don't want to blow their cover," Uncle Vincent told her.

"So how do they protect us?"

"They infiltrate your daily lives and perform usual duties," Miles's father answered.

"Like whom, Pop?" Miles asked.

"Dr. Chancellor, your personal physician, is a Network doctor."

"What about the law firm I retain, aside from NeNe?"

"Network."

NeNe posed the next question. "And what about the law firm that employs me?"

"Network," her father responded.

"Did The Network do a background check on our cousin and the head nanny?" Bella asked.

"Your nanny and cousin Carmen *are members* of The Network," Miles's father responded.

Miles, Bella, and NeNe all slid back in their chairs, mouths wide open. This was serious. The Network had infiltrated their lives, right down to their daily activities.

Feeling the intensity rising within Miles, Bella kept her hand wrapped in his. She knew the unwanted attention of The Network frustrated him. She wondered if he felt his father and uncle had overstepped their boundaries. Miles had fled to California to get away from his family's interference, and now they might be suffocating him again. Bella knew he was caught in his feeling and trying to process the news about the *extent* of The Network's influence on their lives.

She turned her hand to look at her palm, which was reddening and sweating in his grasp, but continued to clasp his hand for support. Rubbing their joined hands with her free one, she tried to maintain her cool before she spoke.

"I like that the nannies are so calm with the babies. That they both have defense skills and training in martial arts is a plus. At first, I had my reservations about the help, but Miles convinced me I was drowning under the mounds of dirty clothes accumulating with two babies." Bella felt the skin of his hand cool a bit as she spoke.

"It *was* my idea to bring in extra help. Thanks for reminding me, Bella." He closed his eyes, but she didn't need to look at him to perceive the sarcasm dripping from his lips.

"It was a good idea." She smiled and kissed his lips, which he kept tightly drawn. "Even knowing that they're Network employees, it's still a good idea to have them. We both reviewed their references, and they were by far the best candidates for the job. I've been calmer around the babies since they came to help, and their feeding and bathing times are things I look forward to. I do plenty of work online. I see on social media the lives of kids who have special talents. That's why I don't want my children to grow up scrutinized by others, used by others for their own personal gains, or treated like lab rats. If this is the price Miles and I have to pay for their safety and their privacy, I'm willing to pay it. I welcome their exposure to a large, loving family that accepts them for who they are because I see the positive effects the love of a large family has had on Miles. I'll just have to accept that some of the members of our extended family may also be members of The Network."

"Thank you, Bella," his father said. "So, son, are you all

right with all of this?"

Miles relaxed his grip on Bella's hand and pursed his lips. "I agree with Bella. I'll do anything to keep my family safe and to create the sanctuary they deserve."

"Bella, one more thing." Uncle Vincent looked directly at her. "You can't share any of this with your mother."

She swallowed hard. Secrets could worsen their attempts to resume the closeness they once shared. There were differences of opinion, but no secrets between the two of them – until now. And this was a big one.

She met Uncle Vincent's gaze. "I understand."

She was now a Moore and not as close to the members of her family of origin, the Wahlbergs. Besides, Miles had warned her prior to their marriage that becoming a Moore meant she would have to accept the benefits *and* challenges of being a member of the family. Family secrets came with the territory.

What else don't I know? she wondered.

Chapter 7

The christening ceremony proceeded as planned. She thought she would be more anxious watching so many people walking around her babies, but her fears were relieved when most of them chose to avoid kisses, at least when she was looking at them. All those in attendance had also agreed to wash their hands or use the hand sanitizers placed throughout the home before greeting each other or sharing in the mutual adoration of her children. Bella tried to avoid hovering, but found it hard not to do so. She liked that her mother was making the effort to spend as much time as possible with the twins before she left for a meeting the next day in London.

Conversation and laughter flowed over the bounty of food and drink. Afternoon turned into evening by the time family members began departing. Miles's parents and his sisters were the last to leave. They remained with them while the other members of the extended family prepared to return to their homes. Bella was exhausted from the full day of family festivities, but she was determined to rise early the next morning to resume her yoga and meditation practice.

She kept her personal promise to get up before sunrise while the nannies cared for the babies.

"Wait for me and we can walk over to the studio together," Miles yelled from the bathroom while getting dressed to go to his office.

She planned to enjoy the sunrise while he took care of business.

They left their home after giving the babies a kiss and walked briskly down the winding drive to the adjacent property. The weatherman had forecasted that nature's show, the day's sunrise, was going to be a glorious one.

"Let's have a meditation practice this morning together." She tried to convince him to join her on the second-story balcony, just off their former guest room overlooking the hill. Bella had always thought it was interesting that the best view of the sunrise was off of the guest room instead of the master suite, but Miles had once told her that the last thing his father wanted to see was the sunrise after playing long nightly sets as a jazz musician in the clubs around southern California. In fact, he and his mother had once teased him and called him Kaiden the Vampire because he didn't rise until late afternoon during his busy touring season.

Miles, on the other hand, was an early riser who required little sleep and often rose at four in the morning to compose songs. Since the birth of their babies, they had settled into a comfortable rhythm of either cuddling and talking with each other at night before they went to sleep or speaking early in the morning before they rose to face the day.

"Maybe later in the week," he responded after contemplating her request. "I have a lot to do this morning, but you enjoy your private time."

"All right, but don't forget about joining me this week. Meditation is a good way to start a busy day." She sighed and kissed him goodbye. On her way to the second-floor balcony, she heard a noise coming from one of the small studio rooms just outside of the private suite.

When she peeked inside the converted recording room, she saw Lil' Pharaoh wearing a headset and mumbling to himself. Facing away from her, he kept his attention on the sheets of music on the music stand and didn't notice that she'd entered the room and was standing behind him. She looked at her exercise watch. She had a few minutes to spare before her sun salutations, so she decided to remind him that he had media sessions today on a local popular radio show.

In a booming voice, he started his rap as the tape rolled.

She touched him on the shoulder, and he hesitated before turning around.

"What you want from me, bitch?"

She looked at him, wide-eyed and filled with anger. Unaccustomed to the venomous words, she reared back her arm and slapped him across the cheek, causing his head to jerk backward.

"What was that for?" He stared at her, keeping his fists at his side.

"You just called me a *bitch*," she said, her chest heaving, her breath quickened by adrenaline and indignation.

He grabbed his cheek, then pointed his index finger at his music stand. "I'm laying some of the lyrics on my tracks. I wasn't thinking about you," he yelled, narrowing his eyes. His chest expanded with each deep breath as he looked at her, but he made no physical attempt to defend himself.

She stepped back, unsure if he was going to calm down. The pounding of her pulse in her ears gradually subsided as she realized he may not have wanted to give Miles another reason to be angry with him.

"I wasn't calling you a bitch, Bella," he repeated as he rubbed his face, which still bore her handprint.

She looked at him, trying to assess the situation. "I'm sorry I slapped you." She tried doing her cleansing breath exercise to calm herself and cupped a hand around her neck to place soft pressure on the throbbing pulse points. "I came to remind you about your interview later today with WCAL. They've given your song a lot of airtime, and we need to make sure they know how much we appreciate their role in making the song a success."

"I'll be there." His response was terse, and he was still frowning as she turned to leave the room. "I'm sorry, too, if you thought I would ever disrespect you. I want to thank you for getting the interview for me. I know how hard it is to get on the morning show at WCAL."

She nodded, but quickened her steps to get out of the studio as soon as possible for her date with the rising sun.

Bella was in her head as she assumed her position on the balcony. Thoughts about her encounter with Pharaoh ran through her mind. She took a deep breath and settled into her practice, mildly irritated that she'd missed the exact moment of the sun rising above the horizon, but its warmth shone on her as she looked up at its bright rays. She was happy with her life, despite its minor hiccups.

After completing her yoga poses for the morning, she closed her eyes and had settled into the meditative portion of her practice when Pharaoh came outside and sat in a cross-legged position beside her, at a safe distance. Feeling his presence, she looked at him out of the corner of her eye before closing them again as she sat with her hands palms-side up in her lap. She continued taking deep, cleansing breaths, trying to focus on the air filling her lungs, but his presence was a distraction. Refusing to acknowledge him before she finished her session, they both sat on their mats for a few minutes without speaking to each other.

Pharaoh was sitting quietly. When she opened her eyes, he was looking at her like a sad puppy. He dropped his head to look at his hands, then slowly lifted his head and turned to face her.

"Are you going to tell Miles what happened this morning?"

"Pharaoh, we both apologized to each other. I accepted your apology. I won't run to Miles with the news that I slapped you if you don't." She smiled at him. "He might not be too happy with me."

Pharaoh took a deep breath, visibly relieved that the misunderstanding wasn't going to be an ongoing issue between them. "I was concerned you might tell him that I called you a bitch." He shook his head. "No, I meant I *didn't* call you a bitch. I did say the *word* 'bitch,' but I wasn't referring to you."

She listened as he tried to dig himself out of the hole that would only deepen if she didn't rescue him. "It's okay, but maybe you should reconsider using that word to describe any female."

"Let's not discuss *that* again. It's just a blow term, you know, to blow off some steam. You can call me one when I get on your nerves. I promise I'll give you plenty of opportunities to blow off steam. It's just a part of my charm," he said with a slight smile on his face.

"I'll pass. By the way, I was meaning to ask why you're challenging Miles so often. He knows what he's doing, and your career will take off under his tutelage."

"His tutelage?" He frowned. "Is Miles the Great the only one who understands music? My father also taught me a lot before—" He stopped talking abruptly and looked away from her.

"I know your father was a musician before he died. Is that why you walk around with a chip on your shoulder sometimes?" She held her breath, hoping her bluntness wouldn't cause him to shut down, but he surprised her by continuing the discussion.

"What would you know about a chip on my shoulder? You're living the glamorous life married to Prince Charming." The sarcasm in his voice didn't escape her.

"My life hasn't been as charmed as you choose to believe. I also know the pain of losing a father at an early age." Her heart rate quickened as she pondered the wisdom of disclosing her past. "I carried that pain for a long time, but at a certain point in my life, I decided I had to come out of the darkness. I felt lucky that I *had* a father who loved me. My father *died*, Pharaoh. He didn't run away or abandon me. He died, and it wasn't his choice to leave me. I knew if he could, he would've come running back to me and my mother." She looked up at the sky and paused.

"I decided I needed to live the life my father would have wanted for me. He loved me unconditionally. He would have wanted me to live my life to the fullest and be happy. I'm living my life in honor of the great man my father was. I was his only child, and I know he wouldn't want me to grieve for the rest of my life."

Lil' Pharaoh looked up at the blinding rays of the sun, blinking back tears that filled his eyes but refused to fall. "I was my father's only child and I know he loved me. I've never told anyone this, but I miss him every day. I guess I get angry anytime I feel like someone's trying to replace him."

"Trust me, Miles has his hands full with being a parent to the twins. He's made it clear he wants no more children. He wants to be a mentor to you, not a father."

"Thanks. I needed this." He uncrossed his legs, and she sensed from the scowl on his face and his stiffened posture that his public persona had returned.

"One more thing before you leave." She gazed at him, capturing his attention. "I'm concerned about you, Pharaoh. I had a good friend, Jason, who many years ago got caught in a bad situation that cost him his life. I don't want your choices to cause you to have consequences you're not able to handle."

He remained silent, then turned his head away. "Don't worry about me." He shrugged. "I'd love to do the trip down memory lane with you and find out more about your friend, but I need to be on time for the interview," he told her as he pulled his sunglasses out of his shirt pocket.

She hoped she hadn't crossed too many boundaries when it came to challenging Lil' Pharaoh, but she was his assigned publicist. He'd told Miles at the time of his signing that he didn't want anyone else to handle his publicity. Lil' Pharaoh had unmistakable talent, but he had a lot to learn about the music industry. He could be a handful for anyone to manage. She was concerned that he continued to surround himself with too many people outside of AriMusic who liked his swagger, not to mention the fact that he always questioned authority. It was one thing to question authority, but another to think he had all the answers.

He got up from the mat and, without warning, leaned over and left a lingering kiss on her cheek.

"What are you doing?" She pulled away and raised her hands.

He caught them midair.

"Let me go," she snarled at him.

"I'm sorry, Bella." He backed away. "You're so beautiful. I couldn't resist." He bit his lower lip. "I promise it won't happen again."

"Like hell it won't." She rose from the mat, her hands balled into fists.

He stood in front of her as if planting his feet to receive a blow.

"I'm not going to slap you again." She pointed her finger at him. "The next time, I'll be all over your ass and you'll be out of here."

"Understood." He placed his glasses over his eyes and left.

Darien told Miles that the interview at WCAL went well. That evening, Lil' Pharaoh returned to the studio, prepared to lay down tracks for his verses on the song "Daddy's Gone, Girl." Miles had discussed his plans to have him sing the male verses while Reagan Madison sang the first three female verses on the collaboration. Initially, Pharaoh had resisted appearing on the song with Reagan, which had angered Miles. Pharaoh didn't even have a good reason, other than he probably wanted to engage in an adolescent pissing contest.

Miles thought he would have to sing on the tracks if Lil'

Pharaoh continued to complain, but earlier that day, Lil' Pharaoh sent a message telling him he'd practiced the song and would be ready for taping that night. Miles didn't know what to make of his temperamental artist, but he decided to go with the flow. The team assembled in the studio with Reagan and Pharaoh positioned at their mics.

Daddy's Gone, Girl

What happens to a girl,
when Daddy's gone?
Her world turned upside down,
what went wrong?

Daddy's not here,
he went away
to Daddy's Gone World.
He left today.

Here today and gone tomorrow,
family left in tears and
feelin' great sorrow.
Did something happen?
Mommy, did you not try,
to tell Daddy,
at least say goodbye?

Pressed to Mommy's breast,
eyes filled with tears,
a brave girl trying not to grieve
or face her fears.
Mommy sighs and shares a fact,

"Daddy's gone, girl,
he's not comin' back."

After several takes, they wrapped up taping for the night. Miles gave Reagan and Pharaoh high fives.

"Now that's what I'm talking about. The two of you were fantastic." He congratulated them on their ability to deliver the vocals he'd hoped for. Their voices blended so well that Miles decided to let them sing the final verse of the song together.

"Pharaoh, your light shines bright, but I hope you now realize the importance of collaborating with others." Miles looked at his protégé, who shrugged and took the mic set off his head before requesting to take a break.

Miles knew Reagan understood this important fact. She'd grown up in the music industry as a child performer signed to an entertainment conglomerate known for turning out child stars, and she'd later worked as one of AriMusic's principal dancers and backup singers on some of his songs. She wanted a solo career, but trusted that Miles knew what he was doing by having her work with others on the compilation project.

Why is Pharaoh having so much difficulty seeing the same thing? Miles wondered what had changed in their relationship while he watched him prepare to leave.

"I think I'm gonna bounce for some fun on the town," Pharaoh announced from the recording booth.

"We'll resume taping early in the morning, Pharaoh," Miles called out to him over the intercom.

"I'll be here." He smiled and hurried out of the room, off to another as yet unknown escapade in the streets of Los Angeles.

Chapter 8

The nightclub atmosphere was electric. Pulsing neon lights bounced off the walls. Fog machines located at the entrance and in several corners pumped white vapor into the air, creating a fantasy atmosphere. The crowd of toned, youthful bodies danced to hard-driving, number-one rap tunes that had been filling the LA airwaves. In small corners of the large space, the smell of alcohol, expensive perfume, and weed co-mingled like spirits meant to control the gathering.

"Hey, Pharaoh." NasXL, a fellow rapper who was with Knight Productions waved him over to his table in the VIP section of the trendy club. Pharaoh had gone to high school with him and several guys in his crew. He and XL had scheduled interviews at WCAL the day before.

"Bruh." Pharaoh walked over and gave him a masculine handshake. Members of Pharaoh's crew followed behind him. He covered his eyes with his hand to avoid the sprays of Morette Champagne that were being showered around the room.

"Just in time for the celebration." He offered them a seat. "I'm surprised Miles let you off the chain. Got tired of being his lap dog?" XL showed his pearly whites as he looked around the table.

Nervous laughter broke out among members of his crew.

"I'm my own man." Pharaoh frowned, rising from his seat.

"I'm kidding." XL got up quickly and extended his hand for a fist bump. "We go way back. Why you so sensitive?" He smiled and motioned Pharaoh to resume his seat. "Sorry. No disrespect intended. Drinks for everyone." He waved his hands. "Order anything." Snapping his fingers, he got the waiter's attention to take Pharaoh's request.

"Who thought we would be enjoying this kind of success?" XL spoke to Pharaoh over the music. "How are things at AriMusic?"

"Great." Pharaoh looked at the fluted glass placed in front of him with bubbles rising to the surface. "Just great."

An imposing figure, a hunk of a man with a broad chest dressed in a suit that didn't hide his muscled legs came to the table. Daryl "Dark" Nyland was the CEO of Nyland Productions. Most of the rappers celebrating their number-one hits had signed with him.

"Dark, you know Lil' Pharaoh." XL rose from his seat to make the introduction.

Dark gave Pharaoh an appraising look before Pharaoh rose to offer his hand. They both nodded before Dark turned and took XL's seat, next to Pharaoh.

Although alarms were going off in Pharaoh's mind as he watched Dark smiling at him, superficially friendly yet mocking, he chose to let caution fly in the wind and picked up his glass. He was here to have fun, away from Miles's constant and watchful eye. Throwing back his head, he took a big gulp of his drink. He had heard others describe Dark as the apple that hadn't fallen too far from the tree. Most of Dark's relatives, including his father, were doing time for crimes, including murder. He knew Dark had come from a bad seed. The DNA of a stone-cold killer and a lack of empathy were his family's legacy.

Dark pointed to one of his men, who got up and went to the DJ's stand. After the man spoke into the DJ's ear, the music changed.

"Whoa." Pharaoh and his crew got up and started throwing their hands in the air. It was one of Pharaoh's mixtapes of music Miles felt didn't fit the brand he was crafting for Pharaoh. The crowd's response was positive as they turned and pointed to the table.

"Go Pharaoh, go Pharaoh," they sang, moving to the beat of the song laced with profane lyrics.

Pharaoh got on top of the table, held his hands up high above his head like a conqueror returning from a victorious battle, and took a bow. He climbed back into his seat after moments of basking in the glow. Fame, for him, wasn't a monster. It was a drug.

"Where did you get that?" He looked at Dark, who was the obvious architect of the moment. "Miles took that tape from me. He didn't like it. Said we didn't need to drop it."

"I have my ways, Pharaoh – people inside AriMusic loyal to me." He took out a cigar and lit it in the smoke-free club. "I disagree with Miles. You see the reception from the crowd. They love it. You'd have an instant hit if you were in my house."

He smiled and looked around at the partygoers, some of

whom were still giving him the thumbs up. "I'm riding with Miles...for now." Pharaoh met Dark's gaze. "I'm still under contract."

"We can change that." Dark flashed one of those smiles again that made the hairs on his arms stand at attention.

Pharaoh brushed his hands over his arms. He had heard of Dark's *unconventional* methods in the industry.

"That man is nothing but trouble," his mother had warned. Pharaoh was underage when she had refused Dark's offer. "Either I sign you with Miles, or you don't sign with anyone."

Pharaoh leaned back in his chair and placed his arms behind his head. The relaxed posture settled the tingling feeling coursing through his body.

"I bet Miles got you saddled with other artists that shine in your light." Dark pursed his lips.

His comment hit a nerve. He really didn't like having to work with Pele.

"Nice guys finish last, Pharaoh."

"What are you proposing?" He inclined his ear to listen closely.

"We should give him an offer he can't refuse," one of the men sitting near Dark offered.

"Yeah, let's have some cold black-steel negotiations," another shouted out and laughed.

Dark looked in their direction as they lowered their heads and cowered. "Shut the *eff up*," he yelled at his associates. "I don't roll like that anymore. I've even cleaned up my speech so I sound more like a businessman." He grabbed his jacket's lapels. "Don't listen to them. I'm proposing that Miles and I have a conversation. That's all." He glared at those sitting at the table, including XL.

"Miles doesn't pack heat." Pharaoh placed his hands under the table to hide the slight tremor. "He won't take kindly to anyone trying to make him a bitch. Listen, I don't want trouble."

"We don't want problems either." Dark placed a hand on Pharaoh's shoulder. "I don't want to see your talent wasted. I'm proposing...an opportunity. You get to write the songs you want to perform and have your crew around you."

"Listen to the man." One of the guys who routinely travelled with Pharaoh hit him on the arm.

"I'll bet they aren't welcomed at AriMusic. Are they?" Dark cocked his head. "How you gonna level up in the game without your crew? All great men cause those loyal to him to rise also."

His crew nodded.

"If you don't think Miles will listen to you, maybe you can whisper something into his wife's sweet ear." Dark smiled. "She's a beautiful woman and I heard she likes young studs."

"I don't want Bella involved in anything that may go down between us." Pharaoh's chest heaved and he pointed at the space between him and Dark. "I'll break off anything we got going together." His anger rose. "Keep Bella out of my business. Let me handle this."

The others at the table shifted their bodies away from Pharaoh, as the vibe had changed.

Dark was silent for a few seconds before breaking into raucous laughter. "Chill out." He placed his arm around Pharaoh's shoulder. "You're so tense." He patted his chest. "Listen, I'm sure you'll handle it. In the meantime, I got a line of Snow White that will chill you out."

"I don't do coke often." Pharaoh pulled away from his embrace.

"Try it." Dark smiled, this time warm and friendly. "I promise you'll like it."

Chapter 9

Bella had settled into a good routine at work. The twins were nine months old and had been sleeping through the night for months. She and Pharaoh spent less time together alone. As he had promised, he made no further attempts to cross the line with her. She decided not to tell Miles about the kiss. Things had settled down, so why give him more ammunition against Pharaoh? There was no doubt in her mind. He would have fired him.

Sitting at her desk, she rubbed her eyes after several hours on the computer. Her morning had been filled with planned meetings and her afternoon was loaded with the unexpected. She looked at her phone, pinging with messages from Darien and Pharaoh.

Darien was irritated with Pharaoh, who refused to wear the clothes from the Ram's Headline that had been picked out for him for the photo shoot, and he wanted her to talk to him. Pharaoh was irritated with Darien, but he wanted her to know that he would go along with the request just for her. She replied to both in a text message.

Okay.

Opening a window on her screen, she reviewed sales projections on the songs "Daddy's Gone, Girl" and "Love's Fury." Based on sales, they were on track with current releases to ship the compilation project platinum. She planned to share the good news with Miles, but in the meantime, she finished returning messages. Alerts from various social media sites began popping up on her screen. She clicked on a few of them with the titles, *Doing double duty: Dancers at AriMusic are Miles Moore sex slaves* and *Ari will never change his ways*. Most of the articles were misleading and sensational reports amounting to lies. She recognized that the pictures were at least five years old, when Miles admittedly had an active social life with multiple women in the entertainment industry.

"I wonder why they're being recycled now?" She raised an eyebrow as she checked the IP address of several of the pictures. Most of them were coming from the same location. She made a mental note to talk to Bradley to check out who was behind this newest smear campaign.

"Hi, Bella." Reagan knocked on the door, which was ajar. "You're busy?"

"Always, but come in." She smiled at Reagan and waved her into the office.

Reagan looked behind her before closing the door. "I'm not one to spread gossip, but you should know Pharaoh has a crush on you." Reagan barely contained her laughter. "Do you think anyone in their right mind would believe he could drive a wedge between you and Miles?"

"Don't believe the things you hear, Reagan." Bella maintained a blank expression. "You know Pharaoh is a natural flirt. That's all."

"I wouldn't even bother you with this, but the second part of the rumor is that the two of you were caught kissing here in the studio."

Shit. Bella stopped typing and stared at Reagan. "Where did you hear this?"

Reagan raised a hand in the air, rotating her wrist. "Girl, let me tell you." She leaned forward. "A housekeeper supposedly saw the two of you, who told another housekeeper, and it got back to Mr. Curtis, their boss. He fired their asses last week, on the spot, for being nuisances to good order, but not before the damage was done."

"I'm not sure why people are trying to cause trouble...for Pharaoh." Bella averted her gaze. "Especially now, after he's been trying so hard to be a team player."

"Speaking of team..." Reagan cleared her throat. "Have you seen the company Pharaoh has been keeping? The pictures of him rolling with Dark's crew have been coming up a lot. Dark is bad news, Bella."

"I've heard he's a bottom feeder in the industry, but we're trying to give Pharaoh more space." Bella swallowed the hard lump in her throat.

"He should know better. Dark and his group are bad news." She crossed her arms. "He promises the world and by the time you figure out he's a liar, it's too late. Anyway, I think you should tell Miles about the rumors before they get to him."

"What do you think will happen if I tell Miles that the rumors are true?" Their gazes locked.

Bella watched as Reagan's jaw dropped before covering her mouth with her hand.

"Miles would fire his ass. That's if he doesn't first get arrested for killing him. It's true he kissed you?"

"Pharaoh caught me off guard and kissed me on the cheek, but I pulled away." Bella blew out a deep sigh. "That was many months ago and he hasn't tried anything since then."

"So why is this surfacing now?" Reagan's phone buzzed before Bella could answer. "I've got to get back to the recording room. Me and Pele got a late session scheduled for tonight." She rose from the chair as Bella came from around the desk for a hug.

Looking toward the door while she hugged Reagan, Bella couldn't answer the question. She knew she needed to find out before things blew up in her face.

"Bye, Bella." Reagan waved as she left the room.

"Bye, Reagan." She waved back. Her thoughts raced, occupied with possible reasons. Someone wanted to create trouble for Pharaoh and between her and Miles.

Looking at her schedule, she saw that she'd planned to set some time aside that week to talk to Pharaoh. He was still wasting too much time partying instead of writing songs. Reagan was right. The company he was keeping was another problem.

Closing her eyes, she rubbed her forehead. She wasn't sure how she would approach Miles with the news.

After shutting down her computer, she headed for the door. Time to put her big girl panties on and face the music.

Chapter 10

M iles looked forward to playing with the twins, but his evening of personal time had been shortened by his delay in getting home. Instead of eating dinner, he headed straight for the nursery. As usual, the twins had begun smiling and cooing as soon as they'd seen him enter the room. They delighted in spending time with their father just as much as he did. After the babies were sound asleep, Bella snuggled with Miles, the two enjoying their ritual of talking to each other before dropping off to sleep.

She laid her head on his chest and played with the light dusting of hair on his pecs. "Were you thinking about me when you wrote 'Daddy's Gone, Girl?'" Her words were slightly slurred.

Miles raised an eyebrow and lowered his head, focusing on her reddened eyes. "No, I was reflecting on how many of the women in AriMusic weren't raised by their fathers. During a recent talk, Pharaoh also mentioned that he hadn't dated many women who'd had fathers in their lives. Can you imagine what it's like to wake up every day and know that your father lived in the same country as you, looked up at the same sun, but made no attempt to be a part of your life?"

"I'm sure it's painful to feel abandoned and not know why your father left. I lost my father, …but I never felt abandoned by him." A tear fell down her cheek.

"That's the same thing Pharaoh said. He didn't seem so angry when we talked. I'll tell you something, Bella, Pharaoh is talented, but he's also tiring." He watched as her mouth opened and heavy eyelids slowly descended. "Is there something wrong?"

"No, just tired." She rubbed her eyes. "I might have had a few more glasses of wine than I usually drink while I waited for you to get home."

It's not like her to drink more than one glass on a weekday.

"How much did you have to drink?" He knitted his brow.

"Maybe two or three little glasses." She held up three fingers.

He buried his lip between his teeth. "You sent a text that there was something you wanted to talk about." He held her tighter. "I'm all ears. Talk to me."

"This should be the happiest time of our lives, Miles." She choked on her words. "We have two happy, healthy babies. Our artists are enjoying chart-topping sales." She raised her head, focusing on his eyes. "Kiss me."

He placed his hands on her face, tenderly cupping her cheeks, and inclined his head. Pressing his lips to hers, he connected with her tenderly before deepening the kiss, enjoying the smooth feeling of her mouth. He didn't let go until they were both breathless.

"Do you know that I love you?" She placed her hands around his neck.

"Yes, I know that, but I also feel something is bothering you." He sighed and loosened her from his embrace. Lying on his pillow, he placed his hands under his head and stared at her. Within seconds, she was asleep. He remained awake, listening to the steady rhythm of her breathing.

Miles gazed at his beautiful wife resting in the comfort of their bed. A smile spread across his face. No matter the problems they faced, he couldn't believe his good fortune. Wasn't he the man who ran from family? The same one who wanted nothing to do with the trappings of family life? Things had changed after he met Bella. He once saw family life as an obligation, an institution set up to persecute those with nonconformist views, and the source of creative suffocation. He felt none of that with Bella and he didn't want things to change between the two of them. She had always encouraged him to embrace the man he was without making excuses or spotlighting his shortcomings.

Maybe she'll remember to tell me what's going on in the morning, after she sleeps off the alcohol. He turned over, feeling drowsy. "It'll be better if we deal with whatever is bothering her in the morning."

Chapter 11

The Cannibals

Cannibals have always existed among the human species.
They're not just flesh eaters.
Instead, they devour your spirit,
chew on your enthusiasm.
Nibble on your dreams,
suck out your zest for life.
They're the source of strife.

Siphoning your energy,
Draining your vitality.
Doing everything they can,
to derail the Master's plan
of Joy for every man,
that's the Master's plan.

CHORUS

Who's your Hannibal?
Cuz he's a cannibal.
Master of the intangible,
he's an animal.

Lyrics by Lil' Pharaoh

For several weeks, Pharaoh's behavior was above reproach. He agreed to all of the changes Miles suggested on his track "Cannibals," including when Miles told him to record the verses in a narrative voice and freestyle on the chorus. He told Miles he didn't have that in mind when he'd written the song, but he did it anyway. His only request was that they complete the track before he agreed to appear in a public-service announcement for an urban cable network.

It was a long night of taping. With the exception of a few studio engineers making final touches to "Cannibals," very few staff members reported in that morning.

Miles had a light breakfast at work and had signed several contracts with venues for the American leg of Pele's tour when his door flew open. An angry Lil' Pharaoh stormed in and stood in front of his desk, looking disheveled in a wrinkled, partially unbuttoned shirt. His eyes were bloodshot, probably from a night of drinking with friends.

The honeymoon was over. Lil' Pharaoh's reckless ways had returned.

"Why does Pele get to go to Hawaii to film their video, but you're sending me to South Carolina to film mine? I don't even want to *do* 'Between the Dusk and the Dawn.' I don't get what you're trying to say." He paused. "Why don't you do the song and I'll do another one of my songs? I'm trying to get along with you, but I have to draw the line somewhere. I should get to go to Hawaii and have some fun. *I'm* the star at AriMusic, not Pele."

Miles took a deep breath before answering his questions. He was trying to get along with Lil' Pharaoh, too, but it was time he redrew some lines.

"Pharaoh, don't ever try this stunt again."

"What do you mean?" Pharaoh stumbled as he looked around for a chair, reeking of alcohol.

"Don't *ever* burst into my office again. Yes, you're a successful recording star with AriMusic, but you'll never disrespect me. Do you understand me?"

Pharaoh jerked his chin upward to acknowledge he heard him and slouched in his chair.

"I need to hear you say this is the last day you're going to come in here with some bullshit."

"Fine. No more bullshit, but I need to know why you made the decisions you made. I don't think you respect me."

Miles suspected that either of the singers, Latifah or Myoshi, had shared the news with Lil' Pharaoh during pillow talk. He'd heard rumors Pharaoh was sleeping with one of the members of Pele. The plans to send them to Hawaii had only been announced late last night, as a marketing strategy, since the group was named for the Hawaiian goddess of fire. They'd been excited, squealing with delight after he broke the news.

"Pharaoh, the Sea Islands – especially the islands off South Carolina – are considered historically gruesome Ellis Islands for African Americans. The lyrics of the song reflect on the experience of an African coming to America. I've assigned the song to you because of your strong vocals and because I felt you could deliver the depth of feelings the song needed. I told you I don't just see you singing about thuggin' or partying. The song will expand your repertoire early in your career, and I think it'll resonate with your fans. I'm trying to lay down tracks that'll reflect your expected growth as an artist. Trust me, you'll want to expand your fanbase, and songs like 'Between the Dusk and the Dawn' will show that you're capable of handling a wide range of topics." He kept his voice tones even.

"And, Pharaoh, I'll say this again. You should try harder to avoid mixing business and pleasure. It's clear to me that you're sleeping with someone in Pele."

Pharaoh rose in his seat and braced himself by gripping the arms of the chair. His speech was mildly garbled and venomous spittle flew as he spoke.

"Back up," Miles warned him. Immediately, Pharaoh maintained his distance.

"What I do with Latifah is *my* business. I don't tell you what to do with Bella. I don't interfere with you and Bella. I'm a man just like you. I let you handle your business, so you should let me handle mine."

Miles looked at him as if he was seeing him for the first time, undaunted by Pharaoh's hostility and poor judgment. It wasn't just the alcohol talking. Pharaoh needed help beyond his capacity to give.

For now, Miles decided it was best not to stoke the flames of Pharaoh's irrational anger.

"Maybe you could use some time off. We've all put in a lot of work trying to get the compilation project completed. I can have my assistant cancel some of your appearances. Talking to a professional about the stress of the industry can be helpful."

"Naw, naw. I can handle it," Pharaoh said gruffly, calming down a bit. "I'll do your PSA, but I want to go back to the old neighborhood. They're having a block party next week. Maybe being around my people, hangin' out and relaxin', is just what I need."

"I was talking about giving you some time off, maybe with your family somewhere outside of the city. I've seen too many folks in this business get caught up in drugs and the party scene. In addition to time with your family, I'm more than happy to arrange for you to spend some time at a facility where you can have around the clock access to a therapist. Don't worry. We have arrangements with places that will protect your privacy."

Pharaoh got up to leave. "Naw, I can handle my own problems. I can stop drinking any time I want. I think the block party and some dancing will do me good. I'll tell them to set up a booth where I can look down on the people, maybe at a park where we can maintain the distance you're always preaching about." He turned and exited without saying good-bye.

Miles shook his head and massaged his jaw. It was constantly tight from his conflicts with Pharaoh.

That evening, just as he promised, Pharaoh was ready for the taping of the public service announcement. He slept off the alcohol during the day and reported to the studio on time for the taping. Looking over the music sheet, he stepped up and took the mic with confidence.

Chapter 12

After spending the entire day before with the twins, Bella had to catch up with work at the office. She delighted that they were now calling her "Mama" often in their sweet little voices. She loved the laughter of her children. The first day she heard them say the word, her heart felt like it would burst with love, overflowing.

"Mama. Mama."

Taking them into her arms, she showered them with kisses. She knew what it was like to be loved and love others, but nothing had prepared her for the warmth of feeling or the joy of hearing the word while being surrounded by her babies. They had also grown fond of some of their stuffed animals in the last month. She giggled when they both extended their little pudgy arms and spread their fingers.

"Figgo, Mama," they both uttered as they crawled in front of her.

She turned around and there were two stuffed bears her mother had given them, dressed in fireman uniforms, on the

73

floor. "Is this what you want?"

She placed the bears on their laps. Bright smiles spread across their faces. She joined them in clapping and repeating what she thought were the names for their toys. "Figgo."

It had been a great day to fill her soul with their love instead of dealing with the conflicts of the adults in her life. Carmen had come in to prepare them for their naps before she got ready for work. *Back to the grind.*

She lifted her head off the page of sales data she was studying at the sound of Lil' Pharaoh's loud voice demanding to speak to her. Miles had insisted she hire an assistant after her uncomfortable meeting with a few of the new prospects who weren't given a contract they desired. She liked that her new assistant, Josi, handled her calls and managed her schedule.

But Lil' Pharaoh hadn't met Josi yet and wasn't familiar with Josi's new role. And, from the sounds of things, their first meeting wasn't going well. Bella rose from her desk to address the situation brewing outside her office. She opened the door and saw Lil' Pharaoh pointing his finger at Josi, who was standing in defiance of his demands.

"It's okay, Josi. I'll see Pharaoh now."

Josi moved to the side to allow Pharaoh to pass by her.

"What's up with Girl Friday? I'm a busy man. I don't have time for her. We need to talk about my appearances. I don't like the schedule Miles has planned for me."

"Pharaoh, Josi has a job to do, and I'd appreciate it if you didn't make things difficult for her. If you need to speak to me, she'll make sure it happens. I'm busy, too. She's just trying to help me maintain some order in my day." She took a breath before continuing. She hated being caught in the middle of two men with big personalities yet again, with one of them being her husband.

"Miles knows what he's doing. I'm sure he's explained his vision for your career to you."

"I thought you'd say that. You always take his side."

"It's not about taking sides, Pharaoh. The fact of the matter is we both work for an organization named AriMusic." She didn't think she needed to remind him directly that her name was Bella Moore, wife of Miles "Ari" Moore.

"Miles told me he wanted me to go to the Carolinas instead of Hawaii."

"Yes, I plan to take the twins to see their relatives in North Carolina. I'll be spending some time with you while the video is taped."

He calmed down and crossed his legs. She sensed he was satisfied with the news.

"There are plenty of resorts in the Carolinas for you and your family to enjoy. Charlotte is also a vibrant city with plenty to do. I can arrange to get you VIP tickets to some of their professional sporting events."

"Now you talkin', girl." He grinned playfully, a look that was as much a curse as it was a gift.

Trouble, she thought as he flashed his wickedly delicious smile. She knew it had attracted the attention of too many women. She raised an eyebrow as she smelled alcohol mixed with the cover of peppermint.

"While you're here, let's discuss the plans for your appearance at your neighborhood block party – which, all things considered, should not be a block party. Instead, I've made arrangements for a limo. You and your mother will go early in the day, stay for about half an hour to meet a select few of your lucky fans, then go home."

"Thanks, but I won't need a limo. I plan to go to a gathering at night. The block party was cancelled."

"I don't recommend that. You have to get used to taking control of your time and stop this attitude of 'I'll see what happens.' I don't want to throw it in your face, but it hasn't been that long since we got you out of that mess at the apartment downtown. That was a PR nightmare. We're still paying the owner of the club and witnesses to keep you out of the media. I don't want to remind the public of that incident."

"I'm taking my mom and my aunts to the gathering. They're worse than you when it comes to suffocating me." He laughed, but his light-hearted demeanor ended when Miles entered the office. "I guess Josi doesn't make everybody knock on the door or make an appointment to see you," he said loudly enough for Miles to hear.

"Josi wasn't at her desk. And no, I don't need an appointment to see my wife." He turned his attention to Bella, who was still seated behind her desk.

Pharaoh didn't look back or greet Miles.

"Babe, I just wanted to tell you I'll be here late tonight, so don't wait for me for dinner. I have a meeting with Darien and Parker. You're welcome to join us, but I'll still need to check in on Pele's taping session tonight."

"Okay, honey. I'm working late, too. My mother is in town. She wants more time with the babies and they'll be spending the night with her. I don't want to commit to another meeting today, so I probably won't be there." Bella looked at her desk and waved her hands over the papers piled high.

"I see your desk is in need of a little tidying up. I'd be glad to help you clear it." He arched his brows.

She bit her lip and briefly closed her eyes, savoring the memory of him taking her on top of a similar desk.

She smiled when she saw that his pants were tented by

his hardening member. He shoved his hands in his pockets right before Pharaoh turned his head and scowled at him as if tasting something sour. At the same time, Bella felt the tingle of an electric charge growing between her and Miles.

"See you later. Love you," he said, and winked before leaving the room.

"I love you, too." She smiled and blew him a kiss.

Pharaoh looked at her and didn't speak until Miles closed the door. His eyes were drawn to narrow slits. The scowl hadn't left his face.

"*Love you*, babe," he said, mocking Miles. "Are you blind to him?"

She pointed to the nameplate on her desk to remind him of her relationship with his boss. "No, Pharaoh, I'm not blind to him, but I *am* married to him – and deeply in love."

"Bella, I've seen his type in this business. They only love you as long as they need you. I know I'm out of line, but men like Miles always have a sidepiece. Maybe not now, but trust me, he's no different than any of the other moguls in this city."

She shook her head in disbelief. He was young and misguided, but she could no longer deny Pharaoh had feelings for her, and his feelings were inappropriate.

"Bella, sorry for the interruption." Josi peeked her head into the office. "Andrew Caughman, one of Miles's new assistants, is here with some papers you need to review and sign."

"Send him in." She held up a finger for Pharaoh to stop talking while Andrew made his way to her desk. "Hi, Andrew, what do you have for me?" She turned to the young man dressed in business attire.

"A few things that demand your attention." He smiled. "Sorry for the interruption." He handed Bella the papers. "You've already reviewed the first contract. It's ready for your signature." He pointed to the paper while Pharaoh resumed talking.

"Don't get mad at me. I didn't invent the game. I'm just telling you how it's played. You may be number one, but that doesn't stop Miles from having a number two." He shrugged as the scowl on his face softened. "Don't say I didn't warn you."

Andrew's jaw dropped. He turned and looked at Pharaoh.

"Pharaoh, that's enough." She slammed her hands on the desk. "Your slights on Miles's character are unacceptable."

"Fine." He rose and stumbled while walking to the door. His mocking tone returned as he turned the knob and mimicked Miles again. *"Love you, Bella."*

She sat there, stunned, as he walked out the door and didn't look back.

Signing the contract in a hurry, she gave it to Andrew.

"Thank you." He took the contract and left, closing the door behind him.

She needed time to gather her thoughts. The situation between her and Pharaoh had taken a turn for the worse. Bigger problems were looming, like how to tell Miles without incurring his wrath that she'd waited to share concerns about Pharaoh she could no longer blame on the alcohol.

Chapter 13

Miles wasn't surprised Bella hadn't made the executive meeting with Darien and Parker, although he hoped she had cleared her schedule to attend. In the interim, something else had come up. He needed to talk to her about what Andrew shared with him after the meeting.

"Is Bella still there, Josi?" His call had rolled over to Josi's desk after Bella didn't pick up.

"No, she packed up her things and told me she was leaving for the day."

"All right, thanks." He hung up and pondered his next move. "Hey, babe." His voice was lighthearted as he practiced. "You'll never guess what happened today." He pursed his lips.

"Hey, babe," he said again, his tone darker. He didn't want to sound accusatory, but he believed Andrew. "You'll never guess what happened today. Something Andrew told me," he spoke out loud. He wanted to get his point across that Pharaoh's behavior was unacceptable without blaming her for it.

"Might as well get it over with. I'll call her on her cell."

She answered on the first ring. "Hey, Miles." Her voice was cheerful, but there was something that rubbed him the wrong way. Before he could temper his response, his anger took control.

"I'm not going to tolerate this shit any longer." He placed the phone on speaker. The volume of his voice was loud and the tone harsh.

"What are you talking about?" Her tone had changed in response to his anger. "I've had a hard day and I don't appreciate you coming at me like this."

He paused and closed his eyes. "Were you going to tell me about the stunt Pharaoh pulled today?"

Bella was silent.

"Let me fill you in." He frowned. His impatience didn't allow more time for her to answer. "Andrew told me that Pharaoh was insinuating that I was having an affair," he roared. "A damn *affair* and you sat there listening. The man accused me on my turf." He ran his fingers through his hair. "In my office and in the studio I built."

More silence before she responded. "I'm not going to deny that he said something to that effect." The sound of her breath was audible. He sensed she was trying to mute her anger. "Did Andrew also tell you that Pharaoh had a smell of alcohol on his breath?"

He was quick to respond. "No more excuses, Bella. This isn't about Andrew. It's about us."

"Tell me what you thought I should have done." Her volume was louder and higher pitched. "Snap my fingers and make him disappear?" He heard the snapping sound of her fingers. "You've always said that we live in a city of fallen

80

angels. Why does it surprise you that Pharaoh is flawed? I admit, deeply flawed."

"We are all members of the fallen, but neither guilt nor rescue fantasies are going to make me bear the burden of his flaws any longer. He betrayed me and you didn't support me. He's out."

"Place me on Facetime," she demanded. "I want us to look at each other before we go down a path of no return."

He turned on the video and placed the phone on a stand.

"Didn't you say that you went out on your own path because you wanted to make a difference?"

He shrugged in response.

"You could have rested on the laurels of your father's fame as a jazz artist, but you created your own space in the music scene."

"What does that have to do with what we're discussing now?"

"Everything, Miles." She drew her hands up in fists. "You told me when I came to work at AriMusic that you planned on signing a few talented artists that other agencies may not have given a chance. You were tired of seeing some young actors and singers in Los Angeles get countless chances to stay in the game, while others were lucky to get one strike before they were out. I told you there were lots of reasons why that happened, but remember this. I haven't betrayed your vision." She swallowed hard, struggling to get out her words. Tears rolled down her cheek. "I also never believed you were having an affair. I know how to tune out the noise."

"What do you expect of me?" He leaned closer to the screen. "I'm tired of this man-child's disrespect."

"This is your business, as you've reminded me today. You decide."

He listened as she took her time speaking.

"He's the artist you signed. You asked for it." She paused again. "You got it. Face the fire, Miles. Goodbye." The screen went blank.

"Dammit, Bella," he yelled at the dead connection. He placed his hands over his ears. He felt alone and abandoned. Thoughts of their conversation ran through his head. He looked at the bar with every drink imaginable. "I need to get out of here." This wasn't the time to drown himself in sorrow.

Chapter 14

Miles didn't want to go home, especially after the blow-up with Bella. He put some papers he had to review later that night in his satchel before heading over to the recording booth. He had planned to share with Bella his decision to join the first leg of the tour with Lil' Pharaoh and Pele in multiple U.S. cities, with the goal of promoting the compilation project. His participation would last for only two to three weeks, but he wasn't sure how she'd take the news. The two of them hadn't been apart for more than a couple days since the beginning of her pregnancy with the twins. The decision had come up earlier in the week, but to share it now would only make things worse between them.

Reagan stood at the mic and smiled as Miles entered the room. She'd written the song "Pastimes" and Miles wanted to reward her.

"Your writing on 'Pastimes' was superb and since you have strong lead vocals on the song, I think we should market it under the name *Pele featuring Reagan Madison.*

FACE THE FIRE

"What do you think about that, Latifah and Myoshi?"

"Our girl hit it out the park with that performance," Latifah remarked.

"She should get the credit she deserves," Myoshi added.

He found it refreshing when his decisions regarding Pele weren't met with discord. He didn't know how much more conflict he could tolerate with Lil' Pharaoh. He took his seat and signaled to Reagan that the recording session had begun.

She was a gifted singer who could infuse her emotions into her renditions and reach the hearts of others. Observing her process, he relaxed as she closed her eyes and sang into the mic.

An ode to the past,
a time that didn't last.
It happened once,
but you hit rewind.
Over and over
in your mind.
That's the sign,
you're a slave to the past,
a time that didn't last.

Too many memories,
flowing down like rain.
Bombarding you,
terrorizing you,
drivin' you insane.

Your hope is in today,
for a love that's here to stay.
Not with those who did you wrong

MICHELE SIMS

Those days are long gone
Those days are long gone

Lyrics by Reagan Madison

He stood and applauded the women of Pele as they jumped up and down and hugged each other. They had created magic that night – they were able to capture the essence of what he wanted to convey in the collaboration project in just one take. He knew the women of Pele were aware that by working together, they were creatively stronger as a group, meaning they'd be able to support each other's aspirations as future solo artists.

He put his hands on his hips, finally accepting the truth as he sat in the control booth by himself.

Despite his efforts, Lil' Pharaoh wasn't going to get it. Miles would stick with his agreement to let him begin work on his own album, starting with the song "Incomparable," but it would be his last project with his protégé. Bella was right. He had signed the contract with Pharaoh with his eyes wide open. As a child, Pharaoh needed direction. Sadly, as an adult, he was misguided.

"I can't do it anymore," he uttered. "I've done all I can for Pharaoh, but we've got too much money already tied up in the Carolina shoot. It's too late to cancel at this point." He scratched his head and decided he'd shift his focus to Pele. He texted Bella. Their last conversation still weighed heavily on his mind.

I'm sorry. Please forgive me.

She didn't respond.

Chapter 15

Miles went home two hours later, tired from another long week. He wasn't looking forward to accompanying Pele to Hawaii, away from Bella and the kids, but he needed to take care of business.

While preparing a drink before bed, he received a text from one of his execs, Brian, who had been working on another project. He said he'd been able to finish his project with his assigned artist earlier than anticipated. He had also confirmed agreements with the video company in Hawaii. The plans for the musicians, make-up, and wardrobe people were set and ready to go.

Before requesting his assistance with the Pele video shoot, Miles had only ever assigned Brian to smaller projects. He was impressed by his willingness to show initiative and by his organizational skills.

Miles: Thanks, Brian. I appreciate everything you've done to make the project a success.

Brian: No problem, boss. Goodnight.

His phone buzzed. It was Bradley. He took a big gulp of his drink. "This can't be good."

He answered the phone. "What's up?"

"Bad news, boss."

"Let me guess. Pharaoh. What's he done this time?"

"I'll give you the short version," Bradley sighed. "Pharaoh was at one of the clubs owned by Dark Nyland – you know, the gangster turned entrepreneur. He has a recording company now. He invited a few rappers, including Lil' DQ from the East Coast. Well, things got a little heated between Pharaoh and DQ on stage. DQ accused him of consoling and taking advantage of Bella after she found out you had a side-piece."

"Shit. Just when I thought Pharaoh was already bouncing on the bottom." He raised his voice. "What was he doing on the stage with DQ?"

"You know he likes to grab the spotlight," Bradly answered and snorted.

"How in the hell did Bella get dragged into this?"

"Pictures of the two of them coming from one of his publicity shoots. The shots are innocent, but in one of them, he looks like he's crushing on her. Anyway, Pharaoh asked DQ in a rhyme what's the big deal? Because he's also been sleeping with his wife at the same time."

"I'll bet it broke loose after that," Miles responded and fell back into one of the seats in his home office before grabbing his drink.

"The bouncers had to intervene, but not before Pharaoh ignited a new round of an East Coast-West Coast beef. We're ramping up security at the studio and around your home. Vehicles with out-of-state tags have been spotted casing the neighborhood. We're running the tags now."

"Thanks for alerting me." He rubbed his cheek.

"It's a good thing you were planning to send Bella and the kids to North Carolina. I'll ramp up security to travel with them."

"I'll let Bella know what happened later this morning. She's in bed now."

"She probably already knows about the brawl in the club." Bradley paused. "As the head of marketing and media, she gets all the alerts on incidents involving the artists that cast a negative light on our organization."

"You're right." He scratched his head. "It wouldn't surprise me if she already has decided how to spin this. I'll talk to you later, after I've gotten some rest."

"This mess is getting old, Miles."

"I know, Bradley. Bye."

He finally crawled into bed early in the morning, hours before dawn. The room was dark, and Bella now lay asleep beneath the covers in her bright-red lace bra and thong set. He spooned next to her, enjoying the warmth of her soft body and how well they fit together.

She stretched and rubbed her eyes.

"I'm sorry," he whispered in her ear. "Please forgive me."

"I forgive you." She muffled a yawn. "If you forgive me for trying for months to handle Pharaoh on my own. I guess you heard about his latest escapade at Dark's club?"

"Escapade? I was thinking it was more of a fiasco." He spoke softly as she smiled against his lips.

"I'm going to surprise you by letting Pharaoh feel the heat this time. If he comes to the Carolina shoot, fine. If not, he can stay and face the consequences by himself. His choice." She wiggled her butt against his growing erection.

He understood that not only did Pharaoh need to learn a

lesson, but he needed to back off a little too. Besides, he had talked to Bradley, who had tightened their security.

"Really?" He widened his eyes. "That's music to my ears." He wrapped strands of her hair around his fingers. "Can I get some tonight?"

She yawned. "Who's stopping you?"

He smiled. "Better hold tight, babe. I'm needing it hard and rough."

He cupped her breast with one hand and tested her heat with the other. Discovering she was wet with desire, he pulled her thong to the side and entered her without further delay. Grabbing her hips and pushing into her with such force, he had to keep a hand on her to prevent them from rolling off the bed. Lifting her legs, he repositioned himself to deliver maximum pleasure then filled her until they were both sweating and panting for a release of sexual tension. Afterward, he held her close and stroked her hair, which was damp against her cheeks. Remaining in a warm embrace, he caught his breath.

She smiled, her body now limber and relaxed as she cuddled into the planes of his chest and drifted off into a deep sleep.

Rumors questioning their love for each other had always swirled around them, since the day they married. He had to admit that some of them had injured his male pride, but he knew the truth. No one had the power to come between them. He trusted her with his heart and soul.

Chapter 16

At the last minute, Miles was able to join Bella and the twins in North Carolina while Brian accompanied Pele to Hawaii to film their music videos. Lil' Pharaoh wasn't enthused when he heard Miles would be joining them, but Miles planned to leave the making of the "Between the Dusk and the Dawn" video to the director and the small creative team assigned to work with Lil' Pharaoh.

Bella was quickly preparing to attend Lil' Pharaoh's video shoot. Tired from their third night of partying with the Moore clan, she'd woken up one hour later than she'd intended to get ready. Since their arrival in North Carolina, she'd had less quiet time with the twins, which was beginning to show on all of them. It concerned her that the babies had become cranky from being passed around to so many relatives.

"Good morning." Miles woke up after she got up. It was unusual for him to stay in bed later than she did. He threw back the covers, revealing his thick morning wood. After pointing to it, he flexed his well-toned chest and placed his hands behind his head.

"Good morning. Stop tempting me, Miles. You know I'm running late."

"That wouldn't be a problem if you hadn't given Carmen and Ms. Burnside the morning off."

"We can handle the twins. Besides, the nannies need time off, too," she said snippily.

Right on cue, the twins started crying in the next room.

"They've gotten plenty of time off since we arrived in Charlotte. There's always someone around here ready to help with them."

"Please go get them. I don't want the babies to wake up the entire house. Ariana is more patient than Ashe during their morning feedings, but he can't wait to be fed when he's hungry," she reminded him as their cries grew louder and more distressed.

"Okay, let me throw something on." Rushing to get into his pajama bottoms, he heard her phone ringing on the desk.

"Hello." She knew it could only be Lil' Pharaoh, so she activated the speaker to talk to him while she looked around the room for her shoes.

His voice immediately filled the room. "Bella, I'm not wearing rags and looking like no slave."

She turned her head in time to see Miles's fists tightening at his sides and his lips drawing tight. Fearing he was about to explode into a volcanic tirade, she said quickly, "Hold on, Pharaoh," and pressed the mute button.

"I. Am. So. Damn. Tired of his shit. Who in the hell told him he had to wear rags or act like a slave? There's always some drama with—" He broke off his tirade after they both realized the babies were growing more distressed in the next room and screaming.

"Miles, please go get the babies while I finish this call with Pharaoh." She tilted her head to the side. "Please? Let me handle this."

He stomped out of the room, and she returned her attention to the phone.

"Pharaoh, there's no need to worry about that. No one will ask you to wear rags. Your presence in the video is the backdrop for the actors playing out the scenes. There will be actors in traditional regal African garb, as well as actors who will be cast as people held in captivity on the ship. I can assure you, you're not one of the actors. You'll only be in scenes in which you're walking down the beach. I'll be there later today. We can have further discussions at that time."

"Why are you still on the phone with him?" Miles returned, holding one twin under each arm, their faces red and tearstained.

Ashe whimpered and reached for Bella as soon as they entered the room. He grabbed her bra as she took him.

"Pharaoh, I have to go," she told him as she cradled Ashe in her arms. She hung up while Ashe eagerly nursed as she continued to walk around the room instead of sitting down and focusing her attention on feeding him.

Both she and Ashe grew frustrated as she looked for her shoes.

He jerked his head back, stretching her sensitive nipple.

"Ouch," she yelled.

"Ashe, did you hurt Mommy?" Miles chided him in a loud voice.

Ariana, who was being held by him, closed her tearful eyes and spiraled into a state of sadness with quivering lips. As Ashe turned his head and saw his angry father's face, he loosened his grip on his mother's breast and convulsed in tears.

"You're scaring the children, when the person you're really mad at is me." She sat down and tried to comfort Ashe. "Please give Ariana to me. I need to just stop what I'm doing and feed my children."

"I'm not angry with you. Give Ashe back to me and allow me to make this right. I need to comfort my son." He reached for Ashe, who fretfully clung to Bella and whined as his father took him and cradled both of his children.

Ariana, who'd stopped crying, stared into his face, as if searching for familiarity between the man who'd just yelled at them and the tender, loving daddy she adored.

He kissed her forehead with a loud smack, causing her to giggle.

Observing the scene between his father and sister, Ashe calmed down and also got a loud juicy smack on the forehead as he squealed with delight.

"Mommy, can we get some Mommy-and-me time?" Miles asked on behalf of the children.

She positioned herself on the bed to resume feeding them and they greeted her with smiles after returning to her arms.

Watching Miles, she knew he'd had enough. She understood he could no longer coddle Pharaoh while yelling at his children in frustration over ongoing conflicts with a man-child. She needed to support him in the plans to end their professional relationship. She knew it was going to happen soon.

Chapter 17

Miles kept his word and didn't interfere in the taping of the video. Brian had arranged for a limo to transport Bella to the shoot off the coast of Sullivan's Island while Miles stayed in North Carolina with the twins. Before the shoot, she met with the team and was assured Pharaoh wouldn't be playing the part of a slave. The crew had hired a 19th century-style ship for the video to slowly travel toward the shore as they filmed Lil' Pharaoh walking along the beach. The director gave him cues, and the camera began rolling while he sang the lyrics.

Somewhere along the way, his ego became less of a problem as he began to understand the meaning of the song. On his third take, his voice became more dramatic, and he delivered the words with passion. She looked on, saddened that despite his huge talent and their previously close relationship, there was little hope for a lasting association between Pharaoh and AriMusic.

MICHELE SIMS

In between the dusk
and the dawn,
I see what you see,
I feel what you feel,
lost in a dream
that can't be real.

Sweating, I'm nervous,
despair and fear,
surrounding us,
drowning us,
on this long, dark journey
to a new world of sour milk
and little honey.

1787, and it's
We the people,
clearly self- evident that
All men are created equal.

1955,
Rosa took a seat,

2016,
Kap doesn't rise to his feet.
In search of liberties,
and answers to tough questions,
many bow,
on bended knees.

The famous,
the nameless,

FACE THE FIRE

murdered, gone.
Lost between the dusk and the dawn.
Hate, never the answer
or the cure for a cancer.

Hope and change.
Concepts so strange?
In the land of the free and
home of the brave.

Politicos alone
can't clean up this mess.
The Berlin Wall or no other wall
can't stop others from
life, liberty, and the pursuit of happiness.

In between the dusk
and the dawn,
I see,
the promise of America,
the mosaic,
a kaleidoscope,
a beautiful tapestry.

Lyrics by Miles

The sun was starting to set, and the tides rose along the stretch of beach. Bella stood at the shores of the Atlantic Ocean, soaking in the smell of salt in the air, watching the pelicans swoop over the water, and delighting in the small roar of the waves as they approached. Sunlight on the water cast narrow bands of golden shadows that seemed to spotlight where she was standing, but her blissful mood was broken by the water wetting her shoes.

She swept her thick, wind-blown hair off her face, backed away from the tide coming in, and turned to the production crew, who was busy packing up the video equipment before it got wet. Carrying her wet sandals, she walked barefoot toward them to offer congratulations.

She was impressed by how well Seth Cannon, the director, handled Lil' Pharaoh's questions and concerns during the filming while adhering to the safety procedures for the staff. She made a mental note to share her observations with Miles after deciding Seth and his team needed to be assigned to Pharaoh's remaining videos to save the company time and money.

Lil' Pharaoh came up to join them. "I had a good time out here today. I should spend more time at the beach instead of the city. It's relaxing." He turned to Seth. "I already saw some of the shots. I can't wait until you pull it all together. When will the video be ready?"

"I have to edit one more video before I start this one, but I should have it completed very soon. We can get together when we all get back to California. Maybe Miles will approve the funds for a big viewing party. You were great today. I'm excited about this."

Pharaoh smiled and went to talk to some of the actors and dancers in the video, especially one of the dancers he'd had his eyes on during filming.

The crew completed packing just as the sun descended beyond the horizon. After another round of congratulations between the crew, actors, and musicians, everyone was ready to leave. The limo driver came to escort Bella back to her car, but while she was leaving with him, Lil' Pharaoh came running behind them.

"Wait up, Bella. I want to catch a ride back to Charlotte with you. That won't be a problem, will it?"

"Keep the partition window rolled down," she muttered to the driver, then turned her attention back to Pharaoh. "No. I thought we would have time to talk before the shoot, but since I was running late, we can use the time to talk on the drive back. Are you sure you want to ride with me?" She paused. "Full disclosure. Our talk may include some things you don't want to hear."

"Consider me warned." He smiled. "I know how to tune folks out when I don't want to hear what they're saying."

"Fine." She placed a hand behind her neck and massaged it. "Then let's go." *This is going to be a long ride.*

Accustomed to Pharaoh's impulsive nature, she knew he could be unpredictable, but he usually wasn't that intrusive when she had work to do.

The driver approached the car first and opened the door for her.

Pharaoh ran over to the other side and crawled into the back of the limo with her while the driver climbed into the front seat and followed the other cars in the caravan of limos, trucks, and SUVs containing equipment and security person-nel. The progression was slow until they reached the highway leading off the island.

Chapter 18

B ella looked out the window at the beautiful scenery of palm trees, sea oats, and grass blowing in the wind. Closing her eyes briefly, she leaned back against the plush leather headrest until she felt Pharaoh lightly pulling her hair.

Her eyes popped open. "What are you doing?"

"You had something in your hair." He flicked the small debris in his hand onto the floor. "Why are you overreacting?"

She grabbed her bags and began searching through their contents. "Don't act like you're clueless."

"You're making more of this than it is." He leaned his head against the leather upholstery. "I touched Queen Bella." He smirked. "I guess I need to be arrested."

She frowned and continued her search for a hair tie. Running her hands through her tresses, she secured them with the tie she eventually found in her bag.

She drew an imaginary line between them. "Pharaoh, I liked being your publicist when you first came to AriMusic.

You were so eager to learn, and you listened to Miles back then. Our relationship with each other worked because we were friendly and easygoing with each other. You understood that, at its core, we have a *professional* relationship."

He looked away and grabbed his throat. "I'm thirsty."

"There's some water and energy drinks in the cooler." She pointed to the small container located on the floor between them.

He looked inside and grabbed a bottle of water.

"Aren't you going to respond to my comments about your behavior that has been inappropriate? First the kiss and now another reason to touch me?" She pursed her lips and gave him a side-eyed glance.

"I heard you." He rolled his eyes. "We have a professional relationship. Why are you riding back instead of flying on the company's jet?" he asked, still failing to adequately address her concerns.

She opted to remain calm and try another approach with him. "It's so seldom we get back to the Carolinas and I just love viewing the coastal regions. Since we have help with the babies, I wanted to have some time to enjoy the scenery. I didn't know Miles was coming with us instead of going to Hawaii. If I'd known he was coming, I would have flown back, and we could have arranged some time at the beach house in the Outer Banks."

"Oh yeah? So, you all have a place at the beach?"

"His family owns a place. We've enjoyed a little time there together. The views are spectacular." She looked out the window as Pharaoh untwisted the cap on his water bottle.

"I'll bet the view is spectacular." He lowered his eyes and kept his focus on the bottle. "I have something to tell you."

Maybe I'm finally breaking through to him.

"Before I arrived in Charlotte, I stopped in Atlanta and went to a club." He cleared his throat. "A friend of mine suggested that I shouldn't punk out and appear like I was running and hiding after the situation at the club in LA."

"Are you talking about Daryl 'Dark' Nyland?" She turned and faced him. "You consider him a friend? How many times have Miles and I told you he was bad news?"

He gulped down the water and looked straight ahead while she glared at him. She knew she was about to hear the real reason he wanted to ride with her.

He wiped away the excess water from his lips with the back of his hand and looked at her. "Don't look at me like that." He folded his arms across his chest.

"How am I looking at you, Pharaoh?"

"Like you're waiting to hear how I fucked up."

She raised an eyebrow. "I'm surprised I didn't get an alert about your appearance."

"Well, it was private, you know, a closed event." He puffed out his chest. "Dark knows how to keep things on the down-low. It's not in the news if he doesn't want it to make the news."

"So why are you telling me this now?" She folded her arms.

"I did an unplugged version of the song 'For the Young G.' I got caught up."

Her breath hitched. She slowly closed her eyes. She knew she needed a measured response, since it didn't take much for Pharaoh to feel closed in and attacked. She also knew Miles would be furious when he found out Pharaoh had performed a song that they were preparing to release on his solo album at the end of the year without permission from management.

She swallowed hard before she spoke. "Was the performance caught on video?"

He snickered. "Like – yeah? Who would miss the opportunity to film me rapping to them? But like I said, Dark told everybody not to post it."

"So, if you're so assured that Dark is handling things…" She paused. "Why are you telling me?"

"You know why. Your uptight husband doesn't like surprises. There's also the matter that I may cost him money. Dark said I would be safe in his cousin's club, but someone in the audience who rolled with DQ was at the party and fired a shot in the air while I was rapping. There was a little stampede. That wasn't my fault," he quickly added. "Dark said his cousin might send a bill for the damages to the club."

Her phone began buzzing with alerts from anonymous sources posting and describing the scene in the club the night before with snippets of his performance.

"Not this time, Pharaoh. We told you Dark is a silver-tongued conman. The company isn't liable for your screw ups," she snapped. Turning away from him, she cooled her anger with the affirmation, *Stay in control, Bella. You can handle this.* Her heart rate gradually slowed as she looked out at the relaxing scenery.

After taking a deep breath, she resumed the conversation. "The song wasn't ready for release, so yes, AriMusic has wasted funds to begin production on a song you released outside of your contract with the company. After the incident in LA, you'll recall that our lawyer, NeNe, reviewed with you the personal liability you assume when you make appearances that are not approved by me or sanctioned by the company. Since you chose to do it anyway, it will be used as grounds for the termination of your contract." She raised her voice. "So yes, you screwed up, and you can't shift your anger or blame to Miles. This is all on you."

She turned away again, contemplating her next move. She needed to find a way to tell Miles, defuse his rightful anger, and not make things worse by getting more hostile with Pharaoh.

"All this heat you're laying on me is getting me hot and bothered." He reached over to alert the driver to pull over at a convenience store they were approaching.

The driver parked before directing his comment to Pharaoh. "Sir, just let me know what you want, and I'll be happy to get it for you."

"Nah, I can get it myself. Besides, I need some air." He got out of the car, slamming the door behind him.

"Ms. Bella, your husband is expecting us back at a certain time. I'm not sure, but I think he has plans for the two of you this evening. Do we need to contact him and tell him we will be delayed?"

She pulled out her phone. "I'll call him."

She found a link of a video of one of the people who was at the Atlanta club the night before, dressed in dark shades and a ballcap. Shaking her head, she began texting. Meanwhile, a small group of girls had gathered around Pharaoh in the store, screaming and grabbing their phones.

Bella: Don't have much time but check out this link of LP. Need to get ahead of this. Call Darien to help identify the Ram's Head jewelry and clothes that LP and people in the group are wearing. Notify a team in the studio in Cali to put together a quick video that looks like an ad with the song "For the Young G" playing in the background. Talk to you about this later. Got to go.

Miles: Wtf?

Bella: Please just do it and release the ad video as soon as possible. Tell the team not to worry about it being a polished production. There is value to filming as if it were impromptu.

Lil' Pharaoh was able to run away from the group with two bottles of soda in his hands. He grabbed the door handle and slid back into the car.

The driver, who'd remained quiet throughout most of the drive, spoke after starting the car and re-entering traffic. "Mr. Pharaoh, that's what I was trying to avoid. It could be dangerous for you to walk around without the benefit of security or at least one attendant at your side."

"I got this, man." He took a sip of the soda and emptied the bottle before saying anything further to Bella. "We good, Bella?"

"No, but the damage has already been done. I just need to figure out how to handle this."

"I have faith in you, girl. You got this. There's no need for further talk about me leaving AriMusic. We're family." He flashed his megawatt smile.

Pharaoh was accustomed to handling women to get the responses he wanted, but she was in no mood to be handled. He'd created yet another crisis, but she made a promise to herself that she wasn't going to correct all of his errors. She was the chief marketing officer and part-owner of AriMusic, not his babysitter.

Despite her awe at Pharaoh's God-given talent, she saw him as an overgrown kid with emotional demands that rivaled her twin babies. She pulled out her tablet and returned a few more emails to distract herself.

"I think I'm going to take Miles's suggestion and take some time off. My mother wanted to go back to the old neighborhood in Chicago and visit family."

"What did you say, Pharaoh?" she asked, looking up from the tablet in her hands.

"I was telling you about my mom. Now she wants to go to Chicago. We left there when I was very young, but she said my father always dreamed of returning after he made it. I'm living his dream, she said, and now the family wants to share in my success. I'm just letting you know I'll be leaving and taking a few days off. Old friends from the neighborhood in Cali will be joining me there. We plan to hang out and have some fun."

All she could think about was that her problem of providing distance between Pharaoh and Miles was solved, not his safety or whether his decision to return to Chicago was prudent given his recent track record. He would be leaving, and she didn't care where he was going. She would find a way to deal with Miles while he was gone, without the possibility of him making it worse. AriMusic didn't need an epic battle fighting Pharaoh in the courts.

"Thanks for letting me know. We all need time to relax. Have fun."

The remaining hours in the car flew by. Pharaoh could be hilarious when he wanted to be, and she couldn't help laughing at his jokes.

Eventually, she thought it was a good time to slip in a comment about all the trouble he had gotten into without facing a defensive rebuttal. "Pharaoh, I'm not criticizing you, but you need to get your shit together."

"My shi-i-it, Bella? Really, girl? You need to be more

decisive when you say something like that. Say it like, 'Pharaoh, get your *shit* together,' not shi-i-it." He pointed a finger in her face and then laughed.

She tried not to chuckle but ended up covering her mouth.

After mocking her, his gaze showed a serious intent. "I'm working on it."

"Do us both a favor and call me if you need advice about anything. I think it's dangerous that you're depending on Dark for guidance. If you don't watch it, that man will kill your career."

Pharaoh shrugged and took a big swallow of soda.

The driver took Lil' Pharaoh to his rented condo uptown before returning her to the guesthouse at the Moore family estate in the suburbs of Charlotte. It was late, and Bella regretted missing her playtime with the twins.

When she opened the door to the guesthouse, she was hit with the sounds of two babies crying at the top of their lungs. *What is going on?* Heart racing as she ran toward the nursery, she opened the door and saw Miles sitting on the floor with the twins in his arms.

He looked up at her, his clothes wrinkled from the twins fisting his shirt and sighed. "Thank God you're home." He threw his head back and blew the breath out of his cheeks. "We had a great afternoon. They were both tired and went to bed early, so I told the nanny she could have a few hours off since they were both asleep. An hour ago, they both woke up and all hell broke loose."

The twins looked up at her, stopped crying, and smiled.

She lowered herself onto the floor and they both crawled to her. It surprised her that they were both attempting to stand with assistance by pulling their bodies up along her arms. Her babies were growing and getting stronger every day.

They bounced up and down, dancing and playing with her as she blew kisses in their faces.

"I need to pee," Miles told her, getting off the floor. His polo shirt was spotted with food stains and milk. "I think I'll change while I'm at it." He pulled the stained shirt away from his chest and over his head.

Despite her fatigue, she looked at his shirtless body and imagined topping him and caressing his broad chest.

He looked at her and ran his tongue along his lips as her nipples hardened and stood at attention through her blouse.

He smiled. "Remember, it was lust that got us in this current situation."

"What are you talking about, *this situation*? You mean the fact that I get to come home to a loving husband and two beautiful, healthy children? Is that the situation you're referring to?"

He smiled down at her, but the warmth of the moment was soon broken by a foul odor filling the room.

She wrinkled her nose. "Before we get too sentimental, could you get two diapers and help me change the twins?"

"Sure thing." He grabbed Ashe, who was closest to him, and quickly cleaned him up. "Now I *really* have to go pee." With a scowl, he left the room with the two soiled diapers.

"Turn the light down before you leave," she called out.

He returned a few moments later, clad in a fresh shirt, and listened to her singing to the babies as they nursed.

FACE THE FIRE

Texas will always be my home
No matter how far I roam
At home in the saddle
Surrounded by cattle
As far as the eyes can see.
Always ready for battle
To defend my beloved
Homeland
Forever wild
Expansive and free

After she finished singing to the twins, he helped her place them in their cribs. The nanny had returned and told them she would take care of the babies for the remainder of the night.

"Ms. Burnside, my mother overheard the babies yelling over the phone and she told me to let you know she's going to come over and help you."

"Thank her for me, but I'm capable of handling the twins by myself. Nonetheless, I'm sure your parents want to spend as much time with them as they can."

"You're right about that. She insisted I take Bella to the beach at the Outer Banks while we're here." Bella started to open her mouth to protest, but Miles continued, "We need time to talk about some things, and I think we could both use some time at the beach. I know how much you love our beach house, but my mother said the house was rented out this weekend to someone who agreed to pay a lot of money to stay there – even though other holdings were available for a cheaper fee. My grandmother's house is available, and we can stay there tonight and Saturday night while my parents bring the babies to us on Sunday for a couple days of vacationing with the family. Don't you think we could use a break?"

She couldn't argue with the plans.

"The two of you can go get packed," Ms. Burnside encouraged them. "I can handle the babies. We can Facetime you tomorrow. They have plenty of stored milk and I'll have them packed to join you on Sunday."

Miles took Bella by the hand and escorted her to the Porsche parked in front of the driveway. He opened the door for her, making sure she was safely in the car before throwing their bags in the back seat, then got into the driver's seat and ran his hands around the leather-clad steering wheel before starting the car.

"Miles, did you buy this car?"

"It's a rental. Besides, I wouldn't make such a large purchase without first discussing it with you. But I *am* thinking about replacing my old Porsche. I wanted to test-drive this one, so strap yourself in, babe. I'm taking you for a ride."

"You work hard, and you earn a lot of money. It's up to you if you want to purchase a new toy."

"Well, toys are always more fun when you play with others. You know I like to share my toys with you. Someday, I'll share them with my children."

She quietly wondered if it was the right time to discuss the issue that had been hanging over them.

"Do you want to talk about Pharaoh?"

"No. I'm not ready to discuss Baby Pharaoh."

"Baby Pharaoh? When did you start calling him that?"

"I'm only sharing what the other artists call him. Let's just enjoy the ride, and you should get some rest. It's been a long day, and I have plans for you this weekend."

She smiled at him and looked out the window as the car cut through the dark-blue night with astonishing power and acceleration.

As they neared their beach house, she stretched and yawned after her nap in the car. Miles had accelerated the vehicle to almost maximum speed when they reached the open highway but slowed down to the speed limit as they got close to the island. He was wide awake and energized, despite the long drive.

"I guess the people renting my parents' beach house are already here. I see lights on in the house."

Bella looked out at the lighted property, but a limo parked in front of the home blocked the view.

He slowed down as he rode by the house and saw figures walking past the window, but neither of them could see any of the occupants' faces, so Miles sped up and drove the short distance to his grandparents' home instead. The living space at his grandmother's home was larger than his parents' house, and it was equipped to sleep more members of the Moore clan. Bella and Miles expected that his sisters and other relatives would join them at some point during their stay.

"So, how did you like the ride?"

"Exhilarating while I was awake." She stretched her limbs. "You've got to get this car."

"I'll do anything to please my lady." He smiled as he parked the car and grabbed their bags. Tossing them over his shoulder, he grabbed her hand to escort her to the front of the house.

While he searched for the keys, Bella stood in the dark, rubbing her arms to generate heat against the cool, night breeze coming from the ocean.

He placed the key in the door, which creaked but opened without difficulty, then placed his hand on the small of her back, gently guiding her into the darkened home. He took his time to turn on the lights.

Her eyes widened as she covered her mouth with her hands and squealed at the surprise.

Chapter 19

The scene was just as he had imagined. His heart leaped as
he looked at the surprise on Bella's face.

Hiring the best event planner in Charlotte had allowed
him to make his vision for that night come true. He moved
over to let her see all the special touches placed around the
room. The heirloom furniture that usually graced the house
had been replaced with small occasional tables and beautiful
cherry-wood buffets holding trays of delectable strawberries
and other fruits, a small oyster bar, and trays of cut veggies
for their delight.

In the center of the room was a large, round table covered
in a white linen cloth, beautiful stem glasses, and gleaming
silverware. The room was fragrant with a multitude of floral
arrangements artfully arranged and accented by the soft light
of candles scattered throughout the space. Instead of two separate chairs, a booth covered in a white satin drape was placed
next to the table. Hoping the event planner had left unlit logs
in the fireplace, he was relieved to see she had remembered

his instructions, because he planned to spend time in front of a romantic fire with his queen.

He looked at her, admiring her beauty, which shone brightly in the candlelit room. A smile spread across his face as her eyes widened and she tilted her head back, just a little, allowing her thick, luxurious hair to cascade down her back as she focused her attention on the details around the room. He loved the glow in her eyes and the roundness of her mouth as she opened it to take in the sights. It reminded him of the time they'd hiked to the top of a mountain in California to take in the awe-inspiring sight of a glorious sunset. He had seen it many times, but it had been different sharing it with her for the first time. It was then that he'd known she was the love of his life.

A tent was erected in the corner of the room, with yards of satin flowing from the top of it down the height of the room and puddling on the floor. The tent was covered on all sides, except for a large opening in front of the fireplace. A small chandelier hung from the top of the tent and gave off soft illumination as they approached it. Large, fluffy blankets and soft pillows were on the floor. Inside the tent was a small table with champagne chilling in a crystal ice cooler, along with crystal flutes.

"Go on in and take a look inside," he told her as he came up behind her.

She walked inside, looked around, and turned to face him for the first time since entering the house.

"This…is so thoughtful of you. Let's skip the foreplay, I'm ready for you now." Wrapping her arms around his neck, she took in his scent of sandalwood and bergamot, mixed with a hint of masculine musk.

He could smell the mixture of *I want you* scents filling the room. It took all the strength he had to resist taking her right there, right now. Instead, he took her into his arms, and lifted her above the thickened erection tenting his pants while she wrapped her legs around his waist. Looking into her brown eyes, he saw the innocence and purity of her spirit that shone through the first time he met her. It was still there some mornings in bed, just as she blinked open her eyes, and when they were home surrounded by those who loved her, but that look of innocence had become increasingly rare after she became his business partner.

He loved her with depths of feeling that just three years ago would have been unimaginable to him. He prayed she wouldn't be tainted by the rough-and-tumble world of the music industry. "I know you've had a long day, but I wanted to let you know how much I appreciate all you do for me, the business, and for our family."

She cupped his face and rubbed her hands along his cheek.

"You're welcome, babe. Let me show my appreciation to you." She leaned in for a kiss. "I love your five o'clock shadow, Mr. Unshaven." Rubbing his cheek, she leaned in again, but he pulled away.

"Not yet, babe – I need to feed you, since I have plans that'll require all the strength you can muster." He placed her on her feet while she pouted in feigned discontent.

"I haven't eaten all day." She patted her growling stomach. "I'm hungry, but I can wait until you fulfill my other desires. Come on, babe. You can't get a girl all horny and pull away –that's cruel and unusual punishment."

He laughed and pulled her to the booth.

"When and how did these get here?" She pointed at the plate filled with seared filet of fish, grilled asparagus, and fingerling potatoes before her. She hadn't noticed the wait-staff he'd hired for the night coming into the room, clad in soft slippers and placing hot plates of food on the table. Her mouth watered at the sight and smell of the fish caught by the local fishermen off the coast of North Carolina. However, not to be deterred by the sight of a meal she loved, she sat in his lap and wiggled her behind against his thick wood.

"The waitstaff placed it on the table while we were in the tent." He swatted her on the butt. "Be still while I feed you."

She rolled her eyes while he gathered a portion of the fish on his fork and placed it in his mouth.

"Mmm, perfect. You're going to enjoy this." After savoring the delicious bite, he put fish on the fork while she opened her mouth and slowly eased the fish off the fork in a sensuous, tantalizing manner.

"Oh my gosh," she said between chews. "This is really good. Okay, we eat first and lovemaking next." She opened her mouth for a few more bites before saying another word. "I can feed myself, you know. Why don't you eat me – I meant eat *with* me?" She giggled and slid off his lap but stayed close to him in the booth.

"This night is all about you, Bella. I'll eat if and what you want me to eat." He raised an eyebrow and took an oyster on the half shell, poured a bit of spicy sauce on top, and slid it down his throat as she watched in amazement. She wasn't accustomed to eating boiled oysters. He lifted the domed lid off a small plate of golden, fried oysters and popped one in her mouth.

"Try these. I think you'll like them. You're getting smaller from all the running around between the job and babies. A little flour and olive oil won't hurt you. They don't prepare seafood the North Carolina calabash way in California. Eat up, it's fantastic."

Taking her time enjoying the flavors of the oysters, she leaned her head back and closed her eyes as a sensuous smile spread across her face. After the third oyster, she dabbed the corners of her mouth with her napkin before placing it next to her plate. Looking up, she viewed him, titillating his senses.

"You're either going to take me now, or I'll need a shower to cool off."

"Have a glass of wine." He laughed and took a sip from his glass. "It's not time yet."

She slid out of the booth. "A shower it is, then. I'll be back."

"Don't wash your hair. It'll take too long to dry. Make it quick or I'll come get you."

"Is that a promise?" she challenged him, sashaying her butt as she walked toward the bedroom. When she opened the door, she let out another squeal of delight. "Come here!"

He joined her in the room to share in her excitement. Rose petals were scattered throughout the room, making a path to the bed, where additional pink petals were placed in a heart shape. Pieces of candy sat in the center, spelling out the letters *M* and *B*. Soft music played in the background, the candles dancing and flickering as if in tune with the music. A small plate of chocolate-covered strawberries was beside the bed and an espresso machine stood ready to produce a delectable drink at the push of a button.

She looked around as he made two small cups and handed one of them to her to sip while they feasted on slices of sweet strawberries.

His blood ran hot through his veins and every nerve along his spine was firing. Biting the inside of his cheek, he inflicted pain to distract himself from the desire to make love to her and release the intense throbbing in his pants. He stopped staring at her lips, trying to dial back the heat.

"So, this is why you held firm and didn't take me out there. You want me in bed. I'm game for it."

He couldn't help himself. Raising his eyes to meet her gaze, he was fixated by her beauty. His mouth watered as she bit off a piece of the strawberry.

"I thought you planned to take a quick shower?"

She huffed at him. "Fine."

Watching as she stomped off to get her bag, he muffled his chuckle, enjoying the view as she stripped out of her clothes and made her way to the bathroom.

"What are you doing to me? Come here," she yelled again.

He took off his clothes, with the exception of his boxer shorts, before joining her in the bathroom. Coming up from behind her, he wrapped his arms around her as she stared at the mirror, which was covered with the words, *I'll always love you*, written in red lipstick.

Tearing up, she covered her eyes with her hands.

"You've gone to such lengths to make this night special, and I've done nothing but complain. It's just that you have all my senses on overdrive. I need a release."

He placed his hand on her legs, which were pressed together. He let out a breath, sympathetic to her attempts to stifle the pressure growing within.

"You have a choice. Either release me now and take me in the shower, or over there on the vanity." Resolute in her decision, she stared at him without blinking.

He shook his head. "No, babe, please be patient. Take your shower, and then let's enjoy the milk bath. I had essence of rose oil placed in the whirlpool. You'll love how soft it leaves your skin. I researched it and it was recommended by a top beauty consultant."

"Fine." She took a deep breath and shook her head slowly in resignation. "You're in charge, so I'll go along with the plans. I'm horny as hell, but I don't want to ruin this memorable night – never mind that it had started just before midnight after a long day of filming." She leaned forward, allowing only their lips to brush each other briefly.

After her shower, she joined him in the whirlpool tub and had to admit to herself that it was relaxing sitting in his arms, feeling his cock throb beneath her. She struggled less as he began squirming and was clearly uncomfortable maintaining his determination to avoid touching her before it was time.

When they got out of the tub, he wrapped her in a thick, Egyptian cotton towel before escorting her back to the bedroom, where he unwrapped the towel and let it drop to the floor. Her mouth opened with uncertain anticipation of what he'd planned next.

Motioning for her to sit on the side of the bed, he poured warmed oil in the palm of his hands, spread it on his fingers, and then started rubbing it on her body.

She closed her eyes, hoping that if she reduced the visual stimulation, her raging need to have him claim her body would calm. It didn't happen.

The tightly coiled serpent within her jumped and hissed as he massaged the inner surface of her legs so close to her sex, tantalizing and exciting all her sensual impulses before he stopped, helped her to her feet, and wrapped a red silk robe around her shoulders. She pulled at the towel wrapped around his waist, but he gently pushed her hand away.

"Tell me you know how much I love you," he whispered into her ear before nibbling her earlobe.

"I know you love me, but maybe I don't deserve all this." She opened her eyes and peered into his brown eyes.

"You deserve this and more. You've given me so much. I want to show a portion of my gratitude to you." He got up and she took his outstretched hand without hesitation or resistance before following him back to the front of the house. This time, a fire roared in the fireplace.

The sounds of the ocean waves lapping upon the shore filled the room through an open window, competing with the sounds of firewood crackling in the fireplace. In the tent, Miles knelt and beckoned her to kneel in front of him. Placing his forehead to hers, he looked longingly into her eyes, removed her robe, and loosened the towel around his waist. Placing his hands on his chest, he began massaging his nipples in a slow circular motion while taking in deep breaths, slowly inhaling and exhaling as he rubbed himself.

"Grab your breasts and rub them," he said huskily. "Watch me and mimic my moves."

He rubbed his abdomen just above his navel, watching to make sure she mirrored his movements, then he rubbed and pulled on his cock, moving it back and forth in front of her. His breaths became labored as he increased the motion of his hands, and small drops of sweat began to pour off their bodies from the heat of the fireplace and the heat of passion building between them. While he looked down at the small triangle covered with hair between her legs, his heart began to pound in his ears.

"Go ahead, baby. Touch yourself between your legs. Seek your release."

"I want you to touch me, please."

"Just imagine my hands touching you."

She closed her eyes and placed her hand between her legs,

imagining him touching her sweet spot and placing his fingers in his mouth as if he was enjoying the taste of her honey. Her heart began skipping a beat, every nerve in her body tingling as her body tensed under her own touch, swaying back and forth. She didn't notice him rise to his feet and pull at a hook that held a swing high at the top of the tent. The mesh swing descended in front of her, complete with back supports wrapped in padded satin, and she opened her eyes as it came down and brushed against her skin.

He lifted her up by the shoulders, pulling her hands in the air just as she was about to find her release.

"Ugh! Let me guess. It's not time." Her lips tightened, and she took in deep breaths to exhale her frustration.

"No, baby, it's time." He grabbed her by the backs of her legs and sat back in the wide chair, which was big enough to support both of them as he placed her on top of him. He grabbed her by the back of the neck with one hand and placed the other hand along her butt. "I'm all yours. Take what you need."

"I need you – I want you," she panted as she impaled herself onto him. Wet juices covered them both as she bounced up and down, then ground against him in a circular motion. The swaying of the swing and sounds of the ocean added to the intensity of the moment. Her vision blurred as she searched for his mouth.

He grabbed her by the back of her neck and guided her face down to his lips before plunging his curled tongue into her mouth and unfurling it in waves, followed by darting movements that took her breath away. He filled her body with every inch of him and she exploded in ecstasy, finally finding the release she craved. She screamed his name, overwhelmed by passion.

"Miles," she called his name between quick, shallow breaths. "I love you so much that sometimes it hurts."

She placed her hands on her heart and attempted to slow her breathing.

He allowed her to regain her breath, but they remained physically joined in the swing.

"Why does it hurt to feel your love for me? I've often felt your heartbeat racing when you're cuddling with me at night and telling me you love me."

"That doesn't hurt, but at times I'm frightened by the thought of living without you. I don't know why I worry about it, but I do. I know my heart would shatter into a thousand pieces if I had to live in this world without you."

He lifted her out of the swing and took her back into the bedroom, still physically connected. Pulling back the covers, he lowered her onto the bed and pulled out of her while she whimpered.

She felt bereft of his presence as he grabbed a cotton towel to clean her before he got under the covers and spooned with her in bed.

He made sure she was securely in his arms before he spoke. "I pledged my heart and fidelity to you when I married you. I love you with my whole heart. It doesn't hurt me to love you."

"It doesn't hurt as much as it frightens me. I was frightened tonight by your show of so much restraint, and for a moment, I wondered if you were holding out because your needs are being met outside of our relationship, or maybe I wasn't turning you on anymore. It's not like I think about it often, but people around us seem to feel the need to remind me that infidelity goes along with loving a megastar." Shaking her head, she tried to banish the words Pharaoh had spoken to her about men with power and their penchant for infidelity.

He turned her around to face him. "You're the star in my life. Marrying you was a life-altering event for me. I wouldn't jeopardize what we have for anyone. It's just you and me when it comes to satisfying my lust, and I could only hold out because I jerked off at least five times today while you were away. Otherwise, I would have succumbed to the sight of your body an hour ago."

She sat up on her elbow and played with his hair with her other hand. "I never told you how you made me feel on our first date. I was very vulnerable, and you made me feel so safe and protected. Tonight, you've made me feel treasured and cherished. Thank you for a beautiful night. I'll never take for granted all the things you do to make me happy."

"You've already shown your gratitude in so many special ways." He kissed her on the lips, closed his eyes, and held her as they both succumbed to fatigue, entwined in each other's arms.

Chapter 20

While Bella slept in past noon, Miles got in a good workout and jogged for about five miles. He returned from his familiar run along the sandy beach, warmed by the bright sun and ocean breezes. He'd grown up there, spending summer vacations and school breaks with his family at the Outer Banks. This was the place and time for him to recharge and unwind – not even Lil' Pharaoh could disturb the peace he found here in front of the ocean.

When he unlocked the door to the beach house and opened it, he found the event planner's employees had restored the décor and furniture in the large room. All evidence of the den of love that had existed the night before was gone. He looked around for evidence that Bella had gotten out of bed while he was out, but didn't hear any sounds of her, so he made his way to the kitchen to get a sports drink.

The windows were shuttered, and the rooms of the house darkened from a lack of sunlight. He couldn't believe she'd slept through the noise of the movers walking through the house, but when he entered the bedroom, he discovered her sprawled out over the bed, asleep on her stomach with the covers around her waist, exposing the lobes of her breasts and her back. Her hair covered her face, and her head was nestled on top of folded arms.

He knelt down to rub her buttocks and kiss her on the cheek. "It's past noon, time to get up. We promised Mom we would call the kids."

She sniffed the air. "Eww, you stink." She squeezed her eyes tight and frowned. "What have you been doing?"

She yawned and stretched before getting out of bed.

He backed away and took a seat in a nearby chair to enjoy the view of her body, her breasts, soft abdomen, and toned legs all on display.

She pointed to her robe on the floor near him. "Throw it to me?" She stretched and yawned again.

"You need to come and get it. I like watching you walk naked toward me." He licked his lips and rubbed his abdomen under his shirt, wet from sweat.

"Were you working out?"

"Yeah, I went for a run along the beach. I need to make sure I'm back in shape."

"May I ask, in shape for what?" She grabbed the robe, flung it around her shoulders, and braced herself for the answer she already knew.

"I need to be in shape for the compilation tour."

"So that's what last night was all about? You planned to get me drunk on love and wine, then slip in that you'll be gone on tour...for how long, exactly? A year? Year and a half, maybe?"

"Bella, let's get washed up and eat a little something before we start this discussion."

He grabbed her by the hand and led her to the bathroom before turning on the water in the shower. He took off his clothes while she brushed her teeth, then came up behind her and helped loosen her robe as they walked to the shower together.

She stepped into the shower. "We won't be in here long."

"I agree with you. I have a full day planned for us today, and I don't want to start it eating a cold breakfast."

"Why are you concerned about a cold breakfast? I'll fix us some hot oatmeal. I'm sure there's some in the cupboard." She turned to grab the soap.

"Don't worry about that. The staff I hired will be here soon, if they aren't already here, to prepare our food. Didn't you hear them this morning, putting the furniture back in the house?"

"I didn't hear anything."

"Didn't you see them last night, rushing around to put out the food and drinks for us? They're good, but I could still see them working behind the scenes."

"Do you mean to tell me that there were people in the house while you tortured me with tantric sex? Do you think they heard me yelling your name?"

He grabbed the soap and lathered it on his body and along her back.

"They left before the fun started. They only came back to take down our den of love before the kids come with my parents tomorrow."

She stared at the tan marble tile in the shower. "I don't want you to leave. I like the time we spend together, both as a couple and as a family. I don't want things to change."

"I enjoy our time together, too, but we have an obligation to our employees to help them develop their talents and expand their careers. It will increase ticket sales if I go on tour with Lil' Pharaoh and Pele. I'm thinking about touring with them for the first few weeks, maybe months, but not a year."

She washed off the soap from her body, stepped out of the shower, and wrapped herself in a towel. "That may not be necessary, especially after I tell you about my latest conversation with Pharaoh. I told him that his appearance at the club in Atlanta was not approved by me. He knows that it's grounds for termination of his contract." She looked at him over her shoulder and turned to leave the bathroom.

Her cell phone rang just as he was returning to the bedroom. He hurried to get to it first – from the ringtone, it was Lil' Pharaoh.

"Didn't you tell him to relay all questions and concerns to your assistant while we're here on vacation?"

"Yes, that was the initial plan, but I told him on our way back from the shoot to call if he had questions. We have a duty to our artists, remember."

He stared ahead, trying not to roll his eyes as she barely contained her sarcasm. He extended his hand with her phone in it but didn't surrender it until it stopped ringing and went to voicemail.

"You can't continue to be available every time Baby Pharaoh calls."

"If you had given him more freedom and let him become the marquee act for the AriMusic tour like he wanted to be, maybe he wouldn't act like the baby you've grown fond of calling him, and just maybe, *you* wouldn't have to go on tour as the headliner."

"I don't have a choice at this point. Pele isn't ready to tour on their own. Can we eat before we go through *this* again?"

"Sure, when it comes to the business, it's always going to

be handled your way, but you didn't have to go to such lengths to convince me your way is the right way."

Huffing, she grabbed her underwear from her suitcase and hastily put it on under her robe, looked for a hair tie to pull her hair up into a messy bun, and then walked past him.

"Well, that went well..." he commented as he watched her head toward the dining room, carrying away his hope of avoiding an argument on an empty stomach.

Seated at the table and facing the cathedral windows, she looked at the unobstructed views of the sea grasses, sand dunes, and ocean before her. She took in a breath, which provided an immediate calm as she savored the fragrant smells of the shore.

With his hair still wet from the shower and droplets of water glistening on his shirtless chest, Miles entered the room. His lounging pants hung low around his waist, exposing the trail of hair that dusted his abdomen. He got two cups of coffee from the kitchen as he padded barefoot across the room before joining her.

"What made you so sure there weren't women from the caterers still here before you came to the table without your underwear on?" she asked as she lifted the cover off her plate to expose the rich smell of shrimp and grits, a favorite of the locals along the South and North Carolina coasts. As she took a bite of her breakfast and looked at him, she realized she wasn't just hungry for the food. Despite herself, she was hungry for his body.

"Jealous, are you, Mrs. Moore?" he responded, looking at

the view before them. "I paid them to keep out of sight while making our stay as comfortable as possible. Most of the food will be prepared offsite, and they'll only clean the place while we're away." He took in a mouthful of food before wiping his mouth with his napkin. "I'm relieved you're still talking to me, so let me state that, for the record, this weekend isn't about my plans for the tour or the business. This is about us. Last night, I wanted to show you how much I appreciate all you do for everyone around you." He took another bite of his food. "I've spent the last few years lusting after your body, and now I've gotten to the point where I can still lust after you but be a little more romantic and show the deep emotional bond I have with you. Even if your body changes after our next baby, I don't want you obsessing over body-image issues. I love your body, but it's the essence of who you are that I love most." He placed his hand on top of hers and looked into her eyes. "Today, it's still about you and me and no one else. I want to show you how much I cherish you. I don't want you to think that I take you for granted. Tomorrow, the family will be here, and we'll spend time enjoying them."

Bella's eyes widened, her fork stopping in midair as she looked at her man, who'd been full of surprises for the past two days. A smile spread across her face slowly. "Are you telling me you're considering the thought of us having a third child?"

"I've already considered it. When you're ready, I'll welcome another child. The twins are a joy to me."

She got out of her seat and flung herself into his arms, welcoming his kisses and the caresses on her back beneath her thin robe.

"I hope you don't want another child in the next year, but yes, I'm agreeing to increasing the size of our family in the future." He matched her passion as he showered her with kisses and plunged his tongue into her mouth.

"You couldn't have made me happier. Just knowing you're open to growing our family in the future is a joy." She gave him one more kiss before returning to her seat. "I'm sorry for thinking you were manipulating me by planning a great weekend to spring your plans on me for a world tour. You said this entire weekend isn't about business, but let's talk about it for a little bit. Why do you think I tried to respond to Pharaoh's whims?"

"I can't say I understood it." He took another bite of his food.

"I was hoping that if he was given more freedom, he would have been ready to be the headliner, and then you could stay home with us as the CEO of AriMusic. I really don't want you to go on the road and leave us. Pharaoh may be difficult, but he's very talented, and he's not dumb. You can't deny the stats, either. The compilation album is on track to make the company a fortune."

"I know he's talented and a money-maker, but what effect do you think it had on the other artists whom we signed at the same time as Pharaoh? Do you think they deserved to be billed below him? Or should we have developed their careers equally and separately? Think about the effect it would have had on your friend Reagan if Pharaoh was given the title of headliner, especially with all the problems he caused."

"I see your point, but I don't want to go on a year-long tour with you – and if you're willing to be honest, you know you'll be gone more than a month."

"We don't have to be apart. I want you and the babies to come with me."

"I'm sure you're aware of the possible negative effects of

travel on the babies. They get very fussy when we change their routines."

"I know, but we can have the road crew set up their nursery on every stop of the tour, just like it is at home. You've seen how fast a good crew can create and take down the contents of rooms. They'll do the same thing to create a home for us on the tour. I want this to work for us. We haven't finalized any plans yet, and I want input from you. I've asked you for weeks to come to the executive meetings, but you've been busy doing your thing."

"You know what I've been busy with. Let's not lose sight of the fact that you could've told me you were discussing terms for another tour."

Just then, his phone buzzed. He answered as she looked on, hoping the call wasn't from his mother about the babies.

"Yeah, I understand, Bradley. You're right. I need to get a briefing from you now. Bye." He ended the call and took a sip of his coffee.

"What's going on? What does Bradley want?"

"There's something going on at the beach house that I need to be briefed on before we occupy it with the babies tomorrow. My parents, sisters, and whoever comes with them will stay here while we stay at the other house. I need to make sure it's safe before tomorrow."

"Do you want me to come with you?"

"No, I'll throw on some clothes and jog over there while you get dressed. We can call the babies when I get back and then," he said, delaying the rest of his sentence until he got close enough to kiss her, "I plan to take you on a ride around the island in a speedboat."

"Okay. I'll be ready when you get back." She extended her neck to receive another kiss.

Chapter 21

M iles sprinted over to the beach house around the corner from his grandparents' home and he was there in no time.

Bradley stood on the front porch, waiting for him to arrive.

Miles slowed when he reached the yard and walked the remainder of the way, suspecting he hadn't heard the end of trouble from Lil' Pharaoh. After they returned to Los Angeles, he planned to terminate him from his contract.

He'd assigned Bradley's men to follow him while he was in North Carolina, and he figured Bradley needed to give him a report without the possibility of Bella overhearing. They shook hands before entering the home.

"What you got?"

"It's not awful news, but you needed to know as soon as possible. Sit down. There are things for you to review on the table."

Miles sat down and began looking at pictures and notes

from a week's worth of surveillance of Pharaoh, starting at LAX.

"I have his phone logs, which showed he made contact with his new agent and Dark Nyland to discuss future plans. The agent represents several artists who record with Dark's company. I'm getting information from people I know on the inside that Pharaoh plans to sign with them as soon as he can. The same agent rented this place – your house – for Pharaoh last night before he left for Chicago."

"Of all of the homes around here, why would Pharaoh want to rent *this* house?"

"It's sick, but I think Dark used Pharaoh to gather information on you and your family. He and a dancer on the South Carolina shoot had sex in the master suite. He left stained sheets as evidence."

Miles tightened his fists. "That bastard. Order a new mattress set and have it delivered today."

"That's not all. We looked at the video recorded on the cameras your parents had installed in the front room. There's no audio." Bradley passed him the video. "He invited several men from Atlanta with him and his LA crew. These guys have reportedly been used by Dark and his family to arrange hits. Yeah, it looks like they're having a party, watching sports, but I think they were gathered to harm or at least scare you and your family." Bradley sped up the time-lapse video, showing the men trashing the house with litter, beer cans, and food dropped on the floors.

"Why is Pharaoh coming in and out of the bedroom? What is he doing?" Miles asked, watching the footage. The men were scattered throughout the house, asleep.

"He left the young woman in the bedroom and got up in the middle of the night to tear up a few pictures around the room. He placed the pictures with Bella in them in his pocket, while also making a point of throwing away any with you in them."

Miles's brow furrowed, but he didn't turn away from the video.

"I hate to tell you this, but your protégé has got to go. He has a sick fascination with your wife."

Miles rifled through the surveillance notes and balled them up before throwing them into a corner of the room. "What the hell!" He got up, his heart pounding with fury, and began pacing to calm down. "I knew he had puppy love for Bella, but *this*?" He paused as various options ran through his mind.

"Wait." Bradley sped up the video again. This time it was Pharaoh coming out of the bedroom to answer a knock at the door.

"What's going on here?" Miles tried to make out what was happening.

"Someone alerted the authorities," Bradley answered. "Pharaoh is speaking to the police on the porch. The cameras on the outside were disarmed, but I found out from a local contact that they told him why they were summoned to the house."

The next frames included moments in which Pharaoh returned to the front room and flicked on all of the lights prior to a flurry of activity. The men grabbed their things and disappeared out the front door. Pharaoh and the woman he'd slept with were the last to leave.

"My contact also told me Pharaoh was given a warning for violating a noise ordinance. After he told the guys, as you saw, they ran. There's no evidence that he was in on the plot to harm you or your family, but we're still investigating."

Miles placed a fist to his forehead. "I need you to discreetly assign a few of the most trusted members of your staff to continue their surveillance of him."

"My men tailed the car with the guys across the state line headed back to Georgia." Bradley rubbed his chin. "Pharaoh boarded a flight headed to Chicago."

"So, it's safe to stay here after we get it all cleaned up?" Miles leaned in closer, observing Bradley's response.

"We've got all the bases covered, boss." He nodded. "I'll call you if something else comes up. Otherwise, I'll debrief you next week when we get back to LA."

"Good. I also want you to keep a security detail on this house tonight."

"That was the plan. The house has already been swept for bugs and other recording devices. It's clean."

"Return the money for the rental to Pharaoh's new agent. If he pockets it without Pharaoh's knowledge, we'll have something on the slime-bag agent too."

"Good idea. We don't owe it to him, but Baby Pharaoh may need to know who he's about to hand his career over to."

"Good work, Bradley."

"Thanks. You're taking this a lot better than I expected. I don't know whether to be relieved or disturbed that this is the calm before the storm. If it was my wife—"

Miles held up his hand, cautioning Bradley to hold his peace, as any attempt to remain in control unraveled.

"She's my wife. I'll handle this my way, in my time." He balled his fists. "On second thought, I need you to help me take the mattress to the firepit in the back of the house."

"We can handle it, Miles." Bradley shifted his weight after Miles turned to go back to the bedroom. Grabbing the side of the mattress, they took it outside to the pit off the deck.

"Get back," Miles warned. His eyes narrowed as he focused on the mattress. Extending his hand, he sent a fiery flame, incinerating it in seconds. Startled by the intensity of the heat, Bradley stumbled away from the blaze. Black smoke rose and a foul smell filled the air. As his security chief, Bradley was aware of Miles's powers, but he rarely displayed them as often as he had in the past few months. Since it was off-season, the other homes adjacent to it were vacant, but they looked around to make sure they were out of view of prying eyes.

"If he was here, I'd kill his ass." Miles's face was bright red as he drew closer to the flames. Sweat dripped off his body. The veins on his arms looked like ropes under his skin. Gritting his teeth, he gave voice to his rage. "He thinks he can have my wife." His chest heaved. "I've got to get control of this." He placed his hands on his sides and slumped back into a patio chair. Minutes elapsed as the remaining pieces of the mattress disintegrated into black ash. Miles got up with Bradley close on his heels.

"I need to get out of here." He went back through the house, preparing to leave.

Bradley nodded. "I'll make sure I haven't missed additional evidence before I lock up, so you probably should get back to Bella before she comes here looking for you."

"I'll tell her. She's not oblivious to Pharaoh's infatuation with her."

"Her love for you may have blinded her to his lust at first, but people in the organization see it, and it's not good. Other people talk and make nasty insinuations."

"I don't care what people say about me, but I won't stand for anyone hurting my wife with dirty lies."

Bradley walked him to the door. "It wasn't a lie that he

tried to kiss her months ago, and now this. I'm sorry that I had to share more bad news with you. You know I'm here for you. I'll follow your lead on how you choose to handle this."

When they reached the door, Bradley stared him in the eye with a coldness Miles had never seen before, but he knew of Bradley's reputation to do whatever he had to do. There was nothing left to say after he gave Miles *the look*. They both understood what it meant.

No man fantasizes about another man's wife without consequences. *No way.*

He pulled the hood of his jacket over his head, tied it at the neck, and said goodbye before Bradley closed the door behind him. Looking up at the sky and at the expanse of ocean before him, he stretched his legs before jogging back to the house, determined to protect Bella and the rest of his family. She was *his* wife, not some other man's wildest dream.

As the wind blew on his face while he ran the short distance back to his grandmother's beach house, he was relieved Bella had finally agreed that Pharaoh could no longer stay on contract with AriMusic. With a steely resolve, he tightened his jaw and drew his brows together. He would solve his problem with Pharaoh. It was just a matter of time.

Chapter 22

Bella pressed Miles about what had taken him so long to return to the beach house, but she was happy he'd returned before the agreed-upon time to Skype with the twins and his parents' dog, Bosco.

"You've had two separate runs on the beach in one day... What did Bradley really want with you?"

"He needed to let me know what happened last night. We can talk about it later."

"What happened?"

"Later, Bella. I promise." He walked away, heading for the bathroom.

"Okay." She shrugged and didn't press the issue any further. Excited to connect with the babies, she blew out a breath, grateful she didn't have to endure the awkward situation of explaining his absence to his mother.

The two of them gathered on the couch in front of the computer screen, which showed the twins crawling all over Bosco, the large German shepherd who sat docile and attentive to them. Bosco had been Miles's constant companion on his tours before he married Bella, and she knew it had been a hard decision to send Bosco to North Carolina to live with his parents after she required complete bedrest during the latter part of her pregnancy. What little time he had left after attending to her, he'd consumed with getting his new venture, AriMusic, off the ground.

"Bosco is family, and North Carolina is our family's home. Besides, my mother could use the companionship now that my father is on a reunion tour with his former band and my sisters are away at school." He'd shared his reasons to take his beloved pet to North Carolina, but she knew he'd also been concerned about Bosco adjusting to having twin babies in the house. She had a mutual love of Bosco but going from just the three of them to a family of five was a lot for Miles to wrap his head around at first. She hadn't been sure if he could handle the stress of Bosco's possible poor adjustment to their new reality.

"It was love at first sight," Alicia now told them, as she doted on her grandchildren, who were dressed in matching blue-and-white outfits as they crawled around the floor. "I prepared Bosco for their arrival by putting dolls in chairs around the kitchen and living area. He's a smart dog – he sensed that they're special to me. It didn't take long for him to adjust to their noises and activities in the house."

"We're glad to hear it, Mami," he said.

Bella nodded in agreement and reached out to the screen to touch the images of her children crawling around the room under the watchful gaze of their grandmother. Her eyes crinkled a little around the corners when they wandered just a little too far off, but they clearly contained nothing short of pure bliss.

"We love you." Bella used her syrupy-sweet Mommy voice and blew kisses to them.

"Dada loves you," he said, to which they stopped crawling, sat on their diapered bottoms, and looked up to smile at the screen. "See you tomorrow."

The twins reached out their hands in the direction of their parents on the screen as Miles confirmed the time of their expected arrival at the house. When he ended the call, Bella pretended there was something irritating her eyes, causing her to wipe away a tear. Feeling a strong pressure in her chest from missing the twins, she placed a hand over her heart.

The aching feeling subsided when he took her into his arms.

"I'm going to shower again, then I plan to take you on a ride around the island in the Porsche. I'm still trying to decide if I want to buy it."

"It's up to you."

He kissed her and left before she could pepper him with questions. She could sense there was something he wasn't ready to talk about.

Later, he had promised her. She planned to make sure he kept it.

Chapter 23

As she sat on the overstuffed couch, trying to read the local news while she awaited his return, Bella knew something was troubling Miles. She'd observed him before they spoke with the twins, looking off into space with a blank stare, oblivious to her presence when she came into the room. She planned to ask him to explain his long absence again upon his return from the bedroom, but she needed to be careful how she approached the issue.

When he returned from his shower, she looked at her man, who hadn't shaved since they'd left Los Angeles. His hair, fuller and longer than before, brushed against his collar, making him hot as hell. He cuddled beside her as she continued to look at the paper.

"Miles, this looks interesting. Do you want to go to the performance tonight?"

He looked at the advertisement for the local theatrical group, but he didn't answer. She watched him stare at the printed page, still lost in his own thoughts, and nudged him with her elbow to get his attention.

"What do you think about attending this show?" she repeated.

"What did you say?" he asked, finally turning his attention to her as she folded the paper and placed it in her lap.

"You haven't been yourself since you came back from meeting with Bradley. Please tell me what happened." She laid the paper on the couch and crossed her arms over her chest as she awaited his answer.

"My mood has nothing to do with that meeting," he told her.

"Then what is it?" She searched his eyes. "You know you can tell me anything."

"I know that, and if I wasn't certain of your love, I would have killed someone by now." He frowned and looked away.

"What's going on? You're starting to worry me." She turned his chin so that he was facing her.

"Nothing, I'm exaggerating." He let out a long, audible breath, releasing what Bella thought might be fatigue and some sadness.

"We just need to get out of here. It's a nice day for a ride around the island. I don't want to waste this day thinking about business, so this is what I propose – let me show you the island, then we'll go to the marina, and have an early dinner afterward."

"Okay, that does sound nice, but we have to talk about this later. Maybe a little fresh air would be good for both of us." She grabbed her blue beach bag, a smart compliment to her nautical, blue-and-white striped cotton top and navy-blue cropped pants, which fit snugly over her firm hips and toned legs. Unfolding her legs, she slipped her feet into matching navy-blue flats she'd found in a boutique in Los Angeles.

His outfit complemented hers. He looked prepared for an afternoon on the water, dressed in a cotton polo, khaki shorts, and tan-colored leather docksiders to match. He got up from the couch, grabbed his phone from the table to check that it was off before he put it in his pocket. Out of the corner of his eyes, he saw her struggling under the weight of the bag, probably filled with an oversized beach towel, a swimsuit, sunscreen, sunglasses, hair ties, and her favorite water bottle.

"Need some help, beautiful lady?" Extending his hand, he took her bag and peered inside to see she had also packed snacks, more things than he'd imagined. "We have everything you'll need on my boat."

"*Your* boat? I thought we were going to rent a boat."

"You'll find out soon enough," he told her, taking her hand as he led her to the car.

"We're gone," he yelled to the house staff, who had maintained a low profile throughout their stay at the beach house.

Escorting her to and then depositing her inside the car, he quickened his steps to get to the driver's side. Adjusting his shades, he started the ignition and roared the engine so loudly it startled her. Flashing a broad smile, he placed a hand over hers.

He was a safe driver who would never put their lives or anyone else's in danger by driving dangerously. Always comfortable behind the wheel, he drove while she relaxed and enjoyed the tree-lined streets, quaint shops, and lovely bed-and-breakfast inns. She thought they were heading directly to the marina, but he made a turn in the opposite direction, heading out of town across a bridge onto an open stretch of highway.

"I'm going to take a detour before we head to the boat," he told her.

"Isn't there someone at the boat waiting for us?" She

pulled a strand of hair out of her face as they drove down the highway.

"Yes, the captain, but I told him we might be delayed. Don't worry about it. He'll be compensated for his time."

She lowered the visor. The vanity mirror lit up while she twisted her hair and fashioned it into a bun at the back of her head. The car climbed to high speed in seconds, and the gravitational force of the car racing down the highway pushed her back into her seat.

Fumbling at first for the button on the side of the door, she raised her window as the wind coming off the ocean began to sting. She swept away strands of hair coming out of the bun and looked over at Miles, who was bobbing his head to loud music thumping throughout the car. He smiled at her and gently swept away the hair that continued to escape from her messy bun.

They hadn't been together in a fast vehicle since the last time they'd ridden motorcycles, just after the start of her first trimester of pregnancy. She'd conveniently forgotten that her husband not only had a need for speed but thrived on it.

Struggling with her decision to remain silent while the needle on the speedometer shifted more to the right, she considered asking him to slow down. The scenery they passed seemed blurred by speed, but the sight of the powerful, vast ocean to her right and her confident husband on her left, smiling and in charge at the wheel, calmed her fears. The car responded with smooth precision to his maneuvers, and in spite of the pain in her knuckles from gripping the sides of her seat, she sensed she was in a machine built for speed and power. Her heart rate slowed, and she managed a slight smile when he kissed the back of her left hand and opened her tightly drawn fist to massage the sweat away from her palm while he let off the accelerator. The car slowed after he turned around and made his way back to the marina.

"I think this car is our new metal, baby. What do you think about her?"

She caught her breath in time to tell him, "I think it's a good car, but you're the expert on performance vehicles."

"In that case, I think I'm going to order this model in this color. I already have enough black-and-red cars."

Back in town, Miles cut the engine and reached over to retrieve the overstuffed beach bag before going to the other side of the car to open the door for her. They walked hand in hand along the wooden pier, past small boats and large yachts. A private yacht with no visible name on its rear floated in the water at the end with its gangplank down. At the foot of the plank, a tanned older man in a captain's hat waited to greet them.

"Welcome, Mr. and Mrs. Moore. I think you'll find the accommodations to your liking. The ship is stocked with the usual supplies, according to your specifications. We'll be departing in a few minutes."

Bella looked around at the gleaming white boat with its dark wooden interiors and brass so shiny it reflected the sun. A second man, Malcolm Brown, was at the controls, wearing a baseball hat with the words "First Mate" in big letters. He waved at them, and they smiled, waving back.

"Cap' Pritchard, we'll be below deck changing into our swimsuits."

Miles led the way with Bella in tow, until they arrived at the master bedroom suite, where a mauve string bikini spread on the bed caught her attention.

"How do you know this will fit me?"

"Darien has your measurements. I had him ship several

suits to North Carolina for you to wear on the boat. There are others in the drawers if you don't like this one, but I thought it would look nice on you. I plan to keep you very wet today."

She held it up for examination. "Pink?"

"Yes, pink. I've grown to appreciate the color on you – baby-girl pink, mauve, or fuchsia. It's all good on you."

She lifted one eyebrow and snickered. "Mauve or fuchsia? You've been talking to Darien about fashion accessories and colors for me?"

"You sound surprised," he noted, falling back on the bed and lying with his hands behind his head, his feet crossed at the ankles. "You have to admit he knows what looks good on you."

She swiped at his feet, which were still in his shoes on the cream-colored duvet. "Shoes, please, sir," she reminded him as she stripped off her clothes and stood before him in her black, demi-cup lace bra and matching panties. "You're sure you prefer the pink set over a black one?" she questioned him before continuing a strip tease in front of him.

Miles sat up on his elbows and loosened his shorts, which were tenting with desire. "Stop teasing me before I come over and ravage your body. We lost some time test-driving the car, so I'll need to sacrifice my lust to make up for it. Hurry, I want to take you out on the jet skis. It'll be fun." He got off the bed and began taking off his clothes, ensuring he returned the favor by allowing her a full view of his raging hard-on. He stroked it until a small drop of precum glistened on its head, while she stood before him, hot with desire.

"Back off," he playfully warned her as she made an effort to move toward him. "I've got to go to the bathroom, and then we need to get back up on deck. We're going to lose more sunlight if we stay down here much longer."

Placing her hands on her hips, she opened her mouth to protest, but instead thought better of it.

"I'll have you begging for me before the night is over," she teased.

After putting on the mauve bikini, and curious about what was in the drawers on either side of the bed, she opened the one closest to her and found a crocheted bathing-suit cover to match her suit. She primped in the mirror and was ready for her water adventure when he returned clad in swimming trunks.

"When did *you* buy this large boat?"

"*We* own this boat now and I've had it for a while."

"I stand corrected. *We* own this?"

"Yes, we do, and I can't wait until the twins get a little older. I'm looking forward to getting them out on the water."

"The Fire God likes the water?" she asked, causing him to chuckle as the boat's engine started up, roaring as they backed out of the marina. She looked around the room at the fancy lantern lighting and the rich oak finish and wiggled her toes against the plush carpet beneath her feet. She knew Miles made a lot of money, but it occurred to her that she'd never seen his complete financial portfolio. It felt awkward not being sure when or if they would ever discuss that aspect of their lives.

His pull on her hand, urging her to come with him above deck, pushed those thoughts to the corner of her mind.

"Come on. I'll share our complete holdings with you soon enough, just not today. I'll be making some other big purchases besides the Porsche, but we can discuss it together later."

She nodded, almost losing her footing as he dragged her away from the bedroom. The old impatient Miles was back, but she loved how he sensed the things that were important to her.

They got back on deck in time to see the pier and the waterside town they'd called home for the weekend as it disappeared in the distance. She looked on while the captain and Miles busied themselves with lowering the two jet skis located aft of the boat into the water. They loosened the tie to her ski first and allowed her to turn on the motor and push away from the boat before the captain helped him lower his ski into the water.

"Bella, wait a minute. I'm not ready to pull off yet."

She didn't need a lesson on handling jet skis. She turned the handle sharply to head out into the open waters, smiling as she heard him shouting across the distance growing between them.

"This is the ocean, not the Gulf. You're not familiar with the patterns of the currents around here," he yelled at her as her long braid loosened, causing her hair to blow in the wind.

She heard his jet ski getting closer, but she increased her speed, heading farther away from the shore with him in close pursuit.

"Bella, this isn't funny," he shouted as she grinned and slowed down.

"You can give it, but you can't take it when I'm in control of the reins," she retorted, allowing him to catch up before speeding off a second time.

"Slow down, please," he called out to her again.

She planned to ride straight ahead for a few hundred feet, turn sharply to create a wave, then head back to the yacht – but she didn't anticipate he would overtake her just as she made her turn, causing a large wave of white water to blind him as he swerved to avoid hitting her.

Looking over her shoulder, she saw him go airborne. His jet ski splashed hard into the water and drifted in the opposite direction, getting carried away by the currents.

"Miles!" she screamed back at him. "Miles, oh my gosh. Please be okay. I'm coming." Refusing to let the tears forming in her eyes blind her, she raced across the surface of the water. Her heart thumped in her heaving chest as she gripped the handles and frantically tried to reach him as quickly as possible.

When he popped up out of the wave and began treading water, she sighed with relief and helped him onto her ski, uncertain if they could recover his jet ski as it floated away.

He slid behind her and moved her hands closer together on the bar so he could take over the controls as she leaned back into his embrace and began sobbing while choking on her words.

"Are you all right?"

"I'm okay. Please stop crying. You'll have ample time for tears while I'm spanking your ass. You deserve one good ass whipping for this stunt," he fumed.

She leaned her round bottom into his crotch and wiggled it against him. "Do you promise?" she asked, wiping away her tears.

"This isn't funny. You're not familiar with the current patterns around here and your reckless behavior was dangerous."

"I may not be familiar with the currents, but you're the one hitching a ride with me."

He leaned closer and whispered in her ear, "Your ass is so mine. It will be on fire when I finish with it."

"Is that a threat or a promise?"

"It's a threat with a promise yet to be fulfilled."

Struggling to open her eyes, Bella awakened to Miles talking in his sleep. They were on the deck of the boat taking a nap on one of the oversized chairs after enjoying a meal and a few drinks.

"I can't do it anymore. I just can't. He wants my wife, and he can't have her."

He settled down before she could touch him to end his nightmare.

Who was the man in his dream and what does he want with me?

Looking over at the clock with its red illuminated numbers, Bella saw that it was five o'clock in the afternoon.

She turned to him. "Miles, why were you so off after your meeting with Bradley? You were having a nightmare. Are the two connected?"

"Bella, can't this wait until later? I really don't want to be analyzed right now."

"Answer me, Miles." She frowned. "What's bothering you?"

"Pharaoh and his buddies rented the house around the corner." He let out a long breath. "Some things were vandalized, but only small things."

Her jaw dropped.

"Bradley is investigating it."

She sat up on her elbows, propped her head on her hand, and looked at him. "Oh my gosh. You're sure it was Pharaoh and his crew?"

He nodded. "We have them on video."

"Now I understand why you were so absorbed in your thoughts. I feel violated just thinking about it." She rubbed her forehead. "Why do you think he did it?"

"As usual, things got out of control," he responded. "Bradley and our people will handle this. We're keeping Pharaoh under surveillance."

She touched his arm, knowing how much his family's beach home meant to him.

"The things that were broken can be replaced, except things like pictures that were ripped."

"So, this was personal and unlike his other parties where the crowd got rowdy?"

"Afraid so." His hands gathered in fists. "He took pictures of you."

"I'm not making excuses for Pharaoh anymore." She covered her mouth with her hands. "He's definitely drinking too much, but this is deeper than an alcohol or drug problem."

"I agree." He grabbed her hand and kissed it.

"Have you spoken to him about this?" Massaging her forehead, she tried warding off a headache.

"Not yet, but you have to promise to let me handle this my way and on my time. Trust me on this one, please. I'll handle it."

She looked at him as his eyes narrowed.

He knitted his brow and tightened his jaw.

"We need to handle this together." She pointed to him and herself. "We're stronger together." She inclined her head, waiting for a response, but he said nothing as he stared at the Atlantic Ocean, its waves growing larger and menacing.

Chapter 24

They sailed back to the marina after a gorgeous sunset, which had painted the sky in yellow, red, and orange hues.

Stopping in the portal of the door before stepping onto the deck, she made eye contact with Miles, who licked his lips and gazed at the length of her body.

"We should be arriving at the marina soon," Miles told her. "I want to make one more stop before we go back to the house."

"What?" She placed her hand on her hips. "We've already had a full day."

"It won't take long. A driver will be waiting for us at the pier, since we've both been drinking, and I don't think it's safe for me to drive. Someone from the crew can take the car back to the house."

She looked back at the captain and Malcolm, the first mate, to wave goodbye and thank them for a great day on the water.

"Did you have a good time?" the driver asked as he stood by the open door.

"We had a great time," Bella responded with a broad smile.

Miles nodded and entered the vehicle after her.

The driver returned to his seat and took them on a short ride. He stopped the car in front of a bar and grill on the other side of the marina.

"I know the owners, and I told them I would stop by when I was back in town. Come on, I promise we won't stay long. The place is new, and they haven't been able to draw a crowd yet." He opened the door of the limo, took her hand, and led her into the bar. There was a very small gathering inside, and music was playing in the background.

He whispered in her ear as they walked farther into the bar that the owners were friends of his from high school. He wanted to introduce them to her and show his support for their venture.

She looked around and saw signs advertising their specialty crafted, local, and imported beers.

"Miles!" a loud, booming voice announced his presence to the room.

They both turned to see a big burly man coming toward them.

He smiled brightly and gave Miles a warm bear hug. "About time you came to check us out. Who's this beautiful woman with you?"

"This is my wife, Bella Moore. Bella, this is one of my forever buddies, Kelvin Davis, but we call him Kell."

"Listen, he's my brother, not my buddy, so I'm going to give you a hug, too."

Bella held the hem of her dress to avoid it rising above her bottom as Kell swung her in the air and placed her back on her feet, causing her to stumble into Miles's arms. Having witnessed his ire in the past when men gave her unwanted attention or came too close, she looked at him, but he seemed not a bit disturbed by Kell's actions. Instead, he laughed as they caught up on old times, keeping her close and playing mindlessly with her hair until it fell out of the bun and onto her shoulders.

After excusing herself, she went to the bathroom to freshen up and get him out of her hair. She relieved herself and ran a brush through her curls before returning to the group at the bar, which had grown by two more members.

"Bella, meet Sam Wilson, another owner. And this is Chelsey Morris, Frank's wife, the third owner and the creator of the best craft beer on the planet."

Bella said hello to all of them. Before long, she started moving to the beat of the karaoke sound of Miles's "House of Shame" song playing in the background.

Frank freed himself from his duties and joined them when they moved to one of the tall tables in front of the stage. He had a mic in his hands and went directly toward Miles, who began shaking his head no.

"Man, I'm glad you came," he greeted him with a bro hug. "The stage is yours. It's been a long time since I've seen you perform."

The others soon joined in, but Miles continued to shake his head and tell them no way. He hadn't shaved in days, and with longer hair, he wasn't noticed by the other patrons, who'd moved outside the bar to enjoy the evening breeze.

Bella took the mic out of Frank's hand and gave it to Miles, batting her eyes and pouting her lips. "Do it for me, baby, please?"

He sighed and took the mic. Once onstage, he belted out the vocals over the music as the crowd turned their attention to the big screens outside, screaming his stage name, "Ari."

The bouncers immediately took to the door to prevent a mad rush from the crowd as the environment became electric with patrons yelling in excitement and pulling phones out of their pockets to videotape their hometown boy who'd made it big.

Bella took another swallow of his beer, which was sitting on the table, and moved closer to the stage to shake her hips and sway to the music. She hadn't heard the song in a long time and always loved his performances of one of his earlier hits.

He swayed in response to her movements and turned on the charm the more she danced and clapped to his performance.

Chelsey and some other women joined in, dancing and singing alongside her.

As she danced to the music, she saw Miles point to Kell and then to her as a man trying to move closer to her didn't escape his attention.

That's my man. She smiled as she saw Kell coming forward to tap the man on the shoulder and urge him to move on.

More people tried to join the crowd after those inside the bar uploaded the performance on social media, but the bouncers at the door continued to limit the size. As others left to party outside, they let more patrons in. The waiters ran around, trying to get the orders that had swelled from those outside the bar, and the DJ added the instrumental version of another song to the playlist to keep Miles onstage for a second performance. When the song "You" came on, he sang it looking at her, while she stole a furtive glance at Chelsey singing all the words. Tilting her head toward Chelsey, she gave Miles the unspoken suggestion to ask her to the stage in time to sing the chorus with him. He came to the edge of the stage and welcomed Chelsey to join him in singing the song, and she surprised the crowd with her beautiful alto voice.

As he stepped back into the shadows, her voice was showcased as she sang the song, looking at Frank and smiling. Their eyes glistened in the dim light. When they finished the song, Miles helped her get off the stage and into Frank's arms.

"Thank you and good night." He bowed to the crowd's applause before returning to the table with Bella and his friends. Frank and Chelsey had already left before he got there, but they'd made sure to tell Bella to thank him for coming.

"Your drinks will always be on the house, man. Thank you for giving this bar a much-needed shot in the arm." Sam gave Miles a fist bump while Kell made his way to the table to talk to Miles before resuming his duties.

"That was a great thing you did for Frank tonight. He and Chelsey are going through a rough patch. Thanks to you, he's probably going to get some tonight."

"Kell, tact has never been your strong suit." Miles laughed and swallowed some of his beer.

"Maybe not, and sometimes I can be an ass, but loyalty to my friends is important to me. You had our backs tonight, and I want to thank you for that. Chelsey is one of your biggest fans, and she knows you came here to help Frank and the rest of us. You realize you placed us on the map by coming here tonight, don't you?"

Miles looked down and shrugged, uncomfortable with the expression of gratitude from a true friend. "Thanks for looking out for my girl tonight. I saw that guy trying to move in on her," he deflected.

"Anytime, man. I got you and added Bella to the list. All of us have been there for each other since we were boys, and I'm glad it hasn't changed just 'cause you're famous."

Miles reached over and gave Kell a bro hug. There would be no more gushing or talk of gratitude between them. Nothing more needed to be said.

"Are you ready to go?"

Bella nodded and grabbed her things while he said goodbye to his friends. They left through the back entrance to avoid walking through the crowd on the outside and made their way back to the limo while she peppered him with questions.

"You all have known each other a long time?"

"Yeah. Frank, Sam, and Kell grew up around here, and I spent many summers here with my family. They accepted me into their group right away. They're a part of some of my greatest memories growing up, including part of the trouble I got into."

"What kind of trouble?"

"Just boyhood pranks, nothing serious." When they made it to the limo waiting for them, he helped her crawl inside the car.

She moved closer to him after he got in the back seat and closed the door. "I've always been proud of you, but your actions tonight got me feeling both proud and so horny I could strip right here and now." She snuggled closer to him.

"What has gotten into you?" Stunned, he hit the button for the privacy screen so the driver couldn't hear the rest of their conversation. "I've never seen you act like my favorite groupie before. I loved seeing you totally free and uninhibited. That really turned me on, and I'd perform free of charge to experience it again."

"Don't get carried away. Your performances cost a fortune to put on and we have to get paid." She laughed. "I always danced with you at home in front of the television before I started coming to your concerts. I didn't like the live fire scenes in your act, and then there was the little situation of our marriage, pregnancy, then placement on bedrest, and two little ones to take care of at home, but I've always loved the way you perform and how happy you make other people. I thought you always knew that." She gave him a kiss and pulled away to unbutton her dress.

"Baby, I'm spent. I don't think I can get it up."

She jerked her head back and opened her mouth in surprise. "I can't count how many times I was told when I started working for you a lifetime ago to avoid disturbing you, that your suite was off-limits, or that you were busy with one of your daily treats. I assumed it meant you were involved in your daily sexual escapades."

He grabbed her and held her close to his chest. "I've never had a woman in my suite until you trespassed on me while I was in the shower. It's an urban myth that I ever spent an entire day fucking some groupie. The truth is I was probably asleep most of the day, trying to recover from a concert."

"Thanks for setting the record straight. I know you've had many women before me, but to be honest, I don't know if I accepted it deep in my heart."

When they finally arrived home after a long day, they snuggled in bed and fell asleep, their limbs entwined.

Chapter 25

Mid-morning, Bella opened her eyes to the cawing sounds of seagulls outside her window and the rhythmic sounds of the ocean waves lapping up against the shore. When she looked around, Miles wasn't in the room.

"He must have left for a run." She stretched to wake up her limbs and headed to the bathroom to wash and put on exercise wear before her session with Reagan in about an hour. They'd agreed to a joint virtual exercise class.

While preparing, she realized Pharaoh hadn't called her in three days.

Silence was golden, but she found his silence unusual. After finishing her bathroom routine and walking back to the bedroom, she reviewed her cell phone log, and found no calls from him. Curious about his abrupt change in behavior, she suddenly saw that her phone was in airplane mode and discovered that Pharaoh's phone numbers were blocked.

The phone immediately buzzed with messages from Pharaoh after she switched it back on.

"Now I know why Miles wanted to use my phone to call Reagan." Fuming, she tightened her fist, her heart racing and almost skipping a beat as she paced the room then stopped in her tracks to concentrate on taking a deep breath in and releasing it slowly to blow off steam. When she smelled the sweat of his body before she saw him, she turned around to face him as he entered the room.

"It's a nice morning and I had a great run, but I'm looking forward to a walk down the beach with you later today."

Bella looked back at her phone and refused to respond.

"Is there something wrong?" He stopped to await her answer as she raised her head and looked up from her phone with slow deliberation.

She hoped she could reduce her hostility toward him if she took her time to answer. "Did you touch my phone? No, don't answer that. I *know* you did. You had no right to place blocks on my phone without my permission."

"I thought you needed the rest, so yes, I placed blocks on your phone." His tone was unapologetic as he left her standing in the room and went to the bathroom to grab a towel. Before returning to the bedroom, he began wiping the sweat off his body. "Do you mind if I take a shower, or do you want to continue this conversation?"

"We *need* to continue this conversation, since you don't get it. You overstepped your boundaries. You don't have the right to decide who I talk to and when I talk to them." She raised her voice, fists tightening at her sides as she tossed her head from side to side.

"You're overreacting. *You've* silenced my phone before when you thought I needed a break. What's the big deal?"

"The *deal* is I asked your permission before I did anything to your phone. Give me the same respect."

"Sooo…let me understand this. I'm not respecting you because I made a decision as the CEO of my company to assert myself. I told Pharaoh not to disturb us, and as I suspected, he tried to call you anyway. In the interest of full disclosure, did you think Pharaoh overstepped his boundaries when he kissed you?" The veins in his neck were visible as he clenched his teeth. "What CEO do you know tolerates what I've tolerated from him?"

"You knew about that?" She stood still in her tracks.

"Hell yeah. Did you really think I don't know what goes on in my company? There are security cameras all around the place." He turned to go to the bathroom but stopped and put his hands on his hips before continuing his thoughts. "Thanks for telling me about that."

"I took care of it, Miles." She placed a hand to her lips. "I know I could have handled it better by telling you." She paused. "That was the night you came home late, and I had a little too much to drink. He never tried it again, so I never mentioned it. Why didn't you tell me you knew?"

"I was waiting to see if you'd come clean about it or if there was more to it."

"What did you conclude?" She reduced the volume of her voice.

"I went through some shit, just thinking the two of you were involved." He closed his eyes. "There were so many pictures of the two of you on social media. I'm a man in an industry filled with alpha males. How do you think that made me feel?"

"I'm sure it was uncomfortable, but I see pictures of you all the time with different women."

"You know those are old photos." He let out a breath. "I was hurt, but I couldn't deny seeing that you got up in his face when he kissed you. Your response wasn't one of a woman who was turned on."

"I'm sorry that I hurt you by not talking about it. I didn't want to argue about a kiss that meant nothing to me."

"Sorry?" He tightened his lips. "Do you realize we don't argue about the kids, money, or our family? All our arguments are about the same thing. *Pharaoh*. Well, Bella, I'm tired of this. Forgive me if I didn't want him to ruin my weekend with my wife."

He raised his tight fists at his waist, closed his eyes, and fiery balls appeared in his open palms before he hurled them across the room. They landed in a roaring blaze in the fireplace in the corner.

Her eyes widened and her heart thumped as she observed his fury, but she didn't flinch. Frozen in awe more than fright, she watched the flames pop and dance in bright oranges and reds.

Watching Miles gritting his teeth and struggling to gain control, her jaw dropped, never having witnessed his explosion of emotions. For the first time, she was aware of just how much his relationship with Pharaoh had disintegrated.

"I'm not afraid of your fiery temper," she said, and surprisingly, she really wasn't afraid. "I know you love me and dealing with Pharaoh has been difficult." She walked toward him and extended her hand to touch his arms, which were bright red as if sunburned, but cool under her touch.

After she placed both hands on him, he began taking deep, slowed breaths. His chest heaved less with each breath as she placed her arms around his waist and leaned her head against him.

He took her into his arms.

"I don't want you to fear me. I need you to love and trust

me." He looked out the window at the ocean waves.

"You have them both, Miles, now and forever. Are you okay?"

"I will be. I'm just confused by your need to run interference when I try to rein in Pharaoh."

"Well, I'm a little baffled that you can't see how often I've averted a crisis by talking to him, even if it's once in a couple days. When I don't talk to him, he turns to people like Dark or members of his crew. Things don't go well for him afterward." She bit her lip. She didn't want to argue about him anymore.

"Bella, he's a big boy. You need to let him own the consequences of his behavior. I don't like what this is doing to us."

The sadness in his eyes pierced her heart and lessened her anger. "I understand your motives, but I'm still angry about your methods."

"Fair enough, but don't ever keep secrets like someone making a move on you from me again." He met her gaze. "I won't stand for it."

"I realize I was wrong. I'm asking you to forgive me." She stared into his eyes. "Are you planning on apologizing for *your* behavior?"

"Would it matter if I only apologized for making you angry? I can't say I regret giving you three Pharaoh-free days. I do accept your apology."

"Well, if you can't offer a full apology, then I need some space to wrap my head around this. Miles, this isn't cool."

"We both need to examine where we are with this issue. You don't think I respected you, and I'm irritated that the two of you don't respect my authority as the head of this company. Pharaoh Little is an *employee*, Bella. Remember that."

He turned to go shower, leaving her to ponder his words,

but she was distracted by her phone ringing in the family room.

"I almost forgot about my exercise session." Hurrying out of the bedroom, she answered the Skype call from Reagan, hoping it would help her recover from the emotional encounter with Miles. Within a few minutes, Reagan's taut body came into view on the monitor, dressed in a blue spandex midriff top and matching spandex pants.

"Hey, girl, missed you out here. What have you been doing?"

Bella pulled her hair up in a high ponytail and caught it with a hair tie. "Well, I need this workout today. I've been drinking too much, eating too much, and playing too much."

"You haven't gotten any exercise?"

"Well, I've been sexing too much." She looked over her shoulder.

"Wow, girl. Your Inner Skank Goddess has finally taken over you. What did you do with my friend Bella?" Reagan threw her head back, laughing. "By the way, sexing counts as exercise. I don't want to get in your business, but Miles seems like someone who likes a good workout." She winked.

"Let's get started before I spill more secrets." Bending at the waist, Bella touched her toes to warm up.

Reagan turned on the music and began stretching. "What's going on?"

"I'll tell you later."

"Let me guess. It must have something to do with Pharaoh."

Chapter 26

I t was early afternoon before she awoke from her nap and showered after two hours of working out with Reagan. Every muscle was sore from the nonstop dancing. Miles had given her space to think, but she was too tired to deal with her feelings.

"Bella, Mom's outside with the kids," she heard him yell through the closed door of their bedroom. "I'm going outside to help her get them in the house."

She opened her eyes, still groggy from her nap. She'd thought they were due to arrive later this evening. Stumbling into the bathroom, she quickly freshened up before going out to greet her in-laws and the babies.

Miles was already outside, helping his family unload the car while the babies remained asleep in their car seats. He made it to the front steps of the house with his hands filled with baby gear and stumbled onto the porch while his mother and Ms. Burnside woke the babies and took them out of their seats.

Carmen had stayed in Charlotte, visiting her sisters.

Ariana reached for Bella and she scooped her up into her arms while they waited for Ms. Burnside, who carried Ashe inside. Lecia followed close behind them carrying their stuffed animals.

"I had to get them here earlier than I'd planned. They were both fretful after the phone call yesterday."

Bella touched each child's forehead, then leaned over to greet Lecia.

"They aren't sick," Lecia assured her. "They just missed their parents, especially Ariana. She's been clingy since you ended the phone call with them."

"I'm glad you remembered to bring their bears." Bella smiled. "They love them, and they call them Figgos," she remarked about the bears dressed in firemen outfits.

"Carmen has been teaching them Spanish." Lecia looked at the bears and handed one to each twin as they took a few steps then crawled on their knees around the floor. "I thought they were saying *fuego*, which is Spanish for fire."

"*Fuego*." Bella raised a brow. "Maybe you're right."

Cade came into the room and made the rounds with hugs and kisses for each member of his family before settling on the couch next to his wife.

Ms. Burnside rolled a stroller in front of the twins. "Do you mind if I take them for their lunch and nap? They were only sleeping for ten minutes before we arrived." Always the diplomat, Ms. Burnside looked at Lecia, then settled her attention on Bella to await instruction.

"Yes, it's important to keep them on their schedules."

The twins were both rubbing their eyes trying to fight off sleep, and they didn't put up much of a fight. They were scooped off the floor without much protest and taken around to each adult in the room to kiss them goodbye.

"I'll be in shortly to help with their feedings," Bella said.

Ms. Burnside nodded at her and departed with the babies in tow.

"I need to ask you two something." Cade raised a finger to address Bella and Miles. "We've been trying to give you the beach house around the corner for quite a long time, and now the two of you surprise us with an offer to buy the place? We're family – why do you think you would have to pay market value for something your parents own?"

Bella looked at Miles and cocked her head to the side. Before she could reveal that she knew nothing about his desire to purchase the house, he answered.

"Pop, we just thought it was the right thing to do. I wanted to give you a fair price for the place."

"Well, since you remodeled it, we both thought it was only fair to reduce the price by the amount you paid for the remodel. Your mother also made a deal with one of the designers you hired to buy the furniture, since you didn't want the furniture in the house – which, by the way, was in excellent condition."

Miles placed an arm around Bella's shoulder, but she reflexively leaned away, wondering how many decisions he had made without consulting her. She furrowed her brow as Miles stood there shifting his weight from one leg to the other, not responding.

"All right, have it your way. I'm not going to belabor the point. Bella, can I borrow my son to go fishing today?"

"Sure, the two of you have fun," she responded, barely veiling her irritation.

Lecia and Cade looked at each other and back at them with nervous smiles.

"Miles, are you up to it, or did the two of you have other plans? Please don't let us intrude. I just thought the women could spend some time together while we spent time on the ocean. I can't tell you how happy I am that both of you decided to continue the Moore family tradition of spending some time here at the Outer Banks."

"We didn't have plans. I'd love to go out fishing with you."

Cade turned to Bella. "So, what did he offer you to get you to spend more time out here?"

She pondered her response, wrinkling her brow as she searched her brain for an answer. "Well, how could I say no after he promised to purchase a ranch for us in Texas?"

Miles jerked his head, startled by her reply. "Bella, are you serious about buying a ranch?"

"Oh yes, babe, very serious. I've always wanted a home in Texas."

"We're city dwellers," he said, laughing with his father.

"You want my son, a Moore man, to be comfortable on a ranch?"

"Miles adapts well to change. It's one of the things I love about him. Can't you see how happy he is being a future owner of a ranch?" She leaned in and kissed him on the cheek, sensing his chagrin as he drew up one side of his mouth and raised an eyebrow.

"He looks anything but happy." Lecia joined in the laughter at Miles's expense.

"Come on, Pops. Let's change clothes and get out of here," he mumbled.

"I need to check on the twins. When I get back, can you help me with my hair, Lecia?" Bella asked.

"Of course. I noticed while you were in Charlotte that

FACE THE FIRE

your ends could use a good trim. I have some tools here at the house. Miles could use a little man-scaping, too, but I doubt he'll let me cut his hair. I plan to do the girls' hair when they come with my parents this weekend."

Miles stopped in his tracks and turned to his mother with a puzzled look. "Mami, how many people are joining us?"

She began using her fingers to count. "Well, your grandparents, the girls, my sister, your great aunt…"

"Stop – please. You're scaring me. We've been trying to spend quality time with just the immediate family."

"You and your father know how much I love being a part of the Moore family, but I want Bella and the twins to know the Tavares family too. Don't worry, most of the family members know you need space to conduct business even on vacation."

Bella shot him a knowing look as Lecia continued.

"What little time you spend here in the Carolinas is most often spent with the Moores, not my family. I think it's time for a change."

"Mami, we *are* Moores. Does it surprise you when we spend a lot of time with them?"

Bella looked back and forth between them, sensing this was a familiar discussion.

Lecia clasped her hands in her lap and blew out a breath. "You're members of the Tavares family too. Don't forget we love you. We want our time with you and your family."

"I'll never forget what you and my maternal relatives have done for me. I'll be fine after some time on the water today. Mami, I promise I'll be gracious and welcoming to everyone."

"Thanks for the reassurance. Sometimes they tell me you don't love them as much as you love your father's people."

He looked up at the ceiling and blew out a breath. "I need to change my clothes. I'll be back."

The thought, *At least your mother wants to spend time with you. Mine is always off taking care of business somewhere in the world*, crossed Bella's mind as she listened to Miles and his parents.

"Bella, can I talk to you in the bedroom? This won't take long." Miles looked at her.

"Sure," she said and walked off without waiting for him.

Bella stood by the bed as he closed the door and came into the room.

"What's going on?" She watched as he searched through the drawers for a new shirt. He pulled off the one he was wearing, exposing his muscular, sun-tanned chest with the light brushing of hair between his nipples.

Stay focused, girl. Don't let his sexy ass distract you.

"I want to give you a friendly reminder while I'm gone with Pops."

"Miles, what are you talking about?" She blew out a breath.

"Promise me you won't call Pharaoh, and I won't complain about buying a ranch I don't want."

"I promise I won't contact him." She pursed her lips. "I don't want to deal with him right now anyway. You bought the boat, and you made an offer on your parents' home without discussing it with me first. As for the ranch, just know there's always a price to pay for keeping me out of the loop."

"Fair enough, as long as you don't start calling me *dude*."

He looked at her out of the corner of his eye with a half grin on his face. "We're getting a late start, so I shouldn't be gone long. Are you sure you'll be okay?"

She turned her attention to one of the babies, who was crying in a bedroom down the hall. "I'll be fine. I need to go check on the twins."

He leaned in for a kiss she planted on his lips just before darting off to check on the babies.

Chapter 27

Thanks for helping me with my hair, Lecia. You have magical fingers."

"You're welcome. I wanted to try a few different products on that thick hair of yours. Do you like the feel of it?"

Bella closed her eyes to focus on the feel of her hair as she ran her fingers through it. "Yes, it does feel silkier to me. I needed the trim. You take so much time with the process of washing and styling hair – the end result is a work of art. Did you learn to do hair from watching the stylists in your family's business?"

"No, my mother taught me at home that grooming others' hair is an act of love. She perfected her techniques in her first shop, and I think that's why she was so successful and ended up expanding the business. She always told her employees that no matter the length, color, texture, or thickness, hair needed to be lovingly cared for. She insisted everyone who came to a Tavares shop left feeling pampered and appreciated. Her patrons cried and protested her decision to retire.

Now, she has time to let others do her hair."

Bella looked up at Lecia. "Did you ever think about carrying on the business?"

"No, my calling has always been healthcare. Mother taught me and my sister her techniques, and we've passed them on to our children to honor our family legacy."

"Miles talked about how he loved having your fingers in his hair as a child. He said he felt so cherished and loved when you did his hair."

"What?" She jerked her head and shoulders back in disbelief. "That little stinker used to run from me every time he had to take a bath and get his hair washed."

"Well, it must be a family trait, because Ashe isn't too fond of bathing, either, but I think I can make him a convert by giving him a good hair massage and shampoo while I bathe him."

"So, what do you think?" Lecia finished her hair and gave Bella a mirror to look at her shiny brown curls cascading down her back.

Amazed, light tears formed in Bella's eyes as she turned her head from side to side to look at Lecia's work.

"I love it. Thank you."

Their attention turned as they heard the sounds of the babies stirring from their naps.

"Do you want to join me and the babies on a walk along the beach?"

"Sure, sounds like fun. We could all use the quiet time together before the Tavares clan comes in tomorrow. Thanks for agreeing to have more company than you planned for. We don't get to see y'all often, and I really want to show off my grandbabies. I have a large extended family. They can be very entertaining after they warm up to you." She leaned in to give

Bella a hug. "It's important to me that you know how much we love you."

"Well, let's grab the babies and their stuff to enjoy a day at the beach."

Gentle winds blew off the ocean and the sea oats seemed to dance in the breeze as Bella looked at the birds flying in formation across the clear blue sky. She listened to the sounds of the waves, seagulls shrieking, and the boats ringing their bells nearby. Smiling and imagining how the melodies of nature must have stimulated Miles's young creative mind, she recalled how he once told her that songs came to life in his head when he walked along the beach. As she pushed the stroller filled with the twins, toys, and towels, she wondered if this scene had provided him with the inspiration to create "Between the Dusk and the Dawn."

Lecia leaned in and locked her arm around her elbow. "I'll give you a penny for your thoughts. You seem preoccupied with something."

Bella stopped pushing the stroller, smiled, and wiped a lock of hair blown by the wind from her face. She looked at her twins' wide eyes and open mouths as they observed the large expanse of water in front of them.

Ariana extended her chubby little hands in the direction of the water, while Ashe bounced up and down in his seat, anxious to be released from the safety belt.

"Oh, I'm just reflecting on how beautiful this area is, and how it must have been fun spending the summers here surrounded by family and friends. My husband doesn't realize he's led a charmed life." She leaned down to lock the stroller before taking the babies out of their seats, while Lecia spread a blanket out for them to sit along the shore.

"In some ways charmed, and in other ways, not so much. He had to fight for the things important to him, like the freedom to be himself. He never would've been comfortable fitting into a mold someone else carved for him. I can say from firsthand experience that Miles never assumed things would be given to him just because he was our son." They sat down to allow the babies to crawl around and enjoy the warmth of the sun. "He believed he had to work hard to get the things he wanted out of life."

Ariana stopped and sat on her bottom, surrounded by her toys, before she finally conceded her mother and grandmother weren't going to let her place the light-brown sandy stuff in her mouth.

They laughed together as they took turns pulling Ashe back onto the blanket. He always preferred exploring his environment through touch and let out a yell when he couldn't crawl to the water.

"Bella, can I ask you a question? It may be a little personal."

"Sure, what's on your mind?"

"I noticed there seemed to be a little friction between you and Miles. Is everything okay?"

"He's been on edge lately," Bella sighed.

"I see tabloids in the grocery store and I wonder if all that tabloid talk about you and Pharaoh is getting to him."

"What tabloid talk?" Bella didn't subscribe to any of the tabloids, and there was only the rare mention of her name on social media sites.

"Well, the old-school social media have you and Pharaoh

romantically linked. Miles probably ignored it at first, as he should have, but he's a man and he has his pride. I can imagine it's painful pushing down jealous thoughts, even though they may be absurd – it's got to be hard thinking someone else is lusting after your wife. I would imagine doubly so since you and Pharaoh work so closely together."

Bella looked at her as if seeing the situation for the first time through Miles's eyes even though he had talked about how it pricked his pride. She'd thought it was just his anger talking. Her hands flew to her mouth.

"He must be burning up inside, wondering if others think he's not man enough to confront Pharaoh. You're a very desirable woman, Bella, and you don't realize your beauty is only outrivaled by your kindness."

"That *does* put things in a different light. Thanks for the insight." She looked away with tears in her eyes. "My mother and I used to have candid talks like this."

"I can see by the sadness in your eyes that you missed those times." Lecia placed a hand on her arm. "That you miss her."

"I do." Bella patted Lecia's hand. "I told her that we would be in the Carolinas. I was hoping she would join us." She buried her lip between her teeth. "As usual, duty called. She told me that as the CEO of her company, she couldn't be a no-show. She had responsibilities. Instead, she continues to ghost on me and the kids."

"I imagine it was tough for your mother being a single parent after your father died."

"It was, but we had each other." Bella wiped away the tear rolling down her cheek.

"We've been blessed to have Cade, but for most of Miles's young life, Cade was touring, and I got tired of being on the road. I became overprotective of Miles once we discovered his condition. Looking back on it, I probably smothered him. For a long time, we were estranged, until you came into his life and reminded him of the importance of family."

Bella turned to face Lecia. "He has told me that many times."

They both grabbed for Ashe, who was trying to make his way to the water by crawling as quickly as he could to the waves coming closer to them. Ariana stayed close by, sitting on the blanket.

"Lecia, I'm happy the two of you are closer than ever. In the meantime, my relationship with my mother has grown more distant." She watched as the tide receded.

"Miles and I found our way back to each other. Circumstances may change between a parent and child, but the bond remains. I'm certain the two of you will find your way back to each other," Lecia assured her.

"The wind is starting to pick up." Bella turned her attention to the scenery in front of them.

Lecia nodded. "We'd better head back to the beach house."

Chapter 28

D o you know how sick I am that this is still happening in America?" Miles stormed toward Cade, who got out of the car with Captain Pritchard following close behind.

"We got here as fast as we could after hearing there was a disturbance and that you were involved in it." He stood in front of Miles, who was blowing out breaths of exasperation.

"What happened?" Cade placed an arm on his shoulder. "Why is Malcolm standing over there in handcuffs?" He pointed to the young man who had been employed by the Moore family for a year.

"I told you I wanted a few more beers from the bar and grill around the corner." He placed a hand on his hip.

"Right." Cade listened attentively.

"Malcolm was admiring the Porsche, so I let him drive."

Cade grabbed his arm and led him closer to where Malcolm was being detained. Cade addressed the officer while Miles stood beside Malcolm.

"I'm Cade Moore." He extended his hand to the officer,

who was wearing dark shades. "This man is one of our employees."

The plastic name tag on his chest identified him as Officer Connor, who gave him an appraising look before accepting the handshake.

"Good morning Mr. Moore." The officer stood tall, looking Cade in the eye.

Miles frowned and placed his finger on the metal links between the handcuffs, breaking one of them by emitting a vertical ray of fire directly on the chain, which hit the ground, causing sparks.

"Ouch, that's hot." Malcolm raised his hands in front of him.

Cade, who had a milder form of Miles's condition that allowed him to withstand high heat, turned to face Malcolm. He cooled off the links by placing his fingers on the cuffs to protect the young man's skin.

"What's going on here?" Officer Connor's jaw dropped. While turning his head, gazing at all of them standing before him, he backed away and placed a hand on his gun, holstered at his waist. "Is this some kind of Houdini trick?"

"It's not a trick, sir." Cade remained calm. "You still haven't told us why you pulled this young man over. Was he speeding?"

"You already know the answer, Pops," Miles spoke up, raising his voice in anger. "A young black man can't have a fancy car and not get pulled over. I gave him my license and the papers on the vehicle. This officer knows who I am. I could see in his eyes that he recognized me, but the car isn't registered to me yet. I told him that I brought it down here for a test-drive and had already made plans to purchase it."

"*Mijo*, calm down."

Several squad cars arrived. Miles recognized one of the officers coming toward them. It was Kell's brother, Brian Davis. His friends Sam, Frank, and Kell got out of their car and came running to the scene while a gathering crowd began chanting, *Free Miles.*

"Are these men being charged with anything?" Brian asked his fellow officer.

"You know there were reports called in last night of suspicious activity by an unwelcomed element on the island," Officer Connor replied. "I haven't charged them with anything."

"This is Miles Moore, a friend of mine. I also know Malcolm Brown. We've been friends for years."

Miles watched as Brian placed a hand on Officer Connor's shoulder.

"Malcolm was at the bar last night," Kell added. "He helps us out when we're busy."

"If you all are vouching for him," Officer Connor cleared his throat, "he's free to go." He took the keys out of his pocket and released the cuffs on Malcolm's wrists. "Sorry for the inconvenience." He returned to his car followed by his peer, Officer Davis.

"Thanks for coming," Miles told his friends.

"We got you," Kell reminded him as they took turns giving Miles fist bumps before they left and the crowd dispersed.

"Pops, I was handling this and—"

Cade raised his eyebrows. "That's not the point. You're my son, and there was no way I was going to stay at the marina and let things go south between you and the police."

The captain motioned for Malcolm to come with him to his car while Cade began walking to the Porsche.

"I wasn't going to do anything stupid." Miles rolled his

eyes.

"He apologized for the mistake," Cade noted. "Let's try to move on."

"I'm supposed to just forget about it?" Miles faced him. "I've seen reports that they've been looking at situations like this for over a decade in North Carolina, dammit… And yet the pattern continues. Blacks are more likely to be pulled over than whites and even more likely to be searched."

"Remember that." Cade placed his hands on the hood of the car. "I'm always going to be more comfortable dealing with the reality that you're alive to fight injustice than identifying your body in the morgue. Let this be a reminder of the importance of having *the talk* with Ashe and Ariana when the time is right."

Chapter 29

Miles and Cade came back shortly after Bella and Lecia had returned to the house. Cade came toward Ariana, who had her arms outstretched, while Lecia held on to Ashe. Miles greeted Bella with a kiss on her lips.

"Looks like someone needs to get the sand out of her hair," Cade said, brushing away sand clinging to Ariana's hair.

"Yes, and if you'll help me, Cade, I'll get both Ariana and Ashe washed up. Bella, do you mind if we get them ready for the evening? Give me about an hour with them."

"Sure, Mami," Miles chimed in.

"Ms. Burnside is here. She probably has things ready for their baths," Bella reminded her.

"I want to do it. It's not that often that we see them, and I want to try a massage technique on them and wash their hair. It won't take long, and we'll see you for dinner. Did the two of you catch anything?"

"We weren't lucky." Cade looked at Miles.

"We bought fish at a local market for tonight. We'll have to buy some more food for tomorrow when your parents and the girls get here," Cade told her.

"Don't worry about it. You know Tia Maria always brings a lot of food with her."

"Tia Maria is coming?" Cade stopped in his tracks, furrowing his brow and pursing his lips.

"I told you the Tavares clan was coming here Sunday, so stop acting as if this is an unexpected invasion by my family." She walked ahead with Ariana in her arms. "Cade, I didn't realize how long your hair has gotten. I'll need to do something with it."

"What's wrong with my vacation hair? Miles looks shaggier than I do."

"Let's go. My hair trimmers are inside." Lecia disappeared into the house with Cade, the twins in their arms.

Bella smiled at the simple way they seemed to handle the little irritants before they grew into big problems. She knew that, given the choice, Cade would have preferred staying in Charlotte at the family's compound, but he also knew how important it was to Lecia to spend time with her family.

When Bella turned around, Miles had a gift-wrapped box in his hands that he extended to her.

"I stopped at one of the shops near the marina."

Gently pushing the box aside, she wrapped her arms around his neck.

He tilted his head and accepted her warm tongue pulsing in and out of his mouth.

Wrapping the hand that held the box around her waist, and with the other on the back of her head, he guided his tongue into her mouth, then sucked her bottom lip with a fierceness that surprised her.

182

"I thought you would still be mad at me. I'm sorry for my behavior."

"Sorry for what, exactly?" she asked after she regained her breath.

"Where do I start? I'm sorry for blocking your phone. I'm sorry for not telling you about Pharaoh until you pressed me about it. I'm sorry for making such a large purchase without discussing it with you first. I just assumed you would love it here just as much as I do, even though we may have intrusions from the family."

"I'll grow to love being here." She gazed at him with contemplative eyes. "After thinking about it, I understand fully why you had more problems with Pharaoh's behavior long before I did."

"Be prepared." He stood before her. "I think things will unfold quickly from this point."

"I agree with you on that, unfortunately." She looked at his hand, which still held a box covered in white paper with a pink bow. "What's in the box?"

"Open it and see for yourself."

She smiled, untied the ribbon, and opened the box to reveal a white pearl necklace resting on satin fabric. Touching the silken pearls gleaming in the glow of the setting sun, she smiled. "Oh, these are beautiful." She lifted the strand off its mounting. "Thank you."

"Beautiful pearls for a beautiful woman. I love what you did with your hair. You should wear it down around your shoulders more often." He twirled a strand of it around his finger. "I feel blessed to have you as my beautiful and caring wife." Smiling, he buried his nose in her hair. "It smells good. It's so soft."

"Your mother did it for me." She touched strands of her

hair. "Actually, your mother did a *lot* for me today."

"You haven't said if you accept my apology." He touched her forehead with his.

"Your apology is accepted." She took her index finger, touching his cheek down to the angle of his jaw, then sealed their bond of understanding with a kiss on his lips. "I've learned from you that I can't control what everyone does, no matter how many times I try to prevent a crisis or hope that things will change for the better. Too many times, things will not get better. As long as we're okay as a family, then I'm okay."

Chapter 30

Remember when I told you about the incident earlier to-day?" Miles came out of the shower with a towel wrapped around his waist. Droplets of water still glistened on his chest.

Bella, lying on the bed, looked up from the tablet in front of her. "Are you talking about when you were stopped by the officer? I'm glad no one was hurt." She placed the tablet beside her.

"I've given it more thought." Using the towel, he dried his hair and body before grabbing the pajama pants he had thrown on the chair.

"It struck me that whether it was how they are trained, or if it was something that came naturally to them, Brian – Kell's brother – and his fellow officer were using the good-cop, bad-cop routine." He sat on the bed next to her. "Brian has always been a good guy with an easy-going nature, but even with Connor's heavy-handed approach, they defused the situation together."

"What are you saying?" She raised a brow.

"What I'm saying is that we all have been trying in our own way to handle the issues at the company with Pharaoh. I've tried talking to him. You've tried talking to him." He placed an arm around her shoulder and leaned back against the headboard. "Bradley is keeping him under surveillance, but we've got to be smarter. Pharaoh has been masterful in playing us against each other. You're the good cop and I'm the bad cop. The 'don't tell Miles' or 'don't tell Bella' routine has worked for him because he realized we're stronger when we handle things as a team."

"I agree." She let out a breath. "We've spent more time keeping things from each other than sharing and making decisions together."

He grabbed her hand and squeezed it. "We've got to stay one step ahead of this situation now that Dark is involved. It's important that we remain united."

"Let's get some sleep." She placed her tablet on the bedside table and pulled back the comforter before getting under the covers.

Miles reached for the lamp. His phone began buzzing before he could turn out the lights. At the same time, Bella's laptop pinged with alerts on the sites she followed.

"What now?" She frowned. Rubbing her forehead, she read the article.

"Let me guess." Miles leaned over with the phone in his hand, looking at the computer screen. "What's Pharaoh doing now?"

"He had an impromptu concert in one of the parks in Chicago and someone in the crowd fired shots."

They looked at the picture of a smiling Dark embracing Pharaoh.

"Has he lost his mind?" Miles paced the length of the bed while his phone kept buzzing. "We didn't request a permit for a concert in Chicago."

"He appeared as one of Dark's surprise performers." Bella kept her head down as she scrolled the screen.

"Yeah?" Miles placed a hand on his hip and barked at Bradley. "I'm going to place you on speaker so Bella can hear."

"He's at it again." Bradley's hard tone revealed his frustration. "One of my men who was assigned as his bodyguard tried to warn him to not take the stage, but he let the chants from the crowd sway him. If he doesn't stop this, Miles, someone is going to get killed. I'm not exaggerating. He ditched his security detail and isn't answering his phone."

"Why am I not surprised?" Miles scratched the back of his head.

Bella's phone began buzzing. She reached for it on the table and placed it on speaker. "Miles, it's Justin. As the tour manager, something must have concerned him to call us this late."

"Answer it," he told Bella. "Bradley, stay on the line."

"Sorry to disturb you, but I tried calling Miles and he isn't answering his phone."

"Hi, Justin," Bella responded. "Miles is here on the phone with Bradley. They both can hear you."

"Hi, everybody," Justin continued. "We've got some serious trouble with the tour. After the incident today, some of the venue owners are saying they don't want more problems and they're threatening to pull out, citing security concerns, while others who fear that there is going to be a split between you and Pharaoh are threatening to pull out because of money they feel they will lose if Pharaoh isn't on the tour. The boy is trouble, but let's face it." He paused. "He's hot right now. Crowds flock to see him."

"I can activate our media spin machine and start putting out press releases immediately," Bella told Justin. "What do you suggest we do about this?"

"I've tried talking to each owner, but they want reassurances from Miles. I can give you a briefing of the concerns of each of the owners."

"Sounds like I'll have to go on a goodwill tour." Miles looked at Bella.

"Your parents are going to be so disappointed if we have to leave." She moved over to make space for him on the bed.

"They won't like it, but they understand that business is a beast. I can't ghost on the people who have been loyal to AriMusic for years."

Bella nodded.

He let out a breath of relief, hoping she understood.

"I'll notify the pilot," Bradley piped up. "When do you think you will be leaving?"

"Tomorrow." Miles closed his eyes. "Justin, get with Bradley to arrange an itinerary. We'll start with the venues on the East Coast first. Bradley, I need you to go back to LA with Bella and the twins." He squeezed Bella's hand and stared into her eyes.

"I thought we were going to handle things together." She looked at him pleadingly.

"I need you to be there for the other performers scheduled for the tour." He hoped his desire that she return to LA while he handled the promoters wasn't sending a mixed message. Yes, their strategy had to be a concerted effort if they were to succeed, but for now, he needed to divide and conquer his adversaries, Dark and Pharaoh.

"We all have to do our parts, but this time we keep each other informed."

Each of them reflected on Miles's words for a few moments.

Bradley broke the silence. "Let me call you back, Justin, so we can coordinate the plans. Bye, Bella and Miles."

"Bye." They hung up their phones and got under the covers.

"The hardest part of this will be telling my mother tomorrow that we're leaving." He let out a long breath. "I'll need your help."

"We'll get through it together." She snuggled into his arms.

He sensed her pulse quickening. He had told her how hard it had been in the past to say goodbye to his mother. Lecia could be a force to reckoned with when it came to putting family first.

Miles and Cade were seated in the study.

Lecia looked around the room. "Where's Bella?"

"She's upstairs, collecting and packing the babies' things."

Lecia's eyes widened as she placed a hand on her chest. "Packing? Why? What are you talking about? We were all having a great time and the family is coming today."

Miles covered his face with his hand, letting it descend to his throat as the tension in the room rose. "Bella," he went to the hallway and yelled to her while remaining at the foot of the stairs. "Can you come down, please?"

"I'll be down in a minute," she responded before taking her time descending the stairs and following him to where his parents were assembled.

Lecia led her to the couch and motioned for her to take a seat. "What's going on? Miles told me you all were planning on leaving."

"Mami, please don't put Bella on the spot. Something happened with the upcoming tour and we had to make an unexpected decision to leave. We barely got any time to relax after dinner last night when our phones started blowing up with information about an incident involving one of our artists."

"Can't someone else handle it? I know you have *someone* on staff with the expertise."

"That would be me, Mami. I need to intervene in this, and I can't handle it from here." Miles grabbed a drink from the bar and sat next to Bella, repeatedly crossing his legs.

"Mami, the babies aren't accustomed to being around a roomful of strangers."

"That's why I want to introduce them to their *family*. Does this have to do with all the family members planning on coming?" She leaned closer to Bella. "We can get a hold of everyone and tell them not to come. We can do that. Right, Cade? I'm sure they will understand, and if they don't, we can address it later. Is there something else you're not telling me?"

Cade moved closer to her and placed his arm around her shoulder as she looked at Miles.

"Mami, Bella and the kids will be flying out of Wilmington International later today, back to California, so we won't be returning to Charlotte." He sat back in his chair, awaiting the eruption of emotions. "I'm going to have the Porsche shipped from here and fly out on business."

"I see." She sat quietly, her eyes welling with tears. She drew her hands up into fists and swallowed hard.

His chest was heavy as he observed her attempting to speak, but no words would come out.

"Excuse me before I say something I will regret," she told them, and fled the room with Cade following close behind.

He came back only minutes later. "I couldn't console her. She's in our room crying. Can you talk to her? She's too hurt and angry right now to listen to me."

"Sure. Bella, please come with me."

He took her hand and led her to his parents' room, where his mother sat on the side of the bed in tears. Bella loosened her grip on his hands to allow him to go comfort his mother as he took her into his arms.

"Mami, I haven't seen you like this in a long time. Why all the tears? I've said goodbye to you many times in the past few years."

"You have, but this time when you leave, Bella will go with you, and my babies will leave me, too."

As Bella looked on, tears began to fall from her eyes as well.

"Alicia, that's right. I'm leaving and I'm taking my family with me."

She stopped crying and looked up at him. As expected, he had gotten her attention. It was easier to cope with his mother's anger than her tears.

"You know I don't like it when you call me Alicia." She narrowed her eyes and dabbed them with a tissue Bella gave her from the box on her nightstand.

"Okay, so now that I've gotten you to stop crying, Lecia, how are we going to handle this?" He smiled and stroked her cheek.

"Don't call me Lecia, either. I don't want the babies calling me by my first name."

"They won't, Mami. You know it hurts me to see you like this, but I have to get back to work."

Bella took a breath before speaking. "I understand your feelings, Lecia, and I'm working through my feelings about his plans to tour again, but you told me before we got married that there were challenges to being the wife of a superstar, and this is one of them. Can we share some good news?"

Lecia sat up and leaned in. "I could use a little good news right about now."

"Miles and I have talked about adding an in-law suite and additional bedrooms for a growing family to the house. I'd love if you'd come to California to help me design the in-law suite and renovate the family suite at the estate next door. We can drink wine and keep each other company while our husbands are busy working on tour. What do you think?"

She dried her tears before responding. "I'd like that, but I need to know why you and the kids can't stay here while Miles handles business. He stopped coming home often years ago. I didn't like it, but I got used to it."

Miles and Bella looked at each other before he answered. "I dreaded saying goodbye to you."

"Like father, like son?" She jutted her chin in the air. "Business before family?"

"Lecia, you're not being fair, dumping old stuff on the two of them." Cade, who was standing in the doorway, pursed his lips.

"I don't mean to be unfair." She patted Miles's and Bella's hands.

"Mami, you know I needed time away to build my own business and establish my own identity."

"Do you know who you are *now*?" She side-eyed him. They both laughed.

"I'm in a good place right now. I have a great family, and believe me, I don't take any of you for granted anymore. I have a woman I love more than life itself and a mother who is an excellent role model of what a good woman looks like. My children are healthy, and we plan to add to our family some-day. I have my priorities straight and I know who I am."

"As for me…" Bella cleared her throat. "Miles and I dis-cussed it. I'm an equal partner in the business and I need to take care of things in LA while he handles business on the East Coast."

"I see." She stood, straightened her back, and smoothed the wrinkles from her dress. "I'm not going to ruin this day, then. I'll enjoy the time I have with you and not give you an-other reason to avoid coming home to North Carolina. You have to promise me that you'll come back on the Apology Tour as soon as possible."

Cade came into the room and looked around at each of them. His wife was no longer crying, Miles and Bella no longer looked distressed, and Bosco was wagging his tail and walking around Lecia to comfort her.

She bent to pet him and looked up at her husband.

Bella tilted her head as she looked at them. "What's the Apology Tour?"

"I'll answer that." Cade took a seat as Miles moved over to the bed, close to Bella. "The tradition started with me, when my schedule prevented me from being with the family during holidays and family events. When I returned home, they called it the 'Apology Tour' because I would come home with presents, or we would go on a trip somewhere, just the five of us. So when Miles's career took off and he couldn't be with us, he came home as soon as he could and spent time with just the immediate family."

"Well then, I'm fine with an Apology Tour – and, to smooth over hurt feelings, we can plan something with the extended family, too. What do you think, Miles?"

"That'll be fine. I've had a great time this week, and it's not like I don't understand the importance of the kids knowing their family members."

"Okay, is this crying-fest over, then? Lecia, I'm hungry, are you good?" Cade embraced her.

"I'm good." Lecia planted a kiss on his lips.

Later that day, their final goodbyes were filled with tears, but after promises to see each other soon, Bella and the kids headed back to California while Miles left for Atlanta.

Chapter 31

The babies slept through most of the trip, lulled by the motions of a gentle flight and by the actions of Ms. Burnside and Carmen, who had taken turns keeping the twins up before their return home.

"Thanks to the two of you, the babies are learning to travel well." Bella loved those two women and was grateful for the care they provided to the family, especially since it was likely they all would be on the road if Miles signed on for another tour.

For a week, she worked from their home office, putting in long hours.

"I'm glad we were able to avert a crisis," Miles had told her the night before, after he returned to California. "Some of the venue owners would not budge on the agreement to have Pharaoh appear on tour. Pharaoh finally called me. We'll have to work out a deal if he's a free agent and wants to appear at some of the stops."

Miles had decided to come into the office later than usual.

Feeling she needed to celebrate a small victory, she'd had her nails manicured the previous day. She spent more time than usual that morning with her hair, coiffed like her mother-in-law had styled it. Her curls were lush and fell around her shoulders instead of in a neatly groomed bun. In a black, A-line, form-fitting dress and ankle boots to match, her fashion reflected a mixture of business chic with a kickass edge to match. She was ready for whatever came her way.

When she entered the studio, she was surprised as she looked around to see new monitors and newsfeeds scrolling around the room, which Miles evidently had installed while they were away.

"Good morning. Glad you all are back," NeNe greeted her as she walked through the main hall with a cup of coffee in her hand.

She moved in a slow circle, observing the changes. "Good morning. Things are different around here."

"Miles gave me the heads-up while you all were still in North Carolina. He said there were going to be some major changes at AriMusic which require my legal expertise and attention, so he set up an office for me here at the studio." Surveying her new look, NeNe gazed at Bella from head to toe. "You really want to give them something else to talk about, huh?"

"NeNe, it's too early for riddles. What are you talking about?" Bella turned to face her with one hand on her hip, the other arm holding her textured black leather designer bag. "I came in early to check my messages before the day got started. What else is there to discuss?"

"I'm not talking in riddles, just giving you a compliment. You look gorgeous in that dress, and your hair is sexy as hell. Did you get a new stylist and fire the old one?"

"I never had a stylist. I dressed myself, but thank you for the compliment, I think."

NeNe blew over her coffee before taking another sip. "Some of the background singers haven't gotten used to me being here yet. And, for the record, you and Miles need to clean house. I can't tell you how often I've heard one of them saying you must be cheating on him with Pharaoh. I think they're the ones leaking those tales to the smut media, because I saw an article that insinuated you were having sex with both of them on a beach in North Carolina."

Bella rolled her eyes and released a cleansing breath. "NeNe, you can't pay attention to everything you see in those lowbrow publications. Everyone knows it's just sensationalism and fake news."

"Understood, but you can't run an organization where information is constantly leaking out. In the event you get sued, negative press doesn't help. The news may not be true, but once it gets out there, the damage is done. Seriously, you've got to address this torch Pharaoh is carrying for you. He's not a child, and his puppy love for you isn't cute anymore – if it ever was. The staff also need to be informed that we're in the process of severing our ties with Pharaoh."

"Don't worry about it. Pharaoh won't be my problem much longer. I need to focus on making this a teachable moment for the other artists. They need to be reminded that granting interviews or making surprise appearances without clearing it with the marketing department won't be tolerated. I understand that our artists are young and may want to spend nights partying at clubs in their old neighborhoods, but we can't risk it if it's dangerous. I got an alert showing pictures of Pharaoh in another brawl two nights ago with a guy. Latifah was there and he placed her in danger too. His bodyguards stepped in and threw a few punches before Pharaoh sprinkled the guy with cash. The caption read, 'This should handle it.' Have you gotten any notifications of pending legal actions?"

"No, but that would be better than this guy handling it by the code of the streets. Trust me, I would keep my distance from him until this matter settles." NeNe paused and took in a deep breath. "We'd both better get some work done while we can. Something tells me this is going to be a day full of surprises, and not good ones."

Chapter 32

Bella settled into her office, spending the first several hours answering emails, text messages, and setting up press releases for some of the artists. When she looked at data from recording sales, she couldn't believe "Between the Dusk and the Dawn" was on its way to platinum status, and "Cannibals" had also surpassed gold status in sales. Reviewing the data again before getting up to find Miles, she saw the flashing lights in the main hall from the monitors.

Pharaoh is the new reigning king of hip-hop. The heir-apparent scores again in his new masterpiece. His iconic sound will make these new releases a must-have for the serious collector.

She read the reviews scrolling on the board around the room and was about to find Miles to share the good news with him when the door opened, revealing a disheveled Pharaoh with red, angry-looking scratches on the side of his face. Clad in dark sunshades, a wrinkled T-shirt, jeans, and leather boots, he stood just inside the door, placing his shades on his head. After reading the news scrolling around him several times, he bolted to Bella, grabbing her in his arms.

A loud thud reverberated through the room – he'd knocked a table over in his race to reach her. She put her hands out to stop him, but he swung her in the air despite her protest.

"We did it, Bella. Baby, we're creating magic."

"Put me down, Pharaoh." She frowned, tilting her head for a closer look at his fading bruises.

Her demands were drowned out by his loud voice echoing off the walls as he swung her around, while she attempted to maintain her modesty by holding the tail of her dress, which rose just below her buttocks. After multiple revolutions in Pharaoh's embrace, she felt a second set of arms on her back, and gave a worried look over at Miles, who released her from Pharaoh's clutches.

He wore no smile on his face. Instead, a look of consternation formed as he held her in a protective embrace while she attempted to stop her head from spinning. Grateful that he was maintaining his composure, she managed a ghost of a smile as he refused to look at Pharaoh, but kept his eyes focused on her.

"Are you okay?"

"I'll be fine." She placed one hand on the side of her face and blinked to relieve her dizziness, then placed her other hand on his chest as he slowly looked up and glared at Pharaoh. Fearing fierce drama between the two of them, she turned to face Miles and planted a kiss on his lips for everyone to see, and to hopefully defuse the situation.

"We did it, everyone. Look at the news scrolling around us." Pharaoh raised his hands in the air. "The media is proclaiming me the new king of hip-hop," he announced to the crowd gathering in the grand hall.

Latifah came up to offer him a congratulatory kiss on his lips, and he returned it, eagerly putting his tongue deep in her mouth while the others looked on.

Bella turned and saw that Miles was still grim-faced.

Pharaoh finally broke the kiss with Latifah, but kept his arms around her. "My crew has started calling me Tut, the boy pharaoh. I think I'll use it as my stage name."

Bella placed her hand on Miles's taut forearm as he made fists at his sides. Although he hadn't said anything to him yet, she feared he would explode in a tirade at any moment.

"We have you branded – no, *promoted* – by your given name, Pharaoh. Not Tut."

"Oh, so I'm *branded* like cattle on your ranch, Miles?"

"Let's talk about this privately." He turned, leaving Pharaoh standing there while the others looked at him.

Chapter 33

Miles looked at the nanny-cam video of the twins playing in their nursery, which warmed his heart with love and reminded him of what was important in his life while he awaited Pharaoh's arrival.

Minutes later, Pharaoh arrived with Bella in tow. It didn't escape his notice that Pharaoh remained standing behind the chairs, just out of arm's reach. He barely acknowledged him, instead looking back at the twins on his computer screen before shutting down the computer.

"There's something you want to say to me?" Pharaoh looked down his nose. "Good, I think it's time we talk, too."

Miles curled his lip as he glared at the man. The time period during which he'd chosen to indulge Pharaoh was over. He had made it clear on several occasions that he expected respect in his office.

"Let's get this over with." Pharaoh offered a watery smile while maintaining a safe distance from Miles.

"Let's all have a seat and discuss things calmly," Bella

said quietly. She often rubbed her forearm when she was nervous, just like she was doing now. She took a seat and urged Pharaoh to do the same.

"Sure, we can talk about things like adults. I have no problems sitting down." Pharaoh pulled out the chair and extended the distance between them before taking a seat. "I have some demands, the first one being a name change. I've already gone on my sites and announced my name is Tut." He leaned to the side of his chair, snickering. "They went wild. My fans loved it."

Miles's chest burned with anger as his mouth filled with saliva. He took a breath, fighting back the desire to spit on Pharaoh.

"I also don't want to go to some of those lame, company-sponsored meet-and-greets where the stuffed-shirt executives from the magazines and radio stations expect to shake my hand, then run for hand sanitizer like I have some disease. I want my music in the streets, where it belongs."

Miles reached over and pressed the call button on the intercom. "Darien, cancel all of Tut's media appearances for the next three days. He doesn't want any more meet-and-greets."

"Who's Tut?"

"Pharaoh's new name is Tut. Bella is here, too. She'll review all his scheduled appearances and assist you in reassigning him to one of our other publicists. That's all for now." He clicked off the speaker and turned to her, surprised she'd gotten out of her chair.

She took her time swaying her hips as she came around the desk.

"I can handle Tut's schedule." With piercing eye contact, her gaze was steadfast as she sat on the arm of his chair.

"Bella, let Darien handle it. Besides, I need your help in

arranging media coverage for Pele, along with individual appearances for Reagan. Her loyalty to the company should be rewarded. I'll also discuss plans later to cover the new artists we're bringing into the company in the next month."

Without forethought, he placed a hand in the small of her back while Bella pleaded silently with her eyes. Their focus only on each other was broken by Tut clearing his throat. Miles knew Pharaoh had gotten the message. *She's mine and always will be.*

Miles looked up at the man who'd once been his protégé. He was angry but saddened at the same time that their relationship had come to this.

"You can play this how you want to, Miles. I didn't say I had a problem with all the appearances Bella scheduled for me, just some of them. But you run this company as you wish, *sir*." Turning his head to Bella, he snarled, "Didn't you just tell me you were a partner in this business, or does he just let you *think* you're a partner? Never mind, don't answer that." He waved his hand dismissively.

"I'm going to get you the shovel I promised you because you just can't help digging deep holes for yourself," Bella snapped.

He sank back in his chair, shoulders slumped.

Miles was going to talk to him about his frequent partying and caution him about mixing business with pleasure, but he couldn't pass on the chance of watching *Tut* fall in the hole and cover his own grave. A slight smile appeared as he settled down to enjoy the show. This was too delicious.

"I want some time where I'm completely off the clock. And if I want to go to a club of my choosing, I'll go. My contract doesn't include how I spend my free time or staying in a bubble you created. I have true friends who've told me I have leverage with this company. After all, I'm your most famous and lucrative artist. I've raked in the most profit for the company."

Bella closed her eyes and threw her arm around the back of his chair. "Please listen to whatever Miles needs to tell you and go. You're incorrect. Miles is still the most profitable artist at AriMusic." She looked at Tut and then laid her gaze on Miles. "Just share what you need to share with Tut. There's no need to waste time."

"No, *you're* wrong." Tut sat up, his back stiffened. "My agent told me I'm the most profitable."

Miles finally spoke. "So, you admit you've broken your contract? You have an agent not connected with the company?"

"I haven't signed any papers, but he's looking out for me. He told me Dark Nyland is ready to offer me a sweet deal whenever I'm free. I told them I'd stay with you as long as things continued to work out for me. Yesterday I heard a new track in the studio that the producers were working on for the compilation project. I tried to get back in the studio an hour ago to start laying down some vocals, but my password didn't work. Can you fix it?"

"There's no need to fix it. Your security account has been suspended. I'll be recording the songs you saw on the music master list yesterday. Those songs weren't written for you."

With more difficulty than Miles had imagined, he maintained eye contact and bit his lip to contain the intense heat rising from deep within his chest, threatening to explode. Taking his time, he spoke in a slow, deliberate manner as Bella arose to face him.

"You've shared a lot with me, Pharaoh – pardon me, *Tut* – so let me be clear. You're in breach of your contract, but I won't begin legal proceedings until you've had time to hire your own lawyers to meet with NeNe. You're now free to negotiate with any agent and to sign any contract you wish. You got what you've been asking for. You're a free agent."

Pharaoh stood, scraping the legs of the chair along the wooden floor, but he made no quick movement toward Miles. "You'll regret this. I promise you will. Bella, I want you to come with me. You can continue to promote my career and leave this bastard. I'll pay you whatever you ask – and, unlike him, I'll respect you."

Bella held out her hands, separating them while trying to be the voice of reason. "Everyone needs to calm down. Tut, Miles, let's not end our relationship like this. We can work out our differences. We have a tour coming up. We need to see if we can negotiate your appearance on some of the stops." She let out a breath and wiped her brow with the back of her hand. "Why are you asking me to leave? You know I belong here at AriMusic and this bad-boy behavior has gone on long enough. Miles has been good to you, and it's time you respect that he's the boss."

"But he doesn't own me, Bella. I'm not his slave!" he yelled back at her, then grabbed his forehead. "I'm sorry. I didn't mean to scream at you."

Miles cut in. "You're right, I don't own you, but I do own your masters, which means I own the rights to everything you've recorded at AriMusic, considering I wrote almost all of your hits."

Bella looked at Miles, widening her eyes as he shrugged unapologetically. He had intentionally tossed fuel onto the fire.

"Okay, you've left me no choice. I can start over elsewhere. I would've used my own music if you allowed it.

You're just jealous of me, Miles. That's what this is."

"Let's end this before I start laughing at your jokes." He smiled and broke out into laughter, holding his belly as everyone else looked on. "NeNe will be available today if you want to discuss legal issues, or you can wait until you hire your own legal counsel. Either way, we'll be in touch." He wiped the tears of glee from his eyes, calming down.

Tut's jaw tightened, and he raised his fists, but Miles didn't flinch. He stepped back, looking at Bradley and another security guard, who had entered the room and were rolling up their sleeves.

"I don't want any trouble," he conceded, backing away from the desk.

"We need to escort you off the grounds." Bradley extended his hand to direct him out of the office.

He followed them, leaving Bella and Miles alone behind the closed door.

She looked at him, tears glistening but refusing to fall. "Be honest with me, did you plan this?"

"No, babe, things unraveled. Although I didn't plan it, I'm not surprised it ended this way. We've been on this road for quite some time, and now we've come to the end of it. I'm not sorry he chose to leave."

"I support your decision, but he's not a bad person, Miles. He's misguided and full of pain. The alcohol and probable drug use aren't helping either. I know he doesn't understand how this business works, but without someone looking out for his best interests, it won't end well for him. I'll talk to Darien about his appearances, and then I think I'm going home to work from there. It's only our first week back and I'm exhausted. Can we go back to North Carolina?" She shook her head as he stood and hugged her.

"Only if you let me have my way with you," he chuckled.

"Come home early tonight and we can make that happen." She flipped her hair and placed her hands on her hips as she thrust her breasts forward.

"Make sure you have your cuffs available."

"Will do, Officer."

He watched her turn and leave.

Chapter 34

Tut: Come with me.

Bella looked at the most recent text from Tut and read it just as another text came in from him.

Tut: I need you.

She knew what she had to do. She blocked his number, knowing that Miles could've ordered his communications to be blocked on all AriMusic company phones, including hers, but he hadn't. He'd showed restraint. She appreciated that he'd learned from his mistakes.

There was enough blame to go around. Tut wasn't the only one responsible for how their professional relationship had ended. She could have been less tolerant of his boundary violations and indiscretions earlier. Maybe that could've helped him understand why he shouldn't have expected special treatment. He was a talented artist in a company full of talented artists. Miles wasn't going to appease him ever again.

It's better to end this now before it gets worse.

Deciding not to obsess over the break with Tut, she didn't

leave the office right away. Instead, she spent the afternoon writing press articles scheduled for release immediately after alerts on the media sites notified her that the news of his departure from AriMusic had broken. Her strategy was to counter all negative press, but she would remain silent until Tut was ready to let everyone know his affiliation with the company was severed.

She knew there was still time for him to come to his senses and realize Miles had been a good mentor to him before making a mess of things in public.

Sure, Tut could get another contract. His departure would cost the company money in sales, but not to the point that the company would go under without its young star. There was so much potential in continuing their collaboration, but the animosity overpowered any good left in maintaining the relationship. Sensing the macho battle between the two men, she felt like something primal was going on between Miles and Tut as they each vied for the role of alpha male.

"Why couldn't Tut see the position of dominance had already been established? Miles was the king of the pride," she fumed. "He's not dumb." She wondered if his *crush* on her had been fueled by someone like Dark, who had manipulated their conflicts into a crazy competition that included Pharaoh trying to take everything that belonged to Miles.

"Miles will always be number one in my heart." She felt the heaviness in her chest as she thought of the plans Miles once had for Tut. Unlike NeNe, he was an employee of the company of which she was part-owner.

"There's work family and then there's genuine family," she reminded herself.

She had the stomach for gut-roiling conflicts of the business, but did she have the heart to endure this level of antagonism?

Taking a cleansing breath, she turned on the nanny cam and smiled as she watched her babies playing with each other and Carmen. They sang, then threw their hands in the air.

Having had enough for one day, she packed up and hurried home.

A week had passed since Tut stormed out of Miles's office, and there was still no word from his lawyers or any announcements in the media of his departure from the label. Bella checked her sites throughout the day, baffled by his silence. Yes, he still posted on his fan sites, and there were several pictures of him making the rounds at clubs in the LA area, surrounded by young men she didn't know. But she couldn't worry about him anymore. He wasn't her client.

She sank back in her chair and rubbed her forearms, feeling an imaginary chill in the air.

"He's up to something, but what?" Tapping her cheek, she wondered about his next move.

At this point, it wasn't clear what worried her more – Tut's future response or Miles's counter-response.

Chapter 35

M iles stared at the image of his children, now a year old. His chest warmed as he remembered the celebration that Bella had planned with balloons that had filled the family room on their birthday. Smiling, he recalled their expressions when they smeared their faces with cake. *That was a good day.*

Ms. Burnside had told him she'd started playing his music, a collection of nursery rhymes he'd recorded just for them when he was away for a few days on a business trip, and they'd cried the first day she didn't play it for them. He watched as they twirled and bounced to the music. "I can't resist my babies any longer."

Song time with Dada was now a part of their afternoon schedule, and he couldn't get enough of seeing them bouncing around and singing with their plastic mics. Ariana was partial to the song "Twinkle" while the hip-hop songs got Ashe up kicking his feet and singing.

Ms. Burnside was in the corner clapping her hands while

Ashe reveled in the attention of his audience of one.

He turned off the computer and notified Darien to hold all calls as he was off for the rest of the day. Bella hadn't fully shared her feelings with him about Tut's departure six weeks ago and frankly, he hadn't encouraged a discussion about him either. Should he fight Pharaoh and keep his masters? He made up his mind that today would be the day, since he couldn't risk having Tut become a divisive issue between them. Her last comment before he left the house earlier that morning had been cryptic. He'd pondered it before diving into work.

"It's not always good to let sleeping dogs lie."

He knew what she was referring to, but he'd grabbed his toast and hurried to the office instead of risking another argument.

After arriving home earlier than planned, Miles looked around the quiet room and went directly to the bar, but he could hear Bella's voice getting closer as he fixed his drink.

"Miles, is that you?"

He took a gulp of the drink and willed himself to remain calm, no matter how heated the discussion became.

"It's me, babe," he answered as she entered the room with a twin on each side.

"Dada," they gleefully shouted, toddling over to him with their arms stretched out wide.

He bowed and looked at a smiling Bella as he scooped them both into his arms. Sighing, he was relieved that it wasn't going to be a showdown. While bouncing them in his arms, she came closer for a kiss. He much preferred the lovefest.

"You're home early. Everything okay?"

"Sure, things are fine. Well, things are still up in the air at the office, but I was more interested in making sure they were fine between us."

"Why wouldn't they be?" She fixed a glass of sparkling water on ice and took a sip as one of the housekeepers came into the room.

"I can serve the dinner you prepared for everyone outside, if you'd like. I take it your plans have changed, and you won't be eating alone?"

"That would be great, thank you." Bella turned to Miles after the housekeeper departed.

He raised an eyebrow. "You cooked today?"

"Yes, I prepared dinner and thought I would be watching the sunset by myself after feeding the kids, but to address your concerns about things still being up in the air, I'm assuming you're referring to Tut?"

"Exactly." He leaned in and looked at her, hoping to read her thoughts.

"Let's wait and discuss things over a satisfying meal. You can see how excited the twins are to see you. They've been asking about you all day."

He looked at them and planted big kisses on the sides of their faces, grateful for their unconditional love. Then he followed Bella to the patio, where their meal of roasted veggies and flank steak rested on warm plates. Bella helped Ashe into his seat while Miles planted Ariana in her chair and pushed it close to the table. Organic finger foods prepared just for them were put on their trays so they could feed themselves.

He felt electric shocks fly between them as Bella brushed

against him to get Ashe out of his arms.

The scent of the food wafted around him. He took in a deep breath to savor the smells while he pulled out his chair and sat down before taking his first bite.

"Gosh, it's good to be home." He let out a cleansing breath. "I needed to get out of the office."

"It's been tough for several weeks." She placed a hand on his shoulder. "I'm glad you chose to take a break."

The food was complemented by fine wine and sippy cups filled with apple juice. They enjoyed the afternoon consumed with laughter and good food before the sun slipped away and took a bow in a curtain of orange and red that stretched across the sky as it descended from view.

Ms. Burnside and Carmen joined them to take the twins for their baths in preparation for bed. Their fussing ceased after he got up to kiss each child.

"I'll read to them tonight. It's been a while since we enjoyed a nighttime story."

"Great," Ms. Burnside responded. "We'll have the children ready for story time in about half an hour."

He nodded before they left with the children. "Bella, if you'd like, you can enjoy some me-time in a nice warm bath."

"That sounds great. I think I'll take you up on the offer. Meet me in the bedroom after you're done with the twins?" She wiggled her brows and he raised an eyebrow.

"I think I can handle that."

Rising from his chair, he smiled in anticipation of the fun he always had reading to his children and ending their reading time with a song.

Tired from reading four instead of two stories, he put the babies in their cribs after he couldn't resist their requests.

"Notha story, Dada."

If he was being honest, he needed the time to call upon his courage. The heated discussion with Tut still played in his mind. He hadn't asked her, but what if Tut was communicating with Bella? Dismissing the thought, he walked to his bedroom to take a shower, but when he opened the door, Bella wasn't in the bedroom.

Before going to the bathroom, he grabbed a pair of lounging pants and looked around their suite, including the bathroom. She wasn't there, either. He turned on the shower and got in, allowing the heated water to flow down his tired muscles. He thought about Bella as his maleness lengthened and engorged with the heat of his blood. She always had that effect on him, filling him with desire as he lathered the soap and rubbed it across his body.

He'd been drawn to her beauty from the first day he saw her, and although her style of dressing was understated, it couldn't hide her beauty, which she seemed unaware of. There was nothing vain about her. The glow of her flawless, youthful skin made him want to reach out and touch her every time he saw her. Her inner beauty had bonded him to her for life and made gazing into her soft brown eyes a delight.

His member was at full length and hard as stone while he imagined cupping her full, perky breasts.

Turning off the water, he grabbed his towel and dried off his body before stepping into his pants and pulling them loosely around his hips. He returned to the bedroom, eager to find Bella, and there she was, sitting in bed under a cream-colored sheet sheer enough to reveal her womanly curves. He couldn't resist her. There would be time to work out their differences later. Right now, their bodies needed to communicate with each other.

He got under the covers and took her into his arms, capturing her mouth with his before slowly releasing her. "I love you. Everything I am and everything I own belongs to you."

"I know that. No matter what happens, it's always going to be me and you." She parted her legs, and the two of them became intertwined as one.

He loved that about them. Regardless of what happened outside of their relationship, their bodies always called out to each other, keeping them so close no one could come between them. He spooned with her after making love, awake and satisfied she was still in his arms. He brushed her hair to the side and felt her smile against his cheek.

"I can't believe you're still awake." He turned her to face him and finally asked the question. "Are you angry with me that I'm not giving Tut his masters?"

She cupped his face. "No, I understand it's business and you had to make a hard decision. I'm only worried we haven't heard from him. I don't know what to expect."

"Whatever he does, we'll face it together. I think he's enjoying his freedom to do whatever he pleases. We're still putting royalty checks in his bank account from proceeds of the 'Between the Dusk and the Dawn' recording. Sales have exceeded my expectations, and he'll need some money during his transition. That's the least I can do, considering there was a time when I had high hopes for him."

"You did that for him?" When he nodded, she leaned forward for a kiss.

"Baby, your big heart never ceases to amaze me. Maybe you're right. He's probably quiet and grateful for your generosity. That's a load off my mind." She snuggled into him and closed her eyes.

He felt her breaths, slow and warm against his skin. He was happy she was sharing her feelings and releasing some of the pressures of the day.

"I don't want it to get ugly between us and Tut, but I won't back down from a fight." He hugged her tight as he made his position known.

"I never imagined you would back down." She yawned before dozing off, asleep in his arms.

Miles stirred as he followed Bella with his eyes. He'd heard her tablet ping with an alert and watched her silently as she grabbed it and snuck out of the room. It was 3:00 a.m. With quiet feet, he padded to her office behind her.

She looked up as he stared from the doorway.

He folded his arms and leaned against the doorjamb. "Were you trying to escape from me?"

"No, I didn't want to disturb your sleep." She placed the tablet on the desk and rubbed the sleep out of her eyes while he yawned and went to sit on the couch.

"Join me over here." He beckoned to her. "We might as well look at whatever it is together."

She got up, walked to the couch, and sat in his embrace before opening the site to discover the bold headline.

Tut no longer entombed at AriMusic.
A new music era for the Boy King starts NOW.

Together, they read the article, which announced his departure from AriMusic and his plans to sign with Nyland Productions.

Bella clicked on the play icon on the attached video, revealing Tut singing a song accompanied by a man playing a guitar. She placed the tablet in her lap, unable to stop glaring at it as she shook her head and placed a fist between her open lips.

He watched as her eyes filled with anger and sadness.

"This song belongs to you, doesn't it? Was this the song he asked you to record? Did he steal this song?"

"Yes, yes, and yes." He rubbed her arms as her chest heaved.

"It's going to get ugly, isn't it?"

"Not if he doesn't forget he signed a legal contract. I plan to remind him if he has forgotten, but first, let me explain something. His actions fall in line with my Plan B. He'll need to come to the negotiation table or else."

"What are you talking about?" She looked into his eyes and smoothed the worry lines from her brow.

"I knew I had to make plans to feed his revenge. He's young, impetuous, and surrounded by men urging him to seek out a way to hurt me. I guess it took him some time to remember the hook and one of the verses I posted on the master list of songs over a month ago. We'll let it play for a couple of days in the media, and then I'll have NeNe send a letter to Nyland Productions of our plans to sue for theft of intellectual property if they record the song for sales and distribution. He's still under contract with AriMusic until he officially meets with our lawyers to formally end our relationship. In the meantime, my producers will take his voice and add it to the song I plan to release as a duet. I know you're concerned the song will fuel rumors he was having a relationship with you, but we have pictures of him with a dancer, who's already agreed to fill the media with information regarding her relationship with Tut. Although brief, it'll serve a purpose. She thinks the publicity will help her career – maybe, maybe not. Our people are spinning the story right now. I'm only sorry that Latifah will be hurt by these revelations." He looked at her with sad eyes. "We're monitoring his social media sites. I don't want you attached to this story. Let our other publicists handle this."

"I understand your position, but I think you're wrong on this one. I can handle it. My absence from this situation will be interpreted as my guilt. I'm the chief marketing officer and this is business. I'll handle it later today, but for now we're both tired. Let's go back to bed."

She got up and extended her hand to him, but it hung in the air as he leaned back into the couch, his lips drawn tight, hands behind his head. He looked at her, but eventually took her hand and got up.

She wrapped her arm around his waist. "We need to get some rest and not waste time disagreeing about how to handle this right now."

"I trust your instincts. I'll go along with this for the moment. But if that bastard spreads any lies about you, he'll live to regret it."

She rubbed his chest to settle him down as they walked back to their bedroom while he held her close in his arms.

Chapter 36

Stop fightin' it, girl
U belong in my world
I make your toes curl
Call me your Duke of Earl and

There's nothin' U can do about it
I never doubted it
I want to shout
about it
I love U
U love me and
There's nothin' U can do
about it

(Sung by Tut / Lyrics by Miles)

Despite hearing the whispers as she passed the open doors on the way to her office, she had more important things to focus on, like delivering a statement timed for a mid-morning release so it could play on most entertainment radio news segments and on television entertainment shows. Next up was reviewing all posts from AriMusic to include well wishes for Tut. Foremost, she needed to make sure it was clear his relationship with AriMusic had been severed. There would be no animosity between their two camps – at least, none for public consumption.

Her morning schedule included a conference call with NeNe and Miles to follow up on legal matters between their firm and Nyland Productions, so they could come to some terms of agreement for termination. NeNe knew the lawyers who handled their legal affairs and was comfortable she wouldn't have to threaten a lawsuit if they released more music stolen from AriMusic. When Bella hung up the phone, she was relieved Tut couldn't extend the growing feud by sabotaging things at the studio.

Turning her attention away from Tut's actions, she focused on the next key step – solidifying the relationship between Miles and his other employees to avoid the development of Team Miles and Team Tut. While they knew Tut was a pain in the ass for Miles, he was well-liked by many of the singers and dancers for his playful nature, and he amused them with his drama. Bella knew he had been tolerated as the spoiled but much-loved *baby* of their music empire, and she needed to address the rumors about the two of them.

Some thought Tut had acknowledged their relationship in his latest song, even if they knew that the truth of their alleged relationship was merely a fantasy conjured in his mind. Her reputation was on the line, but it was more important to avoid animosity toward Miles and quell the rumors that he drove Tut away because he was jealous and felt threatened.

Bella contacted Darien and Parker and told them to remind Miles to send an official statement to the staff and their affiliates, as they were no longer a small organization of musicians trying to make it in the business. AriMusic now had a worldwide presence, and they needed to get in front of the issue to avert a crisis.

After the initial press statements, Bella remained quiet. A week went by before she released another media post. After arguing with Miles, he agreed not to market the complete, longer version of the song "Nothin' You Can Do About It," but even though she'd won the battle, for twenty-four hours she had to endure his aloof demeanor – a change from his usual heated irritation.

And then what she prayed wouldn't happen, happened.

Tut issued another press release in which he named her as his former publicist, an employee who'd provided invaluable service to him, and he wished her well in her future endeavors. Whether or not it was his intent, the mere mention of her name and innuendos in his releases throughout the day ignited a storm of venom against her. When she looked at the responses from his fans, she was disheartened but unsurprised at the hateful words "bitch" and "whore."

It was shaping up to be another morning of poring through social media posts, and a headache was looming until an alert on another media site caught her attention. The announcement that Miles had just been inducted into the

American Great Songwriters Academy Hall of Fame was trending, and all the media sites she followed were pinging and capturing her attention. The news of his induction knocked Tut's departure from AriMusic off the perch of breaking news in the entertainment world.

Smiling through happy tears about Miles's newest accomplishment, she read that he had been a trailblazer for the last decade and that he deserved the award. She took in a breath, grateful that some good news would buffer the tension they were feeling at the estate. She was about to consider taking a break for a midday yoga practice when Miles came storming into her office.

"Bella, you've got to put out a release. If you don't, I will." He threw a copy of a tabloid on her desk. "I told you to let me handle this in the beginning."

Unfurling the paper, she looked at the headline, 'Affair unravels relationship between Miles and Tut,' and then folded the paper. "I didn't know you liked reading reputable papers like *Uncut*." The sarcasm seeped through her words. "Is this where you're getting your news now?"

"Don't make light of this, Bella. I can't have *anyone* calling my wife a whore." He pointed at the paper curled up on her desk. "The reporter said it was payback for my philandering ways. He even interviewed some of my former lovers, who told him I hurt them and now it was my turn to feel the pain."

She sat back in her chair. "So tell me, Miles, what is this really about? Is this about your need to protect me, or is it about your manly pride, all because someone had the gall to print a false story about your wife with another man?" She tried to keep the emotions out of her voice as he found a chair and sat.

He looked at her with sad eyes instead of a glare. "It's

both. My pride is mixed in this, but I'm sad people are dragging you into a shitty affair, which has become more sordid with each passing day. I won't stand for anyone hurting you."

She came from behind her desk and sat in his lap, wrapping her arms around his neck. "I'm not happy about it either but lies won't hurt me as long as we stay together in this and focus on the truth. Please give me a few more days to handle this, and if you're not satisfied with the outcome from my efforts, then we can change things. I'm only asking you to be patient with me." She placed her hands on the sides of his face, drawing him close and sealing it with a kiss.

"You're not my problem, Bella. Tut and his people are my problem. I've been at this game longer than you, and I know how to survive the darts thrown at me. I just want you to let me protect you, too. I'm your husband. I'm bound by my own code of honor." He held her tight, and she placed her head on his chest while soothing him with calming strokes to slow the pounding beats of his heart.

"I love that your intentions are guided by love, and I respect that you know the music industry better than I do, but I understand marketing and the media better than you. This is my job. I'm bound by my own code of ethics to do it to the best of my ability. Let me do my job, Miles."

He repositioned her on his lap, his maleness growing between them. "How can I tell you no when you have me in a compromised position?" He looked from her eyes to his crotch, causing her to smile and plant another kiss on his lips.

She looked down at the bulge tenting his trousers. "I'd love to take advantage of this, since I know how well you deliver a package." She arched her eyebrows and gave him a devilish grin. "But I have one more press release to work on, congratulating you on your induction into the Academy. And then," she leaned in and parted his lips with her tongue, "I'd love for you to join me poolside for lunch so I can finish discussing media plans with you."

"Sure, we both could use a break from the action. Don't you want to go home instead and enjoy lunch together?"

"No, let's have a working lunch and then give all of our attention to the babies this afternoon."

"Okay, I'm game." He lifted her from his lap and stood, patting her on her behind sensually but firmly.

"What was that for?"

"A reminder to my lady of our agreement. If I don't think the rhetoric against you has been dialed back, I *will* do something about it. This trolling isn't playing well with the venues in northern California. They don't like the negative vibes before the tour. I plan to fly up there with Justin tomorrow for a meeting. In the meantime, you have one week to clear up things here."

Chapter 37

B ella looked at her phone buzzing on her desk. Miles's smiling face appeared on the screen.

"I forgot it was my turn to take the kids to their toddler gym class today." He had the phone on speaker while on the private jet heading to San Francisco.

"I can't hear you over the engine noise," she responded.

"I've been having bad connections all morning." He leaned closer to the speaker. "I said I forgot that it was my turn to take the twins to their exercise class today."

"Don't worry about it." She smiled. "I've got it covered. I planned on taking them."

"I called Carmen and she said she could change her hair appointment if you needed her to take the kids." He leaned closer to the phone. "Ms. Burnside has the day off."

"I've got this, Miles. You take care of tour business while I cover the home front." Bradley entered her office. "I've got to go. Love you, bye." She ended the call.

"Tell me what you found." She came from behind the

desk and sat in the chair opposite him.

"I checked the studio's security system after remembering Tut had told me he often recorded tracks early in the morning from home, using the studio's remote-access technology. After monitoring all entry points, I'm one hundred percent sure that our security has not been breached. Everyone's security codes have been changed for added measures."

"Good." She blew out a breath. "What else have you discovered?"

"You were right that the pictures of you and Pharaoh that have been flooding social media were coming from an office inside Nyland Productions. From what I know about how he runs his shop, nothing is released in the media without his knowledge or consent. They're intentionally creating a negative smear campaign."

"Dark is a manipulative bastard." She narrowed her eyes. "I'm not going to let him get away with this."

Her phone rang. The name Pharaoh came up on the screen. She turned the phone so Bradley could see the name.

"Place it on speaker," he advised her.

"Hello, Pharaoh," she answered the phone. She frowned as a lower pitched, hard-sounding voice called out her name.

"Hello, Bella. This is Daryl Nyland."

Bradley sat up in his chair and leaned closer to the phone.

"Why do you have Pharaoh's phone?" she asked in an unfriendly manner. "And further, why are you calling me?"

"I thought we would be hearing from you by now."

She felt nauseated as she listened to his syrupy-sweet voice. Alarms went off in her head. *Snake venom.*

"Tut always said you were the more reasonable one of the two of you." He cleared his throat. "I wasn't expecting to hear from your husband, but I thought, as a full partner in the business, maybe you could convince him that we have mutual interests. In this game, it's always about the money."

"What are you suggesting?"

Bradley gave her the thumbs-up. "Good question," he mouthed.

"I'm suggesting a meeting, today," Dark offered.

"I have an appointment this afternoon." She didn't want to disappoint the twins.

"You can't rearrange your schedule?" His voice was less sweet. "I think we should talk before things get out of control. I wouldn't want you to feel guilty that you could have averted something that didn't have to happen."

She sat up and raised her voice. "Are you threatening me?"

Bradley waved his hand to get her attention and mouthed to her again. "Take the meeting."

"On second thought, I will rearrange my schedule." She paused. "You're right." Her voice was clipped. "I have some things to say to you. What time can I expect you in my office?"

"I hoped we could have a late, *friendly* lunch meeting here. Pharaoh is recording and he wants to attend. I'm sure you understand how important it is to stick to a studio's schedule."

Bella got up from her seat and returned to her desk. She opened the drawer and looked inside. "You tell me the time."

"In two hours?" he offered.

"Fine." She pursed her lips. "There's a fine restaurant across the street from your studios with a private dining room. The owner is a friend of mine. I'll make the arrangements to assure our privacy. Goodbye." She ended the call. The phone rang immediately. It was Dark. She didn't answer it.

"If he wants to meet with me, he'll be there," she asserted.

"I told you to take the meeting because I plan to meet with him. I've been trying to get in touch with him, but he won't return my calls."

Bella pulled out her 9mm Luger and checked it. She had carried a loaded concealed weapon for years.

"What do you think you're going to do?" He stood up.

She delayed answering his question while speaking to her assistant. "Josi, can you call Ernesto's and arrange for a private dining room in the next two hours? Ask to speak to the owner. He owes me a favor." She took her finger off the talk button.

"I'm on it," Josi promptly replied.

"Can you also call Carmen and let her know that I'll need her to take the twins to their exercise class today?"

"Got it." Josi clicked off the speaker.

"A leopard doesn't change its spots." She examined the gun before placing it in her bag. "I know Dark Nyland has a reputation of being a dangerous street fighter who doesn't play fair. If he plans to just talk, we'll talk." She sat back in her chair. "If he has something else planned, he'll find out I'm not easily intimidated. I'm not the one he wants to mess with. Nobody threatens me or my family." She frowned and closed her eyes, trying to tamp down the anger surging through her veins.

"I'm serious." Bradley leaned on her desk. "I'll take a few men and go to the meeting without you. Dark is unpredictable and not someone to play with. You can't go in there like Annie Oakley with guns blazing." He massaged his bulging veins along his temples with his fingers. "You know Miles isn't going to like this. You go to a meeting with Dark and it could cost me my job."

"I'll get Miles on the phone." She pressed quick dial and

the call went directly to voicemail. "I tried." She held up her palms and shrugged. "You can go with me, or you can stay. Either way, I'm going."

Chapter 38

S o glad you could make it." Dark stood up.

Three of his associates were seated at the table when she arrived with Bradley and a member of their security force.

"I see you didn't come alone." He smiled.

"We both had the same ideas in mind." Bella returned his greeting with a slight smile that didn't reach her eyes. "It's good to have witnesses, I've always been told."

"Would you like to order something before we get started?" He snapped his fingers and a waiter appeared.

"No thanks. I'm on a tight schedule." She moved to the side while Bradley pulled out her seat.

Dark observed them and noted the bulge beneath Bradley's jacket. *He's packing.* He quickly raised his chin, motioning to one of his associates as one of the three got up and left the room.

"Let me get right to the point." He rubbed the stubble on his cheek.

"I thought you said Pharaoh would be meeting with us." Bella looked toward the door. "Shouldn't we wait for him?"

"He's running late." He laced his fingers, then cracked his knuckles. "I'm authorized to speak for him since he'll be signing with my label soon."

"You told the lady Pharaoh would be here," Bradley added. "Is that not correct?"

"He's not here." Dark placed his hands on the table, noticing Bella's slight flinch as his hands came down hard on the wood.

"We can see he's not here." She rolled her eyes. "I don't have time for theatrics." She began to rise from her seat.

He noted she placed a hand on her purse as the tension began to rise. He flapped his hands, palms down, motioning for her to sit down.

She complied, taking her time to return to her seat at the long table.

"All I'm asking is that you speak to Miles to see if we can work out a mutual deal to get Pharaoh's masters. He's making a big deal about it." He chuckled. "Hell, I told him he wouldn't get his masters back from me if the shoe were on the other foot, but he won't sign if I don't at least try to work out a deal. He has agreed to come on this tour with AriMusic if in the end he has his masters. I have the papers right here. You can sign them today." He slid several papers in front of her to review. "This shouldn't take long. Everything is in order. It just needs your signature." He offered her a pen.

Bradley, seated closest to the door, began to laugh.

"What's so funny?" Dark's brow furrowed.

"We can take care of this clown right now." One of Dark's men pulled his gun on Bradley. "Nobody disrespects the boss."

Dark looked at the man holding the gun and tightened his jaw.

The cock of a gun's trigger behind him got his attention.

"You shoot him and I'll shoot your boss," Bella warned.

Dark, along with his men, turned and saw she had a weapon pointed at him. She stood erect in a shooting stance. He sensed she knew how to handle a gun and meant business.

"We can solve this the hard or easy way." Her fingers tightened around the handle with one finger pressed against the trigger. "Do you really think I'd sign papers with a silver-tongued con artist?"

Her hostility made him hot under the collar despite his attempts to maintain his cool. *She's being a bitch right now, but I can handle her.* He took in a deep breath. The warmth he had seen in her eyes in the countless numbers of pictures he had scrolled through on social media was not there. He stood still. As he looked at her, memories flashed before him of the same look in his mother's eyes before she shot one of her boyfriends who had abused him.

"That's what's so funny." Bradley uncrossed his hands and opened his jacket, exposing the weapon at his waist.

The second man pulled his gun, pointing it at Bella, then at Bradley, who remained seated. The tension was high. Bradley's man exposed his weapon too. The slightest miscalculation could spell death for any of them.

Dark took his time returning his full attention to the current situation unfolding.

"What do you want us to do?"

Dark turned to the voice of one the men who had been with him from his earlier years when they were hustling on the streets. With his imposing figure, he slowly raised his hands in the air and gazed at Bella. "Unlike you, pretty lady,

I'm unarmed."

"Tell your men to stand down or I'll shoot you," she replied.

His eyes widened as she cocked the trigger. "We don't need to let things get out of hand." He held up his hands higher in the air, exposing old burn marks. "Put your weapons away, fools," he barked at his men, who placed their guns back in the holsters.

Pharaoh came bursting into the room, witnessing the standoff. "Dark, I told you I didn't want Bella involved in any negotiations, and I meant it." He scanned the room, but focused most of his attention on her. "Y'all pulling guns on a woman?"

"You mean the one with a gun?" Dark smirked. "I told you I would handle this." He made fists at his sides. *This little shit is telling me how to run my company.* He tilted his head to the side and narrowed his eyes, struggling to restrain his anger.

"Pharaoh, Daryl said you agreed to perform at all the venues on the tour," Bella addressed him. She concealed the gun in her purse but kept a hand on it.

"I haven't agreed to anything, but I'm willing to do what I have to do to get my masters," he replied.

"It looks like the two of you have things to discuss." She moved away from the table and slowly headed to the door in a manner to ensure no one was behind her. "Call us when you're ready for serious talks with our lawyers."

Dark watched as Bella exited the room with Bradley and his man behind her.

"Why didn't you let me handle this?" His eyes narrowed as he moved closer to Pharaoh. "Didn't you see how she looked at you? She still has the hots for you. I saw it. If I promised her that you would return to her, we could have had her eating out of our hands, but you ruined it."

He turned away from Pharaoh. Raising the corner of his mouth, he smiled.

Chapter 39

A re my two favorite babies ready for their class today?" Carmen asked Ashe and Ariana as they rode safely fastened in their car seats in 'The Beast,' a car specially designed with reinforced armor and a black box like the ones used on all The Network airplanes.

"Yeah." They clapped their hands and kicked their feet in the air.

"We're almost there," Mr. Johnson, the chauffeur, told Carmen. "There must be an accident or construction ahead. A crew member is directing me to detour." He turned off the highway.

Looking out the window, Carmen noted that the security car that had been accompanying them had disappeared. She grabbed her neck, which was throbbing with pain as the car turned abruptly to the right. Something had collided with them, on the driver's side. She heard Mr. Johnson's moans, while attempting to get to the children, who looked, wide-eyed, at her. They moved their limbs and began fretting.

She unbuckled her seat belt and checked on the children while communicating with Mr. Johnson. "I'll call for help."

Just as she was about to hit the emergency button, the door flew open. She grabbed two flares from her seat pocket before a masked man grabbed her by the arms. Fighting back, she kicked him in the groin as he tried to get her out of the car. The children began wailing. Pointing the flares in the direction of her attacker, she looked over her shoulder at the twins and yelled, *"Usa tu fuego. Usa tu fuego."*

The twins understood Carmen was telling them to use their fire in Spanish. Ariana stopped crying first and looked at her brother.

The assailant had pulled Carmen out of the car before Mr. Johnson regained enough presence of mind to press the emergency button on the console. Red lights began flashing in the front and rear of the vehicle.

The attacker, who had returned to the rear seats, fumbled with the belts securing the twins in their custom-made chairs. His vision was obscured by the twins kicking their feet in his face. He backed off, giving them the chance to lean forward and extend their hands in his direction.

"Figgo," they said in unison. The bright yellow and red flames they flung at the man landed on his shirt, setting it on fire. As he stumbled away from the car, screaming in agony, they threw more fireballs, engulfing him in a blaze.

Chapter 40

B ella, are you…all right?"

"We're all right. Miles, you're breaking up again," she responded after he'd tried multiple times to get a good connection while on the plane heading back to Los Angeles.

The first call he'd received, a bad connection, came from Bradley three hours earlier, telling him of the meeting with Dark. His heart had threatened to beat out of his chest as he left San Francisco, frantic to get back home.

"I can barely hear you. I'll call after I land," he told Bella, relieved to hear the sound of her voice with less static interference. His heart calmed knowing his family was safe. After hanging up, he loosened his tie and unbuttoned his shirt, wet with perspiration. The plane landed without incident despite the dense fog. He placed another call while enroute to the estate.

Bradley answered this time on the first ring. "Miles?" His voice was loud and clear.

"What were you *thinking*?" He fisted his hair and tightened his jaw. "Did anyone consider calling me before the meeting?"

"We tried, but you've been having bad reception all day," Bradley told him. "Bella told me she was going to the meeting with or without me."

"Let me get this straight." His breath was shallow and audible. His voice pitch rose. "While you and Bella were in a meeting with Dark, someone tried to kidnap the twins?"

"That's what happened," Bradley answered his boss. "As per our procedure, there was a small motorcade of men that travelled in unmarked cars in front and behind the vehicle carrying Carmen and the twins."

"Go on, I'm listening." He took a gulp of his drink while riding in the back of the limo. "So what happened?" he barked.

"I'm trying to tell you." Bradley kept his tone even. "There was a traffic detour and someone dressed like a member of a highway construction team directed the first car one direction and the car containing the twins in the other direction. They also blocked the third car from following behind."

"So this was planned, obviously by someone who knew the kids' schedule?" Miles tightened his grip on the door's handle.

"We're in the process of finding out who was behind this," Bradley noted.

"We *will* find out." Miles's chest tightened as hot blood coursed through his veins. His phone began to buzz. "It's Bella. I'll touch bases with you later. Where are you?"

"I'm at the studio," Bradley told him.

"Head over to the house. We need to flush a few people out."

"All right, Miles."

He ended the call with Bradley and pressed Accept call.

"I know you're frantic with worry so I thought I would try again." She paused. "Can you hear me this time?"

"I can hear you." He calmed down hearing the sound of her voice.

"I'm all right and the babies are here at home resting." Her voiced choked. "Carmen was admitted, but she'll be okay."

"Thank God." He sat up in his seat and wiped his brow. "I'm almost home. Traffic was heavy, as usual."

"This has been a difficult day." There was silence for a few seconds. "I wanted to tell you that the twins were examined by their doctor with The Network, and they are fine. He was dispatched immediately after Carmen told them that the kids had used their fire."

"What?" He knitted his brow. "Did you say they can create fireballs?"

"Both of them have your powers." She let out a deep breath. "Carmen received a few bruises and a mild concussion trying to fight off the attacker, but it was the kids who subdued him."

"They weren't injured, were they?" He covered his mouth with his hand.

"Not a scratch," she assured him. "I'm in your home office making sure there's nothing about the family, unrelated to business, on your desk while the children are sleeping. Someone in our employ had to have shared information about the twins with those who planned the attack. We have a heavier presence of guards with concealed weapons throughout the house. Mr. Curtis told me there's a vigil of AriMusic staff forming in the foyer. I was on my way to the front of the house."

"Okay, I won't delay you. I'm sure many of them are

genuinely concerned." He rubbed his chin. "I'm less than five minutes away."

"I'll give them some information, but Miles, I'm not up for a long question and answer session."

He sensed the fatigue in her voice. "Trust me. It won't take long." His voice was calm. "We have something we need to do right away, together."

"What are you talking about?" she asked.

"I'll meet you in the foyer. Bye." He hung up the phone. It was his turn to use the element of surprise.

Chapter 41

Miles had entered the house through the rear secret passageway. He flew up the back stairs, heading full speed to the nursery. Only Bradley and a select few members of the staff were aware of the restricted passageways that allowed the family access to the panic room or to exit the home if they came under attack. Members of The Network, including his Uncle Vincent, had designed the home for added security.

He pressed the button, sliding the panel in the wall that opened up to the twins' room. His heart quickened, pounding with anticipation as he tiptoed across the carpet. The babies were sound asleep in the same crib, holding hands.

His eyes moistened with tears he quickly wiped away.

"My babies." He gently smoothed the soft curly hair from their faces before leaning over the crib and placing warm kisses on Ashe and Ariana's cheeks. Ashe stirred and turned his head, but their eyes remained closed in angelic slumber. They both had the hands that weren't joined drawn into fists.

Miles stared at them.

"Thank God." He looked up at the ceiling, painted a light blue with fluffy clouds. "My babies are safe."

Heading toward the door, he ran his hand through his hair. "Time for business." He straightened his back and headed for the foyer. The anger he had tamped down flamed through his chest along with thoughts of seeking revenge against those who had attempted to hurt his children. He took deep breaths through his mouth.

"Use this negative energy to your benefit," he reminded himself. He paused at the top of the stairs to wipe the sweat off his brow. He decided to keep his jacket on to hide the sweat that had trickled from his armpits.

"Never let them see you sweat," he murmured to himself, watching as Bella received looks of concern and hugs.

Mr. Curtis was right. "This *does* look like a vigil showing respect for the nearly departed. How did so many of them know so soon about the twins?"

He cocked a brow as he took one step at a time, contemplating what he would say. He could hear the voices of his parents coaching him about being a leader.

"Lower the volume of your voice," they'd repeated throughout his youth. *"The power of the message is also in the delivery."*

Those gathered turned their heads as he descended, deliberately taking one slowed step at a time.

Bella's jaw dropped as she turned and saw him coming forward.

Plausible deniability, play your role, babe. He hurried after his foot touched the last step. The crowd parted like the Red Sea, allowing him to get to her quickly.

"Miles, I didn't know you were home." She leaned into his embrace.

"I got here as quickly as I could. It was easier to go through the back to check on the babies." He smiled and took her into his arms before planting a kiss on her lips. He kept his eyes open, scanning the crowd around them. While training with The Network, he was given the nickname 'Gator,' because of his excellent peripheral vision.

"You can sense movement like you have eyes on the side of your head," the agent he was assigned to joked with him. *"You'll see your prey before they see you coming. The only thing you don't have is eyes in the back of your head."*

He was on the hunt today, checking the room for expressions that seemed odd. The members of Pele and some of the dancers were sad with tear-stained faces. Members of his household cleaning staff came in to quickly attend to their chores and leave, while others seemed more curious about the crowd of AriMusic staff who had come to the house. He gave a furtive glance to Mr. Curtis, who was also scrutinizing others in the room. Miles released Bella as Bradley entered the space.

"Are you all right?" He stared into her eyes and blinked, squeezing her hands tightly. He wouldn't release them until she blinked back.

"I'm all right." She nodded.

"Glad you're back." Bradley came forward and extended his hand. "Let me fill you in on what we know so far."

Miles shook his hand, squeezing it tightly as he watched Bradley purse his lips. "First, let me tell you what I've been told about what happened this morning." Miles took a step back and directed his comments first to Bella. "I understand that you and Bradley met with Dark this morning. The meeting didn't go as planned and you all ended up in a pissing match."

Her jaw dropped and she backed away.

Undeterred by the reactions of staff members who widened their eyes in surprise and gasped, he continued. "The two of you were discussing business that obviously involved me." He paused and turned to frown at Bradley. "It didn't occur to either of you that I should be included in the meeting?" He placed his hands on his hips and looked between Bella and Bradley.

Miles made eye contact with some of them, who quickly turned away with down-cast eyes and covered their mouths as they witnessed a match between heavyweights.

The volume of his voice increased despite his genuine attempt to keep it under control. "Bradley, you placed my wife's life in danger."

Bradley's voice was measured. "We tried to contact you, Miles."

Miles looked quickly at him, then jerked his head, dismissing his response. He squinched his face as if smelling something sour.

"I know you're upset about everything that happened this morning. I get it." Bella stepped in.

Miles observed her chest heaving as her face warmed with anger.

She pointed a finger at him and narrowed her eyes. "You don't have the right to come after anyone with that tone. You're not helping the situation."

He sensed a genuine pleading in her eyes to stop. He couldn't. He ran his hand through his hair, then tightened his jaw as he faced Bradley. "I don't blame you, Bella." His breath was audible as the tension rose in the room. "I blame myself."

Darien came in from a side entrance and stood at Bella's side. His new assistant, Andrew, lagged behind, busy on his phone. *What or who is so important that he needs to check or return a message now?*

The front door opened. Pharaoh walked in, causing murmurs from those surprised after his dramatic departure.

Latifah walked to his side and hugged him.

"Look at what the cat dragged in." Miles spoke under his breath, but loud enough for Bella to hear. "This isn't a good time, Pharaoh." He held up his hand to stop him. "I know I told you I was open to discussing business, but we have more pressing issues to face."

Pharaoh nodded. "I came out of respect." He looked at Bella and Miles. "I care about lil' man and baby girl. Besides, this isn't about business, this is personal. I have some things I'd like to share in private." He grabbed Latifah and pulled her closer to him.

Miles looked at the young stars. He wasn't sure about Pharaoh's feelings, but it was clear that her eyes were filled with love as she looked at him.

"Thanks for coming, but not now." Miles gave him a dismissive stare. "We can settle things later."

"Maybe you should hear him out." Bella begged with her eyes.

"Not now." He squeezed her hand again.

"Well then, I'll leave you all. Call me." He turned and Latifah followed him to the door.

Bella blew out a long breath and faced the crowd after Pharaoh and Latifah departed. "I appreciate that all of you have come as a show of support, but as you can see, I'm fine." She canvassed the room and offered the staff a warm smile. "The babies are safe, and I need to go check on them." She waved and headed for the stairs.

"While I have you all here," Miles spoke to the staff as

Bella slowly exited the room. "I need to let you know something. I'm trying as hard as I can to save this tour." He delivered a hard gaze. "And I don't know why I find myself fighting against my own staff. Do you all not understand what this tour could mean to all of us at AriMusic?" He placed his hands on his hips and walked among them. "Instead of trying to put our best foot forward, I'm responding to negative press about fist fighting, rap battles that turn violent, gunslinging with the competition, and drugs." He looked toward the stairs.

Bella glanced at him over her shoulder.

Miles walked toward Bradley. "I'll get the full briefing from you." He leaned closer to his ear, but spoke loudly enough that others nearby heard. "I think you should take some time off to consider if you're still the man for the job."

Whispers of surprise buzzed through the crowd as Bradley planted his feet and stared at Miles without saying a word.

Perfect. Miles returned his steely expression. He loved that Bradley had mastered the vacant, soulless expression in his eyes. If he didn't know better, he would have concluded that Bradley was communicating to him, 'You're dead to me.'

"Thank you for your concern." Miles looked at the staff, many of whom cast their eyes at the floor. "My family is fine, and you know what they say in this business." He placed his hands in front of him. "The show must go on."

Pointing at Bradley and Darien, he continued to speak. "The two of you, join me in my study." He waved away Andrew, who was making a move to follow. "The rest of you, back to the studio. We have work to do."

Chapter 42

Bella turned off her reading light and settled in under the covers. A dim nightlight was on near the door so she could see her way to the nursery if the kids cried or called for her.

Miles stretched and crawled into bed. He had been in meetings for hours with Bradley and members of the security team.

"I'm glad this day is over," he told her, covering his yawn. They had made it through a trauma together meant to shake the foundation of their family that hadn't succeeded. The babies were safe, tucked in and resting comfortably in their beds.

"Your parents called, and it took all I had to convince them not to come earlier than they originally planned. I had to put them on Facetime and show them the twins." She loosened the tension in her neck, moving it slowly from one side to the other. "Luckily for me, the twins brightened up the moment they saw them. They were twirling and dancing like nothing had happened. You might need to sign them to a contract. Their showmanship alone was award-winning." She blew out a breath and smiled.

"Thanks for reassuring my parents." He played with strands of her hair. "I meant to call them, but the meeting with the security staff took longer than I expected."

"Miles, there's one more thing." She placed an arm on his shoulder. "Do you think that scene you created after arriving home was necessary?"

"Sure," he said sleepily, trying to focus his attention on her question. "It may have been a little over the top, but I'm convinced what happened to you and the twins was partly an inside job. Bradley and I are flushing out some suspects."

"So, you and Bradley are okay?" She turned to him, watching as he rubbed his eyes.

"We're cool, but he's going to operate in the shadows for a few days or however long it takes to make the connection between Dark and the person or persons who work for us feeding him information. Mr. Curtis has already let go the housekeeping staff members who were under his suspicions before today."

"I agree, there has to be someone on the inside, but what proof do you have before we accuse others of conspiring with Dark?"

"Bella, it's late." He closed his eyes.

"I know it's late, but I have to know." She placed her hands on the sides of his face. "Tell me."

"While I was on the plane, I had time to think." He placed a hand on his forehead. "Bradley said Dark called you to arrange a meeting. He lets you pick the place, but *he* chooses the time." He paused to let out a breath. "This is what I believe that sly fox did to manipulate the situation. He knew you wouldn't come alone. There's no way our team would have allowed that."

"I'm with you on that." She closed her eyes, feeling the pit in her stomach.

"So, if members of the A team came to protect you, that left fewer people to be with the babies."

"You believe he set this up with the help of someone who knew the twins' schedule?"

"Exactly." He searched her eyes. "I just don't know who is involved."

"Do you think *Pharaoh* was involved?" Her chest tightened as she held her breath.

"There's nothing to suggest he knowingly participated in this." He placed her head against his chest. "He has made more than his share of mistakes, but I don't believe Pharaoh is capable of hurting the kids. No, he wouldn't go along with placing the kids in danger. That's not him."

Bella let out a breath. "I received messages from staff members throughout the day offering their support." She buried her lip between her teeth. "If I read correctly between the lines, they think you're blaming me."

He stroked her hair. "Let them think what they want to think. I know it's difficult, but I need your help to let them continue to think that there is a wedge growing between us. You know the truth is that I don't blame you. There is a method to my madness. We have to do anything to get to the bottom of this."

"We're doing good cop, bad cop?" She placed a finger above her lips.

He nodded. "Exactly, but let me offer a word of advice." He gave her a lopsided smile. "Could you stop pointing a finger or a loaded gun in the faces of dangerous men? It doesn't go over well."

"Are you including yourself among 'dangerous men'?" she responded with a cunning smile.

"I can be dangerous when given the right motivation." He placed a kiss on her lips.

"I'll keep that in mind." She nodded. "I know you're tired, but I wanted to let you know that before today, no one other than Darien and members of Pele verbalized their loyal support to us. Now, others are coming forward. They want to see the company succeed."

"It didn't surprise me that it took something like this," he admitted. "In fact, I believe some of them may have thought I got the bad press I deserved. I know there are staff members who sided with Tut. It wasn't until you started receiving bad press and after what happened today that most of them were willing to let you know they would be there for us. Bella, we might both be the brains of the operation, but you're the heart of AriMusic. Our employees weren't okay with all of this."

"I can take anyone coming after me. I'm a big girl. I've known for a long time this industry can be competitive and cutthroat." She choked on the lump in her throat, overwhelmed by emotions as she tried to speak. "Not my babies, Miles. That's a hard line for me. I'll do anything to protect them. Dark and anyone involved will pay for this."

"You can add that to the vows I made to you on our wedding day." He placed his arms around her neck. "They are going to pay. That's a promise." His phone buzzed on the bedside table. He turned to look at the screen.

"What else can happen in one day?"

Chapter 43

B radley's image appeared on Miles's screen. "I have it from reliable sources at Nyland Productions that Dark didn't return to his office this afternoon. I called to arrange a follow-up meeting as a ploy. I was told by his assistant that he wasn't sure when Dark would be returning. We have contacts on the street searching for information on his whereabouts. Sounds like the move of a guilty man."

"Let's not stop until we find him." Miles took the phone and went to sit in a chair by the window.

"While Bella and I were in the meeting with Dark, one of my men placed a tracker on the car of one of Dark's associates. We know Dark routinely has his car checked, but I'm betting they don't check the other cars."

"Good job, Bradley."

"Thanks. We've also gotten threads of information from the staff. Latifah messaged me. She said that she had told Pharaoh about the twins. He didn't come to discuss business. His appearance was from the heart. It was important to her that we knew that."

Miles sighed. "Fine, but how did *she* find out about it?"

"I questioned her briefly," he noted. "I had her on Facetime and she turned the phone away from where she was sitting. I thought I saw a glimpse of Pharaoh in the background. She told me that rumors were spreading around the studio this afternoon, mainly through the housekeeping staff at your house, who had communicated with housekeeping at the studio. Latifah said she overheard one of the dancers talking about it to Andrew, one of the new assistants."

"Mr. Curtis will get with you about the housekeeping staff tomorrow morning." Miles frowned and tightened his grip on the phone.

"We'll find out more about the dancer, but there are a few more things." Bradley hesitated before continuing. "It would be easier to get information from the staff if you resumed a more easy-going approach with them. They care about you, but since you signed several new artists, you haven't been as approachable. You've been more aloof and distant. I'm concerned that the relationships with them will only deteriorate."

"I've increased my professional distance with the artists because they represent the company that bears my name. As I said in the meeting, lack of personal accountability will cast a negative light on all of us. They should see me as the CEO, not their big brother." He looked at Bella, who had turned the light back on and was sitting up in bed.

"I have to protect the brand I've worked so hard to establish. I can't have them thinking their antics or bad behavior will be tolerated. Tut taught me how challenging the work can be with an artist who's not disciplined."

Bradley was silent for a moment as Miles's words sank in.

"Miles, there has to be some balance in your approach to

handling them. They need to see the real you, not just your authoritarian side. You were such a free spirit when I came to work with you years ago. What happened?"

"Life happened. I grew up and took on more responsibilities. I'm no longer the reckless, impulsive person I used to be."

"No, you're not," Bradley agreed.

"Listen, I'll send out a memo tomorrow morning explaining my heavy-handed approach and apologizing in case I offended anyone. I don't blame anyone for this situation. The truth is that I could have handled my relationship with Pharaoh better. Maybe he wouldn't have fallen into the clutches of someone like Dark."

His chest felt heavy with the weight of remorse. Maybe they could build upon the remaining shreds of their relationship, maybe not. He looked over and saw Bella tearing up.

"Bradley, I've got to go." He rose and walked back to bed.

"Call you later. Bye, Miles."

"What's wrong?" He walked across the room and crawled under the covers.

"Bradley is right." She sighed. "You seem angrier. Not so much at home, but at work. Are you comfortable with the way your life has changed with me and the twins occupying such a big part of it? You're pushing other people away. Is that because working with your wife as a partner has been a harder balancing act than you thought?"

He cupped her face in his hands and drew closer to her. "First of all, I love having you as my wife and my business partner. It has its challenges, like employees crushing on you, but we've weathered that storm." He blew out a long breath of air.

"Secondly, you and our babies could never be a burden to

me, if that's what you're asking." He searched her eyes. "Our family life is what makes it easier to bear any burden. The Ari character I once embraced personally and professionally is gone from my personal life, and I don't miss it. I don't play with fire as much anymore, and I don't need to. I like the man I've become. I look forward to raising our babies and sharing life's adventures with you." He kissed her before continuing his confession.

"I know you have concerns about our current work environment, but to be honest, I want the staff to go home to their own families and not hang around the studio playing out their dysfunctions with me. That's the role of family. I feel we need to put our efforts into maintaining a healthy environment at work, where creativity can thrive." He looked away briefly. "I disagree with one thing you said, though. Are you telling me that I'm so distant that the people at work can't see the real me who loves you with all my heart? You can't see it either?"

She nuzzled his nose with hers and smiled. "Of course they see the love in our relationship. I'm just saying respect isn't built on fear. I don't want them to fear you. I've heard whispers of concern about their positions with the company – that if you could let go of a profitable artist like Tut or threaten to fire Bradley, what would happen if they're not profitable or they screw up?"

"I would let them go. I mean, everyone except for you. This is business, Bella." He leaned closer and took her tightly in his arms, while she slowly began grinding her hips against his, increasing the heat between them.

He kissed her hard. "Now *this* is pleasure." They entwined their limbs in a sensual embrace, coming together to melt away the tension of a stressful day.

Chapter 44

I thought you needed to see this. There's a post from Nyland Productions about Pharaoh." Josi pulled up the article on a popular social media site.

"What is he up to now?" Constant sighing was becoming Bella's way of life. Her computer pinged again, alerting them of another video uploaded by Tut's people, the third video they had watched for the day.

Josi took a seat, rolling her eyes as she looked at Tut and his crew. Steadying herself, Bella clicked on the site and played the video of Tut in a club, surrounded by young men and women dancing and drinking without any cares. Miles's music started playing in the background, and several of them made profane hand gestures and yelled, "Take that shit off." One of the men jerked his crotch in disrespect to the music, while Tut smiled and sat back in his booth.

Bella knitted her brows as he made no effort to stop their behavior.

She continued scrolling down through a series of pictures.

She thought a woman in the background looked like a dancer in one of their recent video shoots. Her notifications also began buzzing with images from other sites. There were photos of him with different women on the same day – some on his arm in the morning, others at dinner, and some in his apartment at night. Bella forwarded the video and pictures to Bradley and Miles.

The security team had continued their surveillance of Pharaoh and their search for Dark. He hadn't returned to the office in the last week. He also hadn't been seen in public even though a writer with Nyland Productions had received a songwriter award to be given at the ceremony scheduled for that night.

"Are you planning on doing something about this?" Josi crossed her arms.

"We won't be responding with a post at this time." Bella looked at the screen. "As they say, when they go low, we go high."

"Okay." Josi got up to leave. "If it's all right with you, I need to make some phone calls before wrapping up business today."

"Thanks for monitoring the internet." Bella closed down her computer. "It's better we stay vigilant before his people start trolling us again."

"No problem." Josi returned to her desk.

The remainder of the afternoon Bella spent time returning phone calls, including one to her mother, who had heard about the twins being involved in a car accident.

"Why do I have to hear from an employee coming to Scotland from the States that my grandchildren were involved in a car accident?" Her mother, Joan, frowned at her on the screen.

"The children are fine." Bella bit her lower lip. *They are.*

"Do you need me to come help with them? You're sure they're all right?"

"Please don't worry, Mom." Bella feigned a smile, wiping away the tear in her eye. "We're all fine. I can't stay on the phone long. The ceremony honoring Miles is tonight."

"I won't hold you long." She paused. "I have good news. I've been looking for a farm in Texas so that I can move my operations and spend more time in the States. I'll be closer to you and the kids." Joan beamed. "I want to be a bigger part of the twins' lives."

"That's great," she noted, genuinely pleased. "Let's talk later. Love you."

"Love you more." Joan blew a kiss and ended the call.

With the time she had left in the office, Bella secured additional tickets for staff who wished to attend the Songwriters' Academy Hall of Fame dinner. She told them she would give out free tickets to all who wanted to attend, but she didn't anticipate that fifty staff members would request tickets. At two hundred dollars a ticket, she had to explain to Parker why the expenditure was necessary – and why they needed to rent a private venue for cocktails for the staff prior to the event. With funds for the event secured, she made final arrangements for a glam squad to meet her at the house. The studio and their home had been locked down like heavily guarded fortresses. With the twins protected and their routine resumed, she and Miles felt comfortable going out for the night.

"Life, and the show, must go on," Miles had reminded her.

Chapter 45

Bella had arranged for a private photographer to capture the night's action. She was excited Miles was getting into the Hall of Fame. She'd planned to leave the office earlier to get ready, but was startled by loud sobbing outside her door. Josi was telling someone she couldn't be seen today.

Concerned, Bella got up and walked to the door. It was Latifah. Her eyes were reddened and swollen from crying.

"I really need to see her. I promise it won't take long." She stood in front of Josi's desk with a sad, tearstained face.

"It's okay, Josi. Please let me know when my next appointment comes. Ms. Burnside will call you when they arrive at the house."

"Sure."

"Latifah, come in. What's wrong?"

The young singer joined her in the office and dropped into a chair, sobbing. "You tried to warn me. It wasn't like I didn't know he was dating other women, but so *many* different women. I feel like a fool."

Bella grabbed her hands and held them in a show of support before offering her tissues.

Latifah held her head low, heavy with the grief of betrayal.

Gently, Bella lifted the young woman's chin. Once they locked eyes on each other, Bella spoke to her, one woman to another. "Latifah, now that you know the truth, what are you going to do about it? Are you going to continue a relationship with him?"

"No. I called him and told him we were over. He said I was being loyal to you and Miles to keep my job." She choked on her words. "He took no responsibility for his behavior. I went back online where I saw the photos and many angry posts from women swearing to hurt him if they found him. I told him about it."

"What did he say after you told him of the threats?"

"He laughed at me. He said he wasn't afraid of no bitches."

"I know he hurt you, but now you know the truth. Latifah, you deserve better. I told you as much as I could about Tut because I didn't want to see you get hurt. At least you know why we discourage relationships between artists. It never works out."

"It worked out for you and Miles." She looked into Bella's eyes.

"Yes, but most of the time it doesn't. We both had to go through some painful times to get where we are today. It took commitment, first as friends, then as lovers. Tut isn't ready to commit to anyone."

Josi's voice chimed in over the loudspeaker. "Bella, your appointment has arrived at your home. Shall I tell them you're on your way?"

"Yes, Josi. Latifah and I are about to wrap up our meeting." Bella clicked off the speaker on her desk. "You may not feel like attending the festivities tonight, but it might do you some good to be around Reagan and Myoshi."

"Of course I'm coming to the award show tonight. I wouldn't miss it." Latifah dried her tears with more tissues. "I love the outfits you purchased for us. I'm going to kill it tonight and let Tut see what he's missing."

"I scheduled a photoshoot of candids for Pele. Don't forget your makeup appointment in three hours. You can kill it with your good looks instead of killing Tut." They both laughed.

Latifah rose for a hug. "I plan to have fun tonight. We are looking forward to taping the public service announcement for the Family Matters Council tomorrow. We know how important it is at AriMusic to be good community partners."

"Good. I plan to come in to watch the video shoot. I like the concept of showing how bullying in the home and placing negative labels on children can make it easier to bully others at school. We need to help prevent this."

"Thanks for listening, Bella." Latifah smiled, a little bounce in her step returning as she walked out the door.

Bella went back to her desk with the intent of gathering her things after returning just one more message. She might be disappointed with Tut, but she didn't want things to get out of hand.

"That's surprising." She looked through her notifications one last time. "No more posts about Tut."

Vowing instead to turn her attention back to the artists still under contract at AriMusic, she decided Tut had already consumed too much of her time and energy. She refused to give him any more time out of her busy day.

"Just one more text." She opened a message from her mother and became engrossed in her response about the twins.

Joan: Love the pictures of the twins. They're adorable. Can't wait to see them again.

Bella: They are busy toddlers who bring a lot of joy to our lives. Hope to see you soon.

She didn't notice Miles entering her office, but she felt his presence and smiled as she took in his scent.

"There has got to be some way to bottle your essence." She looked up at him, enjoying the brilliance of his smile as he stood in front of her desk.

He had a cologne collection, but the fragrances didn't smell the same in the bottle as they did on him, the smell of sensual desire.

"Can I help you, babe?" She placed a period on the final sentence before closing out her message. He came around her desk and she stood to greet him with a kiss on the lips.

"I wanted to check with you to see if you're all right meeting me at the cocktail party. I have a meeting downtown, and it would save time if I got dressed at the condo near the venue instead of returning home. If you're uncomfortable walking into the room without an escort, I'll try my best to get back home in time."

"I don't have a problem meeting you there, I'm just a little surprised you kept that condo. I didn't see it on the list of our holdings. I thought you sold it."

"I decided to keep it. The property is on the list of Ari-Music's holdings. I figured we would have occasions where having it would be convenient, like tonight."

"I'll meet you at the party, then. We don't need to start the evening rushing around and feeling frazzled."

She refused to let her insecurities ruin his night. *So what if he kept his old bachelor pad?*

"Bella, I hate to interrupt you, but you're very late for your appointment," Josi's voice chimed in over the intercom once more.

She grabbed her bag and kissed him before running out the door.

"Gotta go. See you tonight."

Short on time, she ran from her office, forgetting both her laptop and phone on her desk.

Chapter 46

The glam squad wasn't happy that she was late, as her failure to show at the appointed time forced them to start their tasks a half hour later than they'd planned. Still, they worked their magic. Her long, thick hair was styled to perfection and the next step – a facial and full body massage – was so relaxing she almost fell asleep on the table.

"Finished," her head stylist announced, before the team of make-up artists and nail technicians left her alone to get dressed. Bella looked in the mirror, pleased with the outcome, especially the sparkly shadow on her eyelids and the kissable ruby lip gloss. Her nails were painted in red-carpet brilliant red. Her squad had given her the look she was searching for – polished but not overdone. She didn't want to seem like she was trying hard to impress or outshine anyone, since this was Miles's special night. Being comfortable in her own skin was always a priority for her.

"On to the dress." She did a happy dance as she recalled the day she'd seen the original design and had the dress custom-tailored for her. It had been the featured dress at a fashion show for a celebrity who'd worn it on the red carpet, and she'd knocked it out of the park, resulting in many orders for the dress's designers.

In its original design, it was a gown with a full, long train, but Bella had it redesigned as a cocktail dress. She loved how the dress had turned out – its sheer chiffon panels crisscrossing in the back were perfect for this occasion. Sleeveless and A-lined, it hugged her silhouette and showed her curves. She accentuated it with diamond earrings and a bracelet to match her diamond ring. After donning her red sandals as the finishing touch to her outfit, she looked in the mirror, straightened her shoulders, and placed her hands on her hips. This dress required attitude, and she was ready to bring it.

She beamed with anticipation for what should be a fun and well-deserved acknowledgment of Miles's talent. She knew there would be deals made, opportunities for networking with others, and schmoozing with the right people. A year ago, she would've dreaded nights like these, but she no longer felt like she didn't have a place in Miles's world. Instead, she embraced it and wanted to share this time with him.

When he'd found out he had won the coveted award, he'd told her she didn't need to attend the show if she was uncomfortable in the spotlight. It wasn't just discomfort. It was her worst fears coming into reality with the scandal Tut's new management was trying to create by making her the subject of unwanted negative press. She had become a part of the story instead of the one who crafted it, but to her surprise, she was unfazed, even amused by it at times. She'd come out on the other side more confident about who she was, without needing others to validate her. Sure, she didn't like how it upset Miles, but he needed to see she could take it – and, if need be, sling a little of it back.

"I plan to let my hair down and have some fun." She danced in the mirror. It had been a long week, and a little partying would be good to shake off the stress. She grabbed her bag and prepared to go peek in on the twins before calling for the limo to go downtown.

"Show time." She snapped her fingers and exaggerated the sway in her hips, walking confidently with her head held high out the door, eager to celebrate.

"You got this, girl." Swallowing the lump in her throat, she refused to lose her composure while calling for the car thirty minutes later than she had intended. She'd been delayed by the twins, who wouldn't let her out of their sight without a fuss. She massaged her forehead. The night wasn't going as she had planned. She'd sung three of their favorite nursery songs, lavished both with hugs and kisses, said goodnight multiple times, and yet they'd still clung to her. She'd eventually given up and left them crying in the arms of their nanny, assuring them she would return.

The chauffeur waited patiently for her to get in the car. Since she couldn't find her phone in her bag, the chauffeur called Miles to tell him she was running late.

The car pulled up to the curb and joined the gathering of long black limousines, their occupants already inside the building.

"Well, at least you won't have to stand in a long line to get in. Just about everyone arrived earlier."

"Yes, that's one good thing. No long lines." She ran her

tongue along her teeth, her mouth dry from nervousness.

"Have a great night." Her driver opened the door and she got out, pausing to take in the scene before entering the venue.

"I will." Her smile was faint as she went inside and walked down the hallway, passing a few people she knew. Waving to others, she quickened her steps to avoid losing more time chitchatting with well-wishers. There would be time for the obligatory cocktail-party banter after she found Miles.

At first, she didn't notice how her dress stood out in a sea of black suits, white shirts, and black dresses until she entered the room where the party was being held. It felt as if time had stopped while heads turned, all eyes on her. A hush fell over the room as she stood at the entrance, searching for Miles.

Standing across the room from her, he turned and faced her for the first time, a smile spreading across his face as they locked eyes.

She sauntered into the room, confident she looked good in her red dress.

The look on his face said it all.

As she took her time crossing the floor to him, she saw him button his jacket and take a long-stemmed red rose out of a large crystal vase next to him. He held it in both hands before taking long strides toward her, meeting her in the middle of the room, where she stopped to let him present her with the single flower.

He stood there with the delicate rose in his hands, speechless. His silent stare spoke volumes and she teared up, a little uncomfortable with the attention, but mostly because she was moved. She knew her husband. He was pleased. He handed her the rose and she sniffed it, drawing in its sweet aroma.

"Words can't express what I'm thinking – what I'm

feeling. You're naturally a beautiful woman, but tonight, in this dress…you're gorgeous. I'm one lucky man to call you my wife."

"Thank you. I'm so happy to be here tonight to share this honor with you."

He came closer to her and looked at her from the crown of her head to her feet, nestled in her strappy stilettos, then touched her hair and pulled it forward to let it fall over her shoulders onto her chest. He played with the strands in his fingers.

"Please don't mess up my hair. It's still early and we're going to be in so many pictures. I don't want my hair looking jacked up," she whispered to him.

He threw his head back, laughing out loud. "I won't mess it up if you'll dance with me. I'm excited and I need a little time to make sure others don't see it."

"Are you nervous? You don't normally get anxious at these events."

He grabbed her close.

She searched his eyes for answers but was distracted by the hardening of his excitement. "Oh, *that* kind of excitement."

They both laughed at their shared private joke while his songs from the Fire God Tour played in the background. He looked at the DJ and yelled across the room, "Play 'Cry No More,'" and stared into her eyes before leaning in to place a chaste kiss on her ruby-red lips.

"I guess I had better not mess up the lips either."

She smiled at him while cameras flashed, capturing images of his wide eyes mesmerized by her, their kiss, and their first dance of the night.

Miles owned the room and shared it with her. This was

their night, and she wanted it to be memorable. While they danced across the floor, others joined in, many of whom came close enough to tell her they loved her dress.

"I need to tell you I uploaded some pictures of Tut earlier today," she whispered in his ear. "They were of him with other women. I don't want you blindsided if they ask if you had anything to do with it."

"I saw the pictures and the comments from the women. I'm more concerned he's surrounding himself with young men willing to be photographed flashing gang signs. I've warned him such behavior is dangerous, but he's no longer my concern."

He held her close as they danced. "Let's head over to the awards show next door."

"Yes, I think we'd better go. Did I tell you how proud I am of you?" She planted a kiss on his cheek and made sure she wiped away signs of stray lip gloss.

They ended the dance and prepared to leave.

"Yes, you've told me. But I should tell you how proud I am to be escorting the most beautiful woman in the room." He locked arms with her and waved goodbye to those staying at the cocktail party, while others left with them to witness their boss receive another coveted award.

Grabbing her hand, he escorted her to the ceremony while she kept her rose in her other hand.

Chapter 47

T ake us back to the condo," Miles informed the chauffeur as he helped Bella into the limo and got in behind her.

"Why are we going back to the condo instead of to the estate? We have people waiting to celebrate with us. Besides, I'm ready to dance." She smiled and shook her shoulders. "I don't want to be late for the party."

"This shouldn't take too long. Don't worry, the fun won't start before we get there."

"It's your night," she sighed, not convinced she wouldn't miss the fun. "Let me see your award notice again."

He handed her the beautiful scroll he'd been presented. The carved crystal award with his name engraved on it would be sent to him later.

She turned on the spotlight in the back of the vehicle and read it once more. "Miles Moore, inductee into the Songwriters' Hall of Fame." She shook as a chill ran through her body. "Just holding this gives me goosebumps. I couldn't be prouder of you. The only thing that's left for you is Mega-

Mogul of the Year – whenever someone creates that award."

He laughed at her and leaned over for more kisses after she returned the rolled document.

"Come here and give me the only award I'll ever need – being the first and only man in your life." He pressed the button for the privacy partition before engaging in heavy petting. They remained locked in an embrace while the driver continued across town.

The limo finally came to a stop, but the driver didn't move the car to the entrance of the condo until the partition came down a few seconds later. He was accustomed to them making out in the back seat, so time was given to reposition clothing and smooth out strands of messy hair before leaving the vehicle.

Miles hit the button again and the motorized partition descended.

"You can pull up to the curb in front of the building," he instructed the driver as they gathered their things. He'd received a tip from Bradley that paparazzi were expecting them to return to the estate, but thankfully none of them were stationed outside the condo.

The doorman opened the door, and they entered the building quickly.

"Good evening, Mr. and Mrs. Moore." The doorman and several staff members greeted them as they crossed the lobby.

He pulled her into the elevator, but he couldn't get the doors to close fast enough before they were joined by four others.

"Lovely dress," two of the women commented before exiting the elevator car.

"Thank you. Have a good night." Bella smiled and pulled at strands of her hair. The women were smartly attired, possibly returning from a night out with their husbands. She looked out of the corners of her eyes and saw one of the men looking intently at her ass.

Miles pulled her in closer – his man-signal to others that she belonged to him.

They finally reached the top floor. He held her hand while searching his pocket for the key.

"The employees knew my name, but I've never been here before. I thought this used to be your crash pad when you were working late downtown." She pressed her lips together. "Oh, I know how they knew me. They must have seen my pictures recently in the tabloids."

"I don't think that's how they know you. We have a membership here. Some of the employees we passed are assigned specifically to our condo for cleaning and maintenance. For security purposes, they've seen pictures of you." He found the key and inserted it into the lock before opening the door and turning on the lights, leaving her standing at the entrance.

She couldn't believe she was seeing a life-sized portrait of herself dressed in the blush dress she'd worn on her wedding day, surrounded by small pictures of her and the kids scattered throughout the room.

"Come in. Don't just stand there," he urged her. "Is your mind at ease now that you know it's not a den of infidelity?"

"I never said that. I trust you."

"You trust me, but it's important to verify. And I trust you, but I know my kind. You're a beautiful woman, and if a dog got a chance to be with you, he would be in your face, tail wagging and sniffing everything he could."

She turned slowly, looking around the room. "Is that a saying in North Carolina?"

"No, it's human nature. Men love sex, and if they can have

it with someone like you, hell, some would sell out their mother." He moved to the bar and began fixing them drinks, then turned and pointed at her dress. "I want a picture of you in that dress. You don't know what you do to me. I'm getting excited thinking about it now."

"Nothing stronger than sparkling water for me. We took plenty of pictures tonight. We can pick out the best one of the two of us together. Why don't you get what you came for and let's get going?"

"I'm not in a rush." He came closer and gave her the glass of sparkling water before swallowing his drink in one gulp and placing the glass on a table nearby.

She took sips from her glass and felt the heat of his presence as he came up behind her and began trailing kisses along her neck while he caressed the lobes of her breasts and moved his hands down to her hips, rubbing his groin against her.

"Miles, we've got to go. It's getting late." She pulled away, but he took her hand and came closer to her.

"I want to spend some time with you alone before we go. We've been through a lot this week, and I need to slow things down."

"Right now, Miles?" She turned to face him, sensing he needed to say something to her.

"It's so natural how we sense things about each other."

She placed her hands on the sides of his face and stared into his eyes. Tilting her head to the side, she leaned in and smelled the aroma of buttercream from the desserts they had consumed earlier. Pressing her lips against his, she plunged her tongue deep inside, eliciting a moan, soft and low in his throat. Her body heated as their tongues warred for dominance while she explored the soft velvety corners of his luscious mouth. Slowly, she pulled away and panted as she caught her breath.

"You know where this is going to lead. We can have more fun at home. Later." She hoped he was satisfied for now.

"You're *my* girl, *my* lover, and *my* best friend. You've shown others you'll *always* be in my corner, and it turned me on tonight."

"I'm glad you're sharing this with me. You know you and the kids are my world, but tonight is your night to shine – really, I'm okay if you want to go."

"You don't understand. None of this would mean anything to me without you."

"Miles, really, I understand." Smiling, she tried hiding her impatience.

Looking up at the ceiling, she attempted to back away from his embrace, hoping to remind him others were waiting for his arrival. Her heart thumped with anticipation as he viewed her with wanton eyes of desire and began removing his jacket.

Oh, no, not now.

"Bella, I need you. I want you right now." He plunged his tongue into her mouth and kissed her until she was gasping for breath, then began nibbling at her ear and along her neck – all the places that made her hot with desire. She couldn't resist watching him take off his clothes. She would deny him no further.

Forty-five minutes later, Bella awoke, naked in bed, and shrieked as she looked at the clock while Miles lay next to her asleep in his birthday suit. She raced to the bathroom and let out a wail as she observed her reflection in the mirror.

"I'm a mess. Look at my hair." She returned to the bedroom and began crying as he yawned, looking at her hairdo in disarray.

"It looks okay to me." He couldn't hold back his laughter as he ducked the towel she sent sailing his way. "Let's take a shower and we can be ready to leave in ten minutes."

"*Ten minutes?*" Her heart pounded as she stomped into the shower, vowing to avoid saying anything to him or letting him touch her for the rest of the night. She would find her dress, and if she didn't feel like it, she wouldn't attend the party. "I'm done," she fumed.

After getting out of the shower and drying off in the bedroom, she searched for hairpins to secure her hair in an updo, since the hairstyle she'd proudly worn earlier was ruined. While she worked on her hair at the vanity in the bedroom, she found some pins in the drawer.

"Miles can be such an enigma," she muttered through gritted teeth.

On one hand, she had to give him credit that he was thoughtful enough to have her usual hair and makeup products in the drawer, but—

"Ten minutes, my ass," she fussed, slamming the brush on top of the vanity and growing more frustrated. To her surprise, she was able to finish her hair in less time than she thought she needed, and tempered her anger with deep breaths when he came back into the room and pulled out another tux from the closet.

Her jaw dropped after she turned and faced him. "I don't believe this. You're going to walk in looking all polished while my dress is somewhere rumpled in a corner?"

He got dressed in silence and left the bedroom in less than five minutes while she finished her makeup and got up to begin the hunt for her dress in the living room. He was seated on the couch, waiting for her.

She looked toward the corner of the room. There was her

dress, hanging from a decorative pole, pressed, and draped in clear plastic.

"You're making this hard for me to stay mad at you, but I'm going to give it a good try."

She walked across the floor in her underwear, took the dress, and climbed into it before locating her shoes.

Rising from the couch, he remained silent as he zipped the back of her dress, then turned her around and gently pulled out wisps of her hair to frame her face. "Perfect, but you're missing one thing." He waited for her to finish putting on her shoes before pulling out a black box with a shiny satin cover.

Despite her best efforts, her anger subsided. "You've earned points for having someone press my dress, and I don't want to argue. Can we call it a truce?"

"I was never angry with you, so I accept your truce."

When she opened the box, a diamond pendant necklace sparkled before her eyes. She draped it across her fingers and moved it slowly while the light bounced off the center stone and danced throughout the room.

"This is beautiful." She leaned forward to kiss him, her anger gone, though she hated that they'd missed the party and had been rude to their guests.

"Let me put it around your neck, then you can gather your things. I know you're ready to leave."

"You shouldn't have," she choked through tears as he placed the jewelry around her neck. "This was your night."

"*Our* night, Bella. I wanted to do this for you – for us. Don't worry so much. I've seen to our guests. The finest foods are being served right now, and I instructed the staff to open up the most expensive spirits I have. I doubled your dessert order so the employees could each bring a guest and share this night with their someone special, just like I've shared this night with you."

"How did you know about the party plans? I didn't tell anyone. Not even Parker and Darien."

"They didn't tell me, but you forgot that a copy of all large expenditures comes automatically to me. I read the line item charges on the bill."

"What?" She placed a hand to her neck. "I thought it was a surprise."

"I needed a little distraction this past week and playing along with the plan was fun. It's still a surprise party, but for Pele, not me. Two of their songs have gone gold, and I wanted to surprise them with a presentation tonight."

"Oh, Miles, they'll be delighted. Let's go. I can't wait to see their faces."

They took the expressway to the estate and, just as he had predicted, the party was still going strong. Music was blaring and people were dancing under a banner congratulating Pele on their accomplishment. Reagan, Latifah, and Myoshi ran up to greet them as they entered the room.

"I have a presentation to make for all of you," Miles said.

Latifah and Myoshi followed him to the center of the room while Reagan and Bella hung behind to chat.

"You look good with your hair up. Classy and messy at the same time – a good just-been-fucked look."

Bella grabbed Reagan's glass and sniffed the contents.

Reagan smiled and continued, slurring her words a bit. "This is the best vodka I've ever tasted. Where does Miles hide the good stuff?"

"I don't know, but let's get you some water and join the others for the presentation. Water, please." She motioned to one of the servers to bring a glass for Reagan while Miles got everyone's attention.

"Pele has just received their first gold record," he informed the crowd as Pele flashed bright smiles and posed for the cameras.

The party resumed after the presentation, and Bella was ready to hit the floor for a dance with Miles. Later, she joined the others while the DJ spun records for a women's-only mix. Dancing with abandon, free to express herself, she didn't care that she was surrounded by professional dancers who could show her a few steps. She even asked for lessons while on the floor.

The highlight of the festivities, videotaped congratulatory messages for Miles, was shown on big screens throughout the room. Josi had given her several of the videos to review, but in the interest of time, she'd approved all of them after viewing the first ten. The music stopped each time so that the noted person congratulating him could be heard, followed by a raising of glasses and applause.

The music stopped again. This time, Tut appeared on the screen.

Bella closed her eyes and held herself while a pit formed in her stomach. She'd made a mistake by not reviewing each of the videos, but it was too late now. She looked at Miles before joining him across the room.

"Let it play," he told her, and she nodded to the technician in the booth nearby. The image of Tut began speaking to those assembled in the room.

"Surprise! First of all, congratulations to the incomparable Miles Moore, the man of the hour. You deserved the award tonight. I'm proud of the time I spent with you. I'm not sure why things had to end like they did between us." He paused and flashed a classic Tut smile. "I know I was an ass sometimes but, man, I was just being me. Good and bad, I just wanted to be free to do me. I know you understand that… Sorry 'bout the shit I pulled along the way, but I got a joint for you that I know will be a hit. I owe you one."

The music came on in the background and an intro in Miles's voice started playing.

"Pharaoh, it's time, drop the verse."

What was the Great One thinkin'?
Givin' me,
and my boys,
six inches to play with,
our favorite toy.

I'm not loved for my brown skin,
nor for my square chin.
No, I'm hated, reviled,
for what I have within.
I have six inches.
The veil of hate,
against me,
still thin.

Six inches of meat.
I savor it.
Enjoy it,
like a treat.
I sing songs about it,
and relish
sexual favors,
in all flavors,

houndin' me to get it.

The music stopped and Tut continued to speak directly to Miles.

"I freestyled those few verses in the club, and they went wild. I think I've got a hit, and I'll give it to you as a way of saying I'm sorry. My mama didn't raise me to be a thief. So – congratulations, and I'll call you tomorrow. I hope you accept my apologies and my call. Love you, man. Peace. Tut, out."

Bella looked at Miles as he stood motionless, looking at the blank screen.

The room remained quiet until he lifted his glass in salute, and the partygoers yelled, "Here's to Tut."

She hugged him, glad that while the two of them might never work together again, this was hopefully the start of a reconciliation. The music began again, and the crowd came back on the floor to dance until the wee hours of the morning.

Miles savored the congratulations from his guests, and Bella kept hugging him, glad the worst of it was behind them...for now.

Chapter 48

Cheers rang throughout the room after Miles announced the studio wouldn't open before one in the afternoon. Everyone had the morning off, since he knew they wouldn't be getting any work done before then. While Bella slept in, he went to the office and enjoyed a special breakfast prepared by Mr. Curtis.

He loved the peace and quiet of being at the estate by himself, except for a few employees.

Sitting at his desk, he recalled looking around the room the night before at the partygoers' reactions to Tut's video. He might never work with him again in the same capacity, but Tut was right – his song was probably going to be a hit.

He sighed, giving voice to his thoughts. "I could have done things differently." He grabbed his cup of coffee and took a sip. "But no one can ever say that I didn't have Pharaoh's back. Too bad I couldn't make him see it." He remained lost in thought for a few moments.

Maybe just on this song, they could work out a deal. At

the very least, he hoped the war of words would end. It was probably in everyone's best interest for him to make a meeting with Pharaoh and begin the process of reconciliation so they both could move on.

After finishing his morning tasks, he took a break at about the same time a group of dancers and singers were reporting to work in the great hall.

As he left his office, he was met with sounds of wailing and distress outside his door. All the way down the hallway to the front of the studio, he saw his employees, some with eyes red and swollen from crying, others hugging and yelling.

"No – no, this can't be true," someone exclaimed through their sobs.

He looked around and saw Bella coming through the door, initially wearing a smile, but slowing her entry as she looked around at the pall of sadness.

"What's going on? I left my phone and laptop in my office, so I've been out of the loop."

Miles shrugged. "I don't know. I was in the office working, and then I heard folks crying."

The news began scrolling on the big newsfeed above them.

'Pharaoh Little, known as the rapper Lil' Pharaoh and most recently as Tut, was found dead last night, the apparent victim of gang violence in LA.'

Bella buried her face in Miles's chest, crying, as his jaw dropped. He stood frozen as a stone, stunned, while the screams and crying grew louder throughout the room. Darien and Parker came running to investigate the commotion and saw the news scrolling across the top of the wall around them. Pele left their recording appointment in the studio and ran into the great hall to join the others in their grief.

"No, no," they screamed as their bodies convulsed in disbelief, hugging each other. The same man who'd wanted to make amends for his mistakes was gone, cut down in the prime of life like too many others.

Pharaoh Little, a rising star and once the pride of the Ari-Music family, was dead.

Bella saw Latifah screaming, unable to be consoled by others. She went to her and took her in her outstretched arms. "I'm here for you, Latifah."

"I'm pregnant," she wailed, collapsing in Bella's arms. "It's Pharaoh's baby."

Chapter 49

Miles turned and walked to the corner of the room with wooden, heavy steps. He stared out the window, only looking back after a few moments to see his wife hugging and consoling as many people as she could. Reagan and Myoshi had joined Bella in comforting Latifah. They took her out of the room, their arms wrapped around her for support and strength.

Looking at the scene in the room, and uncertain of how he could ease the pain of those around him, he turned his attention back to the trees blowing in the wind. The sun was still warm and shining brightly, but he felt frozen and numb as he imagined Pharaoh's body lying on a cold, steel table waiting for someone – his mother – to claim him. He shuddered, unwilling to allow himself to think about the pain she must be feeling.

"Damn." All of a sudden, his head snapped back as reality overwhelmed him with a tsunami of emotions. One moment he was numb, followed by a blazing desire to scream, yell, or punch something. His chest was heavy, then grew tight with pain. He wiped the sweat from his brow. He'd never imagined that life would give him such an unexpected sucker punch in the gut. This one really *hurt*.

Just then, he felt a warm hand on his back. He turned slowly. It was Bella.

"Miles, may I speak with you in your office?" Her eyes were red, her face tearstained.

"Sure, babe." He placed a hand on the small of her back and led her to his office, his steps slow and heavy as he closed the door behind them. Unaccustomed to the heaviness of grief, he broke down, his shoulders laden with remorse and guilt.

She took him in her arms. "I'm here for you. You don't have to be strong for me. We have to be here for each other." She cried with him.

As his tears fell silently, there was a knock on the door. Darien's voice came from the other side, requesting if he could come in.

Bella gave him permission, and Darien closed the door before speaking.

"I have Mrs. Little, Pharaoh's mother, on the line. She wants to speak to you, Miles. I told her this wasn't a good time, but she started screaming on the phone. She said she couldn't go to identify Pharaoh's body alone. She wants you to pick her up at the house and go with her. She believes you were the closest thing to a big-brother figure he had and that she needs you."

Miles looked up at the ceiling and blew out a deep breath.

He went to his chair to grab his jacket. "Tell Betts I'm on the way."

Darien left to relay the message.

"I'm coming with you."

"Bella, I don't think that's a good idea."

"Well, I'm still coming with you. I'll call Ms. Burnside and Carmen while we're in the car to tell them we may be late getting home tonight."

"Bella, please don't make this hard on me. I don't want to argue with you."

"I don't want to argue either. Let's go. We're wasting time."

The limo driver took them directly to Elizabeth "Betts" Little's home, where she was peering out the window, awaiting their arrival. No one was with her as she pulled the door shut behind her and checked to see if it was locked before she got in the backseat of the limo.

"Hello, Miles." She mustered a faint smile for him, but immediately started crying and grabbed Bella. "My baby is gone. Who killed my child?" Wailing, she threw her head back against the seat.

The scene of the women crying and holding each other was overwhelming as he attempted to console them both. He slowly pulled the two of them apart to rescue Bella and to ask Betts questions before they reached the morgue. With both of them in his embrace, he spoke to Betts while she cried on his chest.

"Betts, what did they tell you about what happened to Pharaoh?"

"I – I haven't been told anything. Two policemen came to my door to let me know he was mortally wounded in a gun battle outside a club and left for dead. They warned me he was badly beaten and disfigured before he was shot. I guess that's why it took some time for them to identify him. There were two other men found dead at the scene."

She stopped talking and cried. Miles held her tight while she composed herself.

"They – they were still in the process of trying to find witnesses, but no one was talking."

Again, she convulsed in tears as the driver pulled up to the back of the hospital and let them out of the car. They went inside and walked down a long corridor on the bottom floor, following the signs to the morgue.

"I'm Miles Moore and this is Mrs. Elizabeth Little, Pharaoh Little's mother. You all were expecting us." He showed his identification and was led down another corridor to a small observation room to await the arrival of the steel gurney holding Pharaoh's body. The technician arrived with the gurney, which held a lifeless body under a white sheet. Before the sheet was removed, he prepared them for what they would see.

"His face is swollen and badly bruised with lacerations on his face and neck."

They nodded. The technician waited a few moments before pulling the sheet back, slowly revealing Pharaoh's disfigured body.

Miles stared at the body to confirm it was him, holding on to Betts, who went limp in his arms. Her eyes rolled back, and she gasped for air.

Bella looked away from the once-handsome face of the gifted protégé and rising star, now grotesque and disfigured with blackened bruises from taking many blows and dried blood on his eyes, nose, and mouth. Betts was barely conscious after taking a brief look at her beloved son, so Bella helped Miles drag her collapsed body to the nearest chair. She seemed too overwhelmed with grief to cry, scream, or let out the pain. One look in her eyes and Miles sensed Bella was crying silent tears for her and all the mothers who'd lost their sons and daughters to senseless violence.

He also felt the crushing pain of this meaningless loss. He couldn't allow himself to imagine having to bury either of his children as he held Betts close to his chest and answered as many of the morgue staff's questions as he could. Betts wasn't communicating. She only watched as they covered her son's body and rolled it out on the gurney.

Finally, Miles said, "I'm sure you can understand how overwhelming this is. We'll have to answer any other questions you have later."

The staff member nodded.

"Can we get a wheelchair?"

He and the staff member helped Betts into the chair. Miles rolled her back to the limousine, where the driver assisted him in getting her in the car.

Bella rubbed her arm as she looked at her pain. "Betts, why don't you come home with us?"

"I want to go home. My sisters and my niece Erica are on their way from Chicago. They should be at the house when I get home."

They complied with her wishes and took her back to her home. Her sisters and niece came outside, surrounding her, crying, and drawing strength from each other. The introductions to Betts's family members were brief as they focused their attention on getting her into the house after they thanked them for taking care of her.

Miles and Bella got back into the limo and drove home in

silence. Neither wanted to face their staff right now, so Miles was grateful to see the message Parker had left on his phone. He planned to meet with the staff and would take care of things at the studio while they took care of each other. Miles typed in a message of thanks and informed him he planned to spend a few hours with Bella at the house, while his parents, who were flying into town today, would spend time with the twins.

"Don't forget my parents are coming in. After the incident with the twins and now with Pharaoh, there was no way they weren't flying in to be with us." He looked over at Bella as he completed his text to Parker.

"We couldn't ask for better timing," she murmured. "Lecia and Cade were planning to take them to a house they rented for the week, instead of coming over every day for a visit. Your mother texted me while you were taking care of Betts at the morgue that they'd heard about Pharaoh's murder and didn't want us to worry about the twins for the next week."

He nodded and continued staring out the window as she held his hand. He remained numb and mute, fearful his emotions would overwhelm him.

Then he turned. "I'm glad you insisted on coming, because the truth is, I needed you," he acknowledged, his sad eyes fixed on hers while he worried that she'd taken on too much in trying to comfort the staff and Betts, too.

The car continued until they reached the winding driveway and slowly ascended the hill before the driver came to a stop at their front door. He opened the door and helped her into the house. She perked up a bit and called out to Ms. Burnside, who was in the nursery arranging travel bags for the twins.

"I'll join you upstairs in a little."

"All right," she responded, her eyes still deadpan and emotionless as she ascended the stairs while he went to the bar to fix a stiff drink.

It wasn't that far from dinnertime, but he needed something to take the edge off the events of the awful day.

As he turned up his glass and took the last drop of his drink, he wondered if it was the right thing to let his parents take the children across town instead of remaining here with them. Turning around to head to the nursery, he paused when the doorbell rang and went to answer it instead.

"I wasn't expecting you so soon."

Surprised to see his parents standing at the door, he smiled and leaned into their embrace as they both enveloped him in hugs and offerings of their condolences. He escorted them inside, where Bella was waiting in the hallway. Ever since their recent visit to North Carolina, Bella and Lecia had developed an even closer bond, and she'd told Miles that she'd spoken openly about the conflicts between him and Tut during her last conversation with his parents.

They went to the study and were sitting and chatting when they heard the sounds of laughter from the twins. Carmen had them by their hands as they walked into the room. Ashe broke free from her grasp and ran closer to where they were all seated but was unable to decide who to go to first. Lecia solved his dilemma by scooping him up in her arms and kissing him, then Cade took his turn while Lecia grabbed Ariana, who gave her grandma kisses on her cheeks.

"Come on, you two. Let's get washed up before dinner," Bella told the twins.

She offered for Lecia to join them while Miles looked at them, knowing the routine at the house was important to her.

"We'll be back soon. Cade, you and Miles can enjoy some quiet father-son bonding time," Lecia encouraged them, following Bella as she took Ashe, grabbing Ariana before leaving the room.

Chapter 50

M iles looked over at Cade. "Can I get you something to drink, Pops?"

"I'll wait until dinner and have some wine. So...you were at the hospital when I texted you? What did you find out?"

"Nothing more than what I told you in my text. Pharaoh – well, he wanted to be called Tut – was at a club last night and was nearly beaten to death before he took a bullet to the chest, which ultimately took his life. A fight happened outside the club. I'm not sure what started it. No witnesses have come forward yet. They're assuming it was gang violence, but the authorities don't know that for sure."

"I see. Well, you've done more than most CEOs, considering he didn't work for your company anymore."

"Technically, he was still under contract, Pops. He hadn't come in to finalize termination of his agreement, and I don't think he hired a lawyer. He had some lowlife as his manager, that's all I know."

"Son, I would advise you not to get involved in this situation. It sounds like it might get a little messy, and you have the safety of your wife and children to think about. Your mother and I will be here for a week to help wherever we can. I'm sure you'll be attending the funeral with Bella."

"Yes, I plan to attend, but I'm not sure if Bella should go and get caught up in the odds of violence."

"You can't protect her from the painful side of life, but if you think there's a chance of gang retaliation, maybe you shouldn't go either."

"There's that possibility, but I can offer my security force to his mother. I also plan to make sure this snake of a manager doesn't claim money that doesn't belong to him. Betts and I have had our differences, but she deserves to have someone looking out for her."

Miles helped his parents get the kids in the car. He and Bella said goodnight after an evening of delicious food and reminiscing about better times. He was glad they'd come to help with the kids. It had been a long day.

After the activity in the house died down, he spent a little time in his home office working on contracts while Bella retired to bed. Afterward, he was surprised to find Bella in the dark, sobbing in bed. She was still dressed in the attire she'd worn at dinner.

"Please don't cry. I know it's been difficult for you trying to comfort so many people, but I'm here for you." He went to her side and rubbed her back, but her sobs were unrelenting. "I hold myself accountable for some of your pain. Too many times you were unfortunately caught in the middle of conflicts between me and Pharaoh."

She stopped crying to listen, but didn't lift her head from the pillow.

"I'll own that I played a role in the collapse of my relationship with Pharaoh... I just couldn't cope with his antics anymore, but you've got to know I never wanted anything like this to happen to him. I'm going to miss him, too."

"Miles." She lifted her head slowly off the pillow. "I'm going to miss him, but I'm crying for *all* the Pharaohs in this country. This incident is a painful reminder of the grief I felt after losing my childhood friend Jason, who died from a gunshot wound to the chest. It was gang-related, but he was just in the wrong place at the wrong time."

Miles got in the bed with her and took her in his arms. "You've never shared this story with me. Tell me about him."

"He was twelve and I was eleven when we first met. I was a naïve little girl, just relocating to LA from a small town in Texas and still missing my father when he took me under his wing. The kids who bullied me because I dressed and talked funny stopped after he adopted me as his kid sister. He let me be me, but called me on it when he thought I was acting too dorky. For my part, I helped him with his homework and made sure my mother packed enough food so I could share it with him. His family was going through tough times, and there were times when there wasn't enough food to feed four kids. He walked me home from school and stayed after school with me when I started joining clubs and becoming more social. The mean girls liked that I could introduce them to him because he was a handsome fella and had a way with girls at an early age."

He stroked her hair and stayed quiet, hoping she would

continue.

"Anyway, he took a package from an older kid in exchange for some money and unfortunately walked into the middle of two guys fighting over turf and was shot. He died on the spot. I don't think anyone was ever charged for his murder. Just another kid lost to the violence of urban warfare. I never cried for him because I was too numb to feel anything. I placed him deep in my heart next to my father, but I think I'm running out of space in my heart to contain the wounds of my past. Sometimes I feel like I can't breathe, and my heart is heavy in my chest. I'm sick of the same old narrative where we, as a community, have to say goodbye to our fathers, sons, and lovers way too soon."

"I can't say I've lost anyone to gang violence or had to deal with the loss of my father." He hugged her tighter. "But I wish I could carry that pain for you." He held her tight. "I do know the pain of grief. I lost a friend whom I met while we were both in the hospital as kids. We had the same genetic condition. That time in my life was painful, but this..." He paused. "Nothing could have prepared me for this."

The tears began falling again. He wasn't sure if it was seeing Bella in so much pain, or their raw emotions, but he couldn't hold back as the dam of intense feelings broke. Sobbing and convulsing with the heat of anger and the choking sensation of remorse, he broke down again. Moments passed as he tried to regain his composure but couldn't. His mind filled with thoughts of Betts and how difficult this must be for her.

"Have you heard anything from Betts?"

"No. She hasn't contacted me since we returned home." She dried her eyes.

"Okay, we need to get some rest so we can be there for

her. I'm going to help you out of your clothes, get out of mine, and then hold you close to my heart so that you'll be reminded that while I'm on this planet, there's a heart that beats for you. There's a heart that loves you and will share your pain." He helped her out of her clothes and crawled into bed next to her as she held on tight. He placed her head against his chest to comfort her and to hear the beat of his strong heart.

"I love you, Miles."

"I love you, too, Bella."

She smiled and looked up at him, trying to make light of the heaviness of their discussion. "Miles, does that mean you'll get on the back of my bike sometimes and we can ride together?" She stroked the hair on his chest and waited for his answer.

"No, babe, I have my own bike. I'll ride or die beside you, not behind you."

"Fair enough."

They both yawned and fell asleep in each other's arms, uncertain of what tomorrow would bring.

Chapter 51

Cry copious tears.
Cry for the lost years.
Cry that you once celebrated,
the day of his birth.
Cry that he's no longer
here on earth.

Cry when you don't hear,
'I'm sorry for your loss' as if
it doesn't matter,
but are peppered with political slogans
like All Lives Matter.
Cry because it makes you sadder.
Cry tears because
you only wanted others to hear
Justice wasn't blind
nor was she fair.

MICHELE SIMS

So cry for a while
like you've never cried before.
Wail and mourn
until your eyes are sore
Cry for the good times
you'll have no more.
Cry because your heart is broken
and forever torn.

Lyrics by Miles

Bella looked out the window of the limo, letting the music take her back to the sad day when they laid Tut to rest. She teared up a little as she recalled the pain in Betts's eyes, but she was glad so many of her family members had come to the service to comfort her.

It had been a month since Miles had sung his hauntingly beautiful rendition of the song he wrote for Pharaoh's services. The song was playing through the speakers of the luxury vehicle as he typed the changes he wanted to make on his tablet. The song had been well-received, so he'd decided to add it to the Tribute to Tut project he planned to drop in a few months after so many of his fans wrote on social media their desire to have more of his music. Tut had died before his solo project was released, and Miles wanted to make sure it reflected the essence of Pharaoh, the complicated but talented young man he'd once nurtured professionally.

Betts hadn't contacted either one of them until the night before, when she'd asked that they come to her home for a talk. When she told Miles about Betts's request, he'd insisted on accompanying her.

She looked at him, busy at work.

"You didn't have to come with me today. Betts is proba-bly lonely now that her family has returned to Chicago. I could hear the sadness in her voice. It was obvious she was crying. This isn't a professional call I'm making as a repre-sentative of the company but a visit, one mother to another."

"That's what I'm worried about."

"What do you mean by that?" She tried to contain the heat rising in her chest.

"Betts is a persuasive woman, and I want to make sure she doesn't use her grief and your sadness to place you in an uncomfortable position."

"Miles, sometimes your suspicious nature can be tiring." She rolled her eyes and turned to watch the scenery as they drove to Betts's home.

"I know. I live with it every day." He closed his tablet and looked at her as she sat back in her seat with her arms folded.

The car pulled up to the curb and they got out to walk hand in hand up the driveway to the front door.

Bella rang the bell and mouthed the word *behave* to him before Betts appeared at the door.

When the door opened, Betts smiled at Bella, initially fail-ing to acknowledge Miles standing at her side.

"Thank you for coming, Bella," she said as she opened the door wider, followed by a tense pause. "Miles, I didn't know you planned to come. We all know what a busy man you are."

"I had some time available this morning and wanted to check on you," he responded as she hugged Bella but made no effort to make physical contact with him.

"Come in, both of you. Can I bring you some refresh-ments?"

"No, thank you," they both replied, and she led them to an area in her living room where two wingback chairs were pulled close to each other.

Miles looked around and pulled over a third chair to join in the conversation.

Bella looked at Betts, a proud woman in a black shift dress now too big for her across the shoulders. With dark circles around her eyes, she looked worn by the weight of grief. She was smaller than she'd been a month ago.

"Are you taking care of yourself, Betts? Have you been getting some rest?" Bella asked as she pulled the chair closer to touch her on the knee and caress her shoulder.

Miles sat on the other side of Bella, farther away from Betts.

"As good as can be expected, considering what I've been going through." A tear slipped from her eye.

"Oh, Betts, I'm so sorry for your loss. We both are." Her sad eyes met Betts's as she hoped to share the burden of her grief.

"I'm sure you are, Bella. Thank you for coming today. I asked you here because I went through some of Pharaoh's things. I found a necklace I thought he may have wanted you to have." She reached for a white box on the table in front of them and handed it to her. "Open it."

Bella looked at Miles before opening the box and pulling out a gold chain with a pendant monogrammed with the letter *B*. Holding the necklace in the air, she contemplated what to say while he looked at her with a tremulous smile spreading across his face.

"He wore that chain many nights, almost like a good luck charm, but he didn't have it on the night he was killed, for some reason. I want you to have it as a memento of my late son."

Miles took the chain hanging from Bella's hand to

examine it closer as Bella sputtered, searching for the words to respond to Betts's generosity.

"Betts, this has the letter *B* inscribed on it. It's probably a tribute to you. He loved you dearly," Miles interjected, leaning over and looking directly at Betts.

"Yes, Betts. It was probably his way of keeping you close. Miles is right," Bella said, rubbing her throat. "I couldn't possibly take something as sentimental as this. We have many pictures at AriMusic as wonderful memories of the time he spent at the company."

Miles placed the chain back in the box and set it on the table.

"I'm not concerned about company souvenirs. I wanted you to have something with a personal connection to my son. I encouraged his decision to sign with AriMusic because I thought he could benefit from additional guidance. Miles promised he would take him under his wing." Betts paused and sat back in her chair. "Look at where that got him."

The air in the room cooled and then heated in a manner of seconds as Miles's chest heaved, but he didn't respond. The minutes ticked by.

Bella didn't know who to touch first, but settled on touching Miles's knee, although it didn't stop him from a counterattack.

"Your son was provided with professional guidance. I never agreed to raise him. That was your job." He pushed back in his chair as Betts burst into tears.

Bella turned to face him, her eyes shooting daggers at him. She grabbed the box of tissues on the table and got up to console Betts, still in tears.

"I-I did the best I could after his father passed, but how do you say no to anything your million-dollar baby wants?

He was the center of my life. I know I spoiled him."

"We all do the best we can with our children. We're not perfect parents either," Bella consoled her.

Betts looked up at her and began to smile a bit as she dried her eyes. "Yes, you're right. Tell me about little Ashe. Pharaoh always talked about your handsome little fellow. He loved that boy."

Bella sat back in her chair, grateful that the emotional storm had passed.

"He loved you and that boy."

The truth is out. Betts identified the elephant in the room.

Bella closed her eyes and grimaced. She didn't know what was yet to unfold, but she knew Betts was still grieving and not filtering her thoughts very well. She could only hope Miles understood that, too.

"My son has a twin sister. Ariana and Ashe are both well. I agree that there are many artists at the company who love Bella. She has a way with people – I've often told her she's the heart of the company."

She'd been holding her breath and, in that moment, felt comfortable letting it out.

Good, he's taken the high road.

"Yes, you're one lucky man with your profitable company, your beautiful wife, and healthy children you're blessed to see every day. That's the second thing I want to discuss. A month has passed, and not a word about who may have killed my child. The police have no clues, and no one has come forward as a witness to the crime. Could you use your pull to get some information for me?"

He looked at Bella, raised his eyebrows, and crossed his arms again while leaning forward to hear her answer.

"Betts, you haven't heard anything? I'm sure they're still

looking for the perpetrators."

"If they are, no one is sharing the information with me."

"I'm sure we could make some calls and inquire into his case, couldn't we, Miles?" She tilted her head and looked in his direction.

"Sure, but I'm hearing from my people that the word on the streets is that no one is talking. Don't worry, I'll have them stay on it. I've had contacts looking into the case and I'll let you know when I hear something. I'm sorry we can't stay longer. We need to get back home. The children are expecting us to accompany them to their tots' exercise class. They've been looking forward to it." He rose and extended his hand to Bella to help her out of her chair.

"Yes, we should be leaving. Betts, I'm glad you reached out to me. I've been concerned about you."

Betts rose and held Bella tightly, averting her gaze from falling upon Miles.

Bella extended her hand to him and looked into his eyes, which were slightly glazed from tears that he refused to let fall. She squeezed his hand in empathy, knowing it wasn't only Betts who was hurting. They said their goodbyes and returned to the car waiting in the driveway.

Once inside, she pressed the button to raise the partition before she spoke.

"I know Betts hit you where it hurts, and you struck back – but I know you didn't strike as hard as you could have. She's still in pain, and she's angry."

"Does that give her the right to spill her anger onto me? I didn't kill him." He made a fist and looked away.

"She knows that. Grief can make you angry at the world. I understand. I've been there. I think she gives it to you because she knows you can take it. Who else is left in her life to help her bear her pain? Her husband and her son are both gone. Can you understand that?" She eased into his arms.

"I couldn't give any details, but as I said, I'm already looking into Tut's murder. I didn't want to make more promises I can't keep."

The car sped along the highway as she looked up at him. "I'm not holding you to anything, but I do know we have associates who can find out what really happened." She swallowed the lump in her throat. "I'm tired of one of America's common narratives – another black male dead on the streets, and so what?"

Miles's genetic anomaly gave him powers that most men did not have. Only something or someone with supernatural abilities could change things – or at least slow down the carnage that could possibly affect her own children someday.

"I know you're trying to live a *normal* life, whatever that is," she sighed. "I never thought in a million years I would be the one to ask you to use your gift."

He looked off into the distance. She could tell he was silently contemplating his options. Trying not to think of the consequences, which could spell danger for all of them, she wrapped her arms around his waist.

Chapter 52

"What do we know so far?" Miles gave Bradley a hard gaze and sat back in the chair in his personal study at the estate.

Bradley passed him the pictures and notes from the investigation. "I think we're closing in on Dark's current hideaway. He's been on the move since Pharaoh's death, but we have an informant close to those in his inner circle. Also, the tracker that we placed on the car of one of his most trusted associates has led us to a location we think he goes to meet up with Dark."

Other than Bella, leaders of the security staff, and Mr. Curtis, most of the employees in the organization thought Bradley and Miles were at odds and their relationship was strained since the attempted kidnapping. Miles had given Bradley's assistant the job of acting Director of Security at Ari-Music while Bradley worked undercover with The Network.

It was a quiet evening at the estate. Most of the staff had left for the day.

As head of the housekeeping staff at the estate, Mr. Curtis had resumed the role of providing services for their personal suite after he terminated the employment of those found guilty of passing information to housekeepers at Nyland Productions.

Bella joined them in the room. "Has the man involved in the kidnapping been cooperative?"

Miles looked at her as she wrung her hands. The attacker had sustained second and third degree burns from the twins fighting him off. Aware that she was concerned that the man would divulge information about the twins, Miles wanted to reassure her, but Bradley spoke up first.

"He has implicated Dark and his people in the attack on the car. He wanted to send you and Miles a message, not kidnap the children. He thought roughing up Carmen and letting the two of you know how much of a threat he could be if he didn't get his way would make you all agree to release Pharaoh from his contract and get his masters. He also wasn't planning to agree to let Pharaoh tour with Pele."

"That bastard," Miles snapped, pounding his fist on the desk. "I knew Dark was behind this. Now we have proof."

Bradley continued. "He's aware of all of Dark's favorite hiding places. We plan to hypnotize him if necessary. I'm sure he'll reveal those places when we finish with our extensive *interrogation*. Luckily for him, he sustained a concussion when he was thrown back by the fireballs from the twins. He has no recollection of the *fuego*, but the plans are that he will disappear before he has a chance to warn Dark. We put out word on the streets that he was killed in the attack."

"About the *fuego*, how are you planning to explain the fire at the scene?" Bella asked, then turned to Miles.

"I had the car custom designed with a black box similar

to the one they use on airplanes. Bradley and his team have analyzed the recordings and it revealed that Carmen had trained the twins to use their *fuego* or fire. She also used the flares placed in the vehicle, so the local authorities thought the fire was caused by those high-powered flares used in emergencies. We have been able to quash most of the press about the *accident*."

She let out a breath and threw her head back. "I'm relieved. I don't want anything to get out about the twins' powers. I'm still angry thinking that Dark placed our children in danger. If he could do this to toddlers, there's no doubt in my mind." She tightened her fists around the chair's arm. "He had something to do with Pharaoh's murder."

"We're all on the same page." Miles looked at Bella.

"My guys won't rest until we find him and uncover the evidence of his guilt."

Miles looked at Bradley. That vacant look of a trained professional who would stop at nothing to uncover Dark's crimes had returned.

"Sometimes you have to do bad things for the greater good," Bradley had told him. Miles was determined to bring Dark to justice.

"Are you willing to go all the way with this?"

"Pharaoh and I didn't end on good terms, but he deserves justice." He fumed, consumed by his thoughts. "I will also get my revenge, by any means necessary. This is personal."

"Agreed. This is personal." Bradley rose and crossed his arms. "You say when you're ready to roll, and we roll."

Miles nodded. "Soon, very soon."

Chapter 53

Groggy from a night of sensual passion, Bella stirred, still sweaty from the effects of hot sex with Miles. After her third orgasm, he'd told her he was still horny. She smiled blissfully.

"You've always had such a high sex drive," she had told him before falling asleep.

She touched his pillow upon awakening. It was cooled by his absence, which triggered her to sit bolt upright, yelling out of fear held deep within her.

"Miles, Miles!" She let out blood-curdling screams.

He ran into the room and discovered her in bed, eyes wide, her torso rigid and motionless as he stood before her.

She looked straight ahead, unable to see that he was there with her.

Taking her into his arms, he began to rock her. "Bella, wake up. I'm here. Were you having a bad nightmare?" He stroked her hair, which was wet from sweat as she convulsed in tears. "I was in the bathroom. I haven't left you."

"I couldn't escape from a dream that you had been killed." Her heart was beating wildly, her skin flushed as anxiety coursed through her veins. She snuggled into him.

"Breathe, Bella, just breathe."

She took in a deep breath, and the spicy smell of his aftershave on clean skin calmed her once more. Her breath slowed as he held her close. She knew his decision to actively participate in bringing Dark to justice was opening old wounds that had scabbed over, but not really healed. It was as if he was opening the vein of her past losses and causing emotions to pour out like water from a dam now breached, and threatening to overwhelm her defenses. She remained in his arms while he rocked her.

"I'll call off the mission. It's killing me to see you in pain."

She said nothing for a few moments, but grabbed him tight around his waist. "I can put the pain of the past behind me. You explained to me why you personally need to face Daryl Nyland. I know I can get through this as long as we stick together."

He looked down at her and lifted her chin. "Let me be clear before you agree to this. I'm not going to put you in danger, and if you think you're going with me to meet with him again, you're wrong. I need to focus on getting information from him, not on keeping you safe."

"So my choices are either to have you call it off, or stay here and worry about you?"

"You also have the choice to trust me and let me proceed with the plan I devised and trained others to accomplish."

"Miles, I don't think you understand that the little I've heard about Dark is disconcerting. He's a killer who's known to be deadly, even to his friends. He's not dumb. He's survived a tough background growing up in the hood."

"I didn't grow up in the hood, but please don't think I'm a choirboy. Bradley and I both share a pattern of not talking about our past. I had a volatile temper at one point in my life and did things I'm not too proud of. I've encountered men like Nyland, and I've learned to sense their weaknesses."

She looked up at him for the first time. "Okay, Miles. I trust you."

"Are you feeling better?"

"Yes, I'm better. Thanks."

He slowly released her from his embrace. "I need to mention, before I forget, that I got a text from my father saying they'll be in town later today. It seems you told my mother I was looking into Pharaoh's murder."

"She knows you and I couldn't lie to her." She got out of bed and gathered her underwear, which was strewn on the floor around the room, before heading to the shower. He followed her into the bathroom.

"Call her and tell her I'm letting security handle it. We don't need more people underfoot while I finalize the plans."

"I called her, but she still wanted to come. She said she missed the twins and wanted to spend more time with them. I'm certain she's worried about you and me."

He sighed as he paced the floor. "This could still work out. My parents can stay with you, either here or at the Ari-Music estate in the guest quarters, while I visit Mr. Nyland. I tried contacting his people again. They refused to meet with us. If he has someone watching me, I'm sure he thinks I wouldn't strike while my parents are in town. This could work in our favor."

She got in the shower while he took off his lounging pants and came in behind her.

The bathroom heated with thick steam and smelled of

fragrant bodywash that they took turns massaging on each other's bodies. When Bella jumped into his arms, he instinctively pushed her back against the cool tiles while stimulating her breasts and groin with the heat of his body.

She leaned into him and rubbed against him. "I could stay like this forever."

"Let's enjoy this while we can. We have an hour before the world comes knocking on our door."

She smiled and kissed him. "Miles, if I told you a million times that I love you, it still wouldn't be enough."

"And I'll never get tired of hearing you say it."

Chapter 54

I t took her several days to discover more about the elusive Daryl Knight. She planned to spend the afternoon finding out as much as she could about him before dedicating her evening to entertaining her mother-in-law. Lecia and Cade had arrived the night before.

"Cade and I are comfortable in the guesthouse," Lecia had assured her. "You and Miles will have the house to yourselves – you know we don't mind keeping the kids. With everything going on, I'm sure it's been stressful for the two of you."

"We're good, considering it all." Bella raised her cup to her mouth and lowered her eyes.

"He seemed a little tense last night." She paused. "I'm so glad you love my son and, more importantly, you understand him. I have to be honest, sometimes I don't know what motivates him, but I won't meddle. Let's switch gears and talk about something more pleasant. I brought a few cute outfits for the twins. Let's go to my bedroom and look at the things I purchased while the kids nap."

Bella agreed and they set off to enjoy their few hours of peace.

"I'm glad you came, Pops. You and Mami can keep Bella company while I visit Mr. Nyland. I know you still have friends at the top echelon of The Network who have told you about the plans. My staff at AriMusic have been informed I will be out of town on business."

His father had worked in various operations in The Network years ago.

"No problem, son. We'll stay with Bella. I know the men you're taking with you and they are competent and well-trained. I had my reservations about including Bradley, but he's proven himself ready for the task. He's loyal to you, he's done his homework, and he showed me the blueprints of every room in Nyland's compound. The Network agents will provide security around the perimeter of the compound and embed themselves in Bradley's forces. I'm comfortable with the plans. Are you sure you don't want me to come?"

"No, as I told Bella, I got this. There'll be increased security here and at the studio. Just act like everything is the same as usual. You can go back to the house and take it easy while I spend the evening recording the final tracks of the song I plan to include on the compilation album. I'm also busy working on the tribute album. Thanks for playing on one of the songs – I can't tell you how much I enjoy it when we collaborate together."

"I liked working with you, too. I looked at the hook and wondered why you and Bella aren't singing that part together. I've heard her singing to the twins and she has a good enough voice for background vocals and minor lead vocals."

"She should be here in a few minutes. I'll ask her. I agree with your idea to sing the chorus together, but you know she doesn't like the spotlight."

"You're persuasive when you want to be. I'm certain you'll find a way to convince her."

"Convince me of what?" Bella asked as she walked into the room and hugged her father-in-law before kissing Miles.

"I think that's my cue to depart. I need to get my fix of hugs and kisses from the twins before your mother tires them out."

"Pops, please convince Mami to stay put until you hear from me tomorrow morning."

"I'll try, but you know your mother." He got up to leave. "I'll talk to the two of you later."

"Bye, Cade." Bella turned to face Miles. "What do you need to discuss with me?"

Miles closed the door behind his father, ensuring some privacy for them. "I want you to look at this sheet music. I can't decide who I want to sing the hook, but in the meantime, sing it with me."

She took the sheet from him and began humming the words. After she became comfortable with the verse, she sang the melody.

"I'm going to record the verse, and when I signal you, join in and sing the hook with me. I'll start with announcing the song title." He hit the record button and began speaking into the microphone.

"First take, 'You Bring out the Best in Me.'"

FACE THE FIRE

From now until eternity
you'll always be
the one for me.
If I travelled many miles away,
if I looked for a thousand years and a day,
I would never find,
a girl as good as mine

You're my best friend,
my enduring hope
the star in my favorite dreams,
the one where I fall hopelessly in love it seems."

Hook: (he pointed to Bella, who began singing with him)

"Together we
created the best version of me.
The two of us,
we're magical,
like stardust."

He cut the mic and smiled at her.

"We sound great together – you make it magical. I re-mixed the hook of the song we sang at our wedding reception. You sounded so good that day, even without practice. I don't think I need to ponder who's going to sing the female vocals on this song. It's clear to me the part goes to you."

"Is that what you and Cade were discussing before I came into the room?"

"Yes, and if I told you so before we recorded the hook, you would've clammed up and not delivered such a natural, heartfelt recording. Please appear on the album with me? I'll never ask you to do a live, public performance of the song – that is, if you don't want to."

"Well, that's a fair compromise. You can use our recording *only* if you promise to look for someone else if you ever do the song live."

He got up from his seat, lifted her off her feet, and swung her around in a circle.

She grabbed her head once he put her back down to stop it from spinning.

Chuckling, he kissed her on the lips. "You don't know how happy this makes me. Music has been my mistress for so long, and sharing my love of making music with you gives me joy I can't put into words." His chest felt heavy. He swallowed hard, trying to keep down the feelings of anticipation tinged with anxiety.

"I'm glad I could make you so happy."

He looked at her and pondered. *This seems like a good time to tell her…*

"I wanted to record the hook tonight." He buried his lip between his teeth. "Just in case things don't go as planned." He let his gaze linger despite feeling the burn of salted moisture gathering in his eyes. He rubbed away the tears that he wouldn't allow to fall and dismissed the thought that they could be spending their final moments together.

No, I can't go there.

"You said you wanted to share some things about Nyland with me. Have a seat, I'm listening."

Her jaw dropped as she stood there in disbelief.

"Is something happening tonight?" She plopped into the seat closest to her. He remained silent as she gathered her thoughts and bit her lip to fight back tears.

"First, tell me what you came across in your research."

"Well, his music production studio is a front for his real business of gun trafficking. Despite California's anti-trafficking laws, he has people bringing in guns from states with less restrictive laws. He's affiliated with gangs and knows about everything that happens on the streets of LA, so you're right. He will lead you to Tut's killer – or killers. I won't be surprised if he pulled the trigger. Wherever he is, his fortress is probably heavily guarded with assault weapons. I knew he was bad, but he's despicable." She narrowed her eyes. "There was also something that I recalled after I met with him. He wears long-sleeved shirts even on LA's hottest days. Mr. Nyland has a long scar on his arm. I saw it and I discovered it wasn't from a fight, but from an accident as a child, when he was burnt playing with matches."

"Interesting." Miles stroked his chin. "You've done your homework, as I knew you would." He knew that researching Dark, no matter how bad the information, had kept her busy and calmed some of her fears.

"My mouth is so dry," she told him.

He could see it was difficult for her to speak.

"It feels like my tongue is stuck to the roof of my mouth." She swallowed hard. "I'm having problems with all of this, but it's important that you know that I still support you, despite knowing how lethal Dark is. He's a dangerous man, but I'm placing my faith in you, Miles."

"Thank you. Your faith in me means a lot." He placed a kiss on her lips.

They looked toward the knock on the door. The twins entered, accompanied by Ms. Burnside and two men assigned to their security detail. She took them out of their stroller, and they scampered to their parents.

Ashe kissed them, but diverted his attention to all the

knobs and brightly colored lights on the control board.

Miles scooped up Ariana and sat her on one knee so she could join Ashe playing with the board. They played for about a half hour before he announced he needed to get back to work and kissed them goodbye. He started with Ashe. "It's time to go bye-bye. Dada has to work."

Ashe went without protest to Bella, who gave him to Ms. Burnside to return him to the stroller.

Miles kissed Ariana, and she began crying when he attempted to raise her off his knee. "Be a good girl. Dada has to work, but I'll be back."

He saw Bella, out of the corner of his eyes, turn her head, unable to hold back tears.

Ms. Burnside distracted the twins and stopped their tears from flowing by promising their favorite snacks awaited them in the kitchen.

Miles turned to Bella after they left, holding her in his arms and cupping her face in his hands.

"I'm okay, Miles. Your words to Ariana flooded me with too many memories, but I won't dwell on that. I'll focus my energy on waiting for the moment you return to us. Our love is strong, and you've promised you'll always find a way back to me."

"I love you. I'll call you as soon as I can. I promise."

She loosened herself from his embrace and looked at him one final time before leaving. "I love you, Miles. I'll let you get back to work."

"I love you more, Bella."

She kissed him one last time. He wished they could stay like that for eternity – one enduring kiss of warm lips joined together, hesitant to part. He wiped away one of her tears as she loosened her embrace, went to the door, and waved one last time. He smiled and waved back.

After she closed the door, he heard her footsteps hurrying down the hall, allowing him to avoid saying the dreaded word.

Goodbye.

Chapter 55

Wearing a black leather jacket, dark jeans, and black leather boots, Miles walked into the office of the notorious Mr. Daryl "Dark" Nyland, accompanied by Bradley. An imposing figure of a man sat behind his desk, frowning, almost growling.

"What the hell are you two doing in my office? I thought you weren't speaking to each other anymore." He slammed his fist on his intercom. "Jalen, get the hell in here and get these bitches out of my face."

Miles stood just out of his reach, close enough to observe his actions. "Jalen isn't available, Dark."

As he attempted to open the top drawer of his desk, Bradley drew his gun in warning. "I wouldn't do that if I were you. Push away from the desk and raise your hands. We aren't here to kill you. We just want to talk."

Dark pushed back from his desk. "Well, talk, dammit. Miles, you and your henchman break into my office and pull a gun on me? I won't forget this."

Miles opened his jacket. "I'm not armed, and you don't need your gun. I just need to ask you some questions, but I don't plan to be patient with lies. Come, let's sit in these two chairs."

Dark came out from behind the desk and sat in one of the chairs Miles had positioned for their conversation while Bradley went behind the desk, his weapon still drawn, and secured two guns in the top drawer.

Miles remained standing until Bradley walked back across the room to take his post at the door.

"You wouldn't return my calls, so I had no choice but to pay you a visit," Miles began.

"Where are my people? I don't understand how you found me or got in here."

"Stick to the subject, please. What do you know about Pharaoh's murder?"

"I ain't telling you shit. I'm no snitch."

Bradley cocked his gun loudly enough for Dark to hear and pointed it at him.

"I told you I'm not going to accept your refusal to help me."

A noise came from the other side of the door. Bradley and Miles turned their heads in the direction of the noise, and the distraction gave Dark enough time to draw a small gun out of his jacket.

Miles saw the flicker of light bouncing off the weapon and threw a fireball at Dark, causing him to drop the hot steel weapon on the floor, fiery red with intense heat.

"Ouch. Shit, what are you trying to do? You injured my hand." He grabbed his hand and writhed in pain. Spittle shot from his mouth, his chest heaving. "What the hell are you, some dragon freak?"

"Something like that, but I need you to tell me what you know about Pharaoh's murder."

The noise on the other side of the door got increasingly loud and Bradley looked at Miles. His brow furrowed, but he stayed in position at the door.

"Bradley, go check what's going on. I've got this." He turned his attention back to Dark after Bradley left to search out the noise.

"Start talking, Dark, I'm listening. It's only going to get worse from here."

An inverted grimace spread across Dark's face as he sat back in his chair. "A punk hanging with DJ Dazz shot Pharaoh. Pharaoh was getting loud in the club and disrespecting Dazz. He told him that he could have any girl, including the girls with Dazz and his crew. They hadn't forgotten how Pharaoh dissed their friend Lil' DQ in Atlanta. When Pharaoh stepped out of the club with one of Dazz's exes, he was ambushed by some gangbangers who were just going to rough him and his boys up, but things got out of hand. They carved up his face to send a message to the other boys in the hood and dropped his body. Consider it an accident."

"No, I consider it murder. Why did the local authorities not report that his body was found in the back of the club? The way he was disfigured, it looked like a crime of passion, not a gang-related murder."

He shrugged. "I guess it didn't fit the narrative, so they were silent about it."

"Yes, of course, the narrative – and I guess the fact that you told your contacts at the police department to sit on it so they wouldn't expose your people's involvement in it ensured Pharaoh's murder would become a cold case. I don't believe that's all there is to this story, but if you insist, you can come with me and tell it to the police. I know his murder would not have occurred without approval from you. I guess you were okay with him helping me in a hostile takeover of your company."

"If that's true, his ass needed to die," Dark yelled, leaning over as if he would pounce on Miles, who sat calmly goading him into a confession. "He came in here trying to change how I do business, disrespecting me. Who did he think he was, a god?" He fumed. "I told you Miles, it was an accident. All Pharaoh had to do was take his beating like a man. I didn't tell him to fight back." Dark laughed, loud and menacing. He looked up at Miles, who didn't blink or waver in his goal to get him to confess.

He knew Dark was from the streets and was sizing him up the whole time. Dark had boxed in the youth league years ago and was known to take a punch at people from time to time. It was obvious that Dark had already estimated his size, his assumed strength, and his probability of physically taking him down.

Miles had been sizing him up at the same time. He looked him straight in the eye, one warrior to another. Despite Dark's attempt to demonstrate prowess by crossing the large, roped guns posing as biceps across his chest, he also revealed the pools of sweat forming under his armpits, which reeked. Miles saw the veins pulsating along his neck between his collarbone and his jaw.

Dark wiped his hands on his thigh, although his voice remained strong and commanding. "I ain't going no-damn-where with you – and, matter of fact, I plan to show you who's in fuckin' charge around here." He stood up, almost two inches taller than Miles, and attempted to lurch toward him, but was thrown back into the corner by the force of a second fireball.

Miles took off his jacket and ran to him to throw it around Dark's left shoulder to put out the flames, while Dark yelled, wild-eyed and hysterical, in the corner.

Miles attempted to help him to his feet, but Dark was still in the mood for a fight. He tried to put Miles in a chokehold, but he broke free as the embers from the fireball caught the curtains on fire and set them ablaze. Smoke and fire filled the room, while Dark struggled to get to the door, less interested in subduing Miles.

"Fire, fire! Let go of me, you crazy-ass freak. I need to get out of here," he screamed.

Miles smiled at him and continued to pin Dark to the floor. "We're not leaving until you agree to tell the authorities what you know. You ordered the hit on Pharaoh, and you know who pulled the trigger."

Dark began struggling less, the wild flailing of his limbs and jerking of his torso stopping as he began to choke and wheeze, unable to catch his breath. "I told you, I ain't no snitch," he managed to get out in between bouts of coughing.

"No, but you're getting ready to be one dead bitch if you don't agree to talk. I'm going to walk out of here with you, dead or alive, and tell all I know about your involvement in Pharaoh's murder. I'm going to tell the biggest drug dealer in this city all the details of your involvement in his cousin's death last year – and you know he's going to torture, then kill, everyone in your family to retaliate. Your choice."

"O-Okay, okay," he sputtered, heat engulfing them before he collapsed on the floor, unconscious.

Bradley and three other men burst through the door, wearing gas masks and carrying fire extinguishers to put out the flames spreading around the office. They helped Miles pull an unconscious Dark outside the deserted building. Federal agents also affiliated with The Network had rounded up all of Dark's men under the guise of an early morning drug raid, and the men were placed in unmarked vans and taken in for questioning. It would be days before any of them were released.

Dark eventually gave up information that led to the arrest of the man who had shot and killed Pharaoh. He also confessed to ordering the hit.

Miles wasn't sure if the man identified as the gangbanger had actually carved up Pharaoh's face, or if he was just the one who'd agreed to take the fall.

Dark said the man who shot Pharaoh, killing him, didn't get orders from him to disfigure the young star's face. He had his own beef with Pharaoh.

Before Miles could contact Bella, the news of the break in Pharaoh's case was on television. It was three in the morning, but he knew she'd be up worrying about him.

After he got in the backseat of the limo with Bradley in the passenger seat beside the driver, he picked up his phone and called her.

"Miles, is this you?"

He could hear the tension in her voice. "Yes, Bella, I'm safe and on my way home."

"Thank God. I was so worried," she sobbed softly.

"Don't cry. I'm on my way home to you. I love you."

"I love you, too. I'll be up waiting for you."

The limo turned into the driveway and made its way up the winding road leading to the front of his home, past the guards standing sentry outside the tall, wrought-iron gates. Before the car came to a stop, the front door opened, and Bella came running toward the car.

Miles stepped out, smiling at Bella, and tried to brace himself for impact, but she slowed her pace as she saw him standing in front of the limo.

She came up to greet him in her yoga pants and top, then stopped in front of him.

At first, she remained motionless with tears in her eyes, then extended her hand to his cheek. Without warning, she flew into his arms. They got into the car together, and she remained in his embrace while Bradley raised the privacy screen, allowing for their reunion.

The car stopped in front of the house and Bradley got out to open the door for them.

Miles extended his hand and escorted her into their home after telling Bradley they would talk later in the day. He and Bella went upstairs, where they took a shower together.

In bed, Bella curled up into his arms, exhausted and ready for sleep. They were planning to meet with Betts later in the day, and chances were, the day would be a busy one.

He looked into her eyes as she turned and cupped his face.

"Miles? I have to tell you something."

Miles sat up, listening.

"I'd like to visit Pharaoh's remains…to finally say goodbye and tell him that he will get the justice he deserves." She choked on the sentiment and tried to swallow the dry ball of emotions in her throat.

"Of course, babe. Getting justice for Pharaoh is important to me too." Safe with her in his arms, he kissed her until she fell asleep.

Chapter 56

After napping the entire drive across town to Betts's house, Miles and Bella bumped heads and repositioned themselves while they slept propped against the plush leather headrests, wearing dark sunglasses. The back of the limo was cool, and sunlight was blocked by the heavy tint on the windows. Bella wore makeup to cover the visible dark rings around her eyes, but Miles didn't care about his appearance. He wasn't clean-shaven, and he planned to keep his shades on at Betts's house.

"Bella, we're both still exhausted. Let's go back to the house and reschedule this meeting for later," he pleaded, kissing the back of her hand.

"Miles, we're almost there. I don't want to disappoint Betts."

They arrived at the grand home Betts had once shared with Pharaoh and he extended his hand to help her out of the limo. As they walked up to her door, hand in hand, she reassured him they were in this together – and she made him promise to ignore Betts's irritation, no matter how she baited him.

Bella rang the doorbell, and this time, Betts came to the door with a bright smile on her face.

"I'm so glad you came today. Please come in."

She surprised them with a change in attitude, and even hugged Miles after she hugged Bella. She escorted them to her study, offering them chairs next to each other.

"Thank you both for coming. I wanted to tell you in person how grateful I am for giving me some closure on Pharaoh's murder. Miles, you cleared the stain on his name. I knew he wasn't involved in gangs, nor did he hang with gangbangers. My boy never even owned a gun."

Miles offered a slight smile as Betts took a breath and looked down, her eyes focused on an imaginary stain she swiped at with her feet.

"I was rude to you the last time you were here. I apologize. My behavior was unacceptable and misdirected. I was angry, Miles." She looked up at him and wiped away tears. "I lost the one person in this world who meant so much to me." She closed her eyes and lowered her head. "Lord, give me strength." Taking a break, she took a breath as her composure returned. "I needed to release some of my anger, but I needed a safe place. Miles, you've always been someone who has made me feel safe. You're strong, and I was wrong to attack you, but at the same time I knew you could handle it." She leaned forward and peered at him. "I want to make amends. Please forgive me."

She sat back and waited for his response.

Bella turned to give him her hand for support.

"I accept your apology, Betts. I know this has been hard on you." He grabbed Bella's hand and she nodded in agreement.

"Thank you, Miles. Your forgiveness means a lot to me." She grabbed a large envelope off the table and handed it to him. "Pharaoh gave this to me for safekeeping, but he asked me to give it to you if something happened to him. He said this contains the tracks he was working on – and I think he said something about a measurement? Six inches? He laughed and told me you'd understand what he was talking about. He didn't have time to upload everything he was working on, but I think they're all there in the envelope." She extended the envelope to him and placed her hand on top of his.

"Thanks, Betts. He did upload some of the tracks on the AriMusic remote-access system, but I'll look this over soon."

Faint smiles passed between the two of them.

"So, Bella, how are you and the twins?"

"We're all fine, thanks for asking, but I'm concerned about you. Have your sisters returned to spend more time with you?'

"No, I told them both to stay home. I'm fine. I didn't want to deal with them, but it was good to see my niece Erica. Miles, did Pharaoh ever tell you about his cousin Erica? That girl can sing."

"I don't recall him ever mentioning her."

"Oh, well, you should check her out."

The conversation lulled, and Miles finally sat up, breaking the uncomfortable silence that filled the room.

"Betts, there's no good time to share this with you, but now that Pharaoh's murder investigation is moving along, this time is as good as any to tell you that he was expecting a child with one of the singers, Latifah Elliott. She told Bella after Pharaoh passed, but I already knew since she was concerned about how her pregnancy would affect the tour. I urged her to talk to Pharaoh about it. He reached out before his death to our lawyer NeNe and had papers drawn up claiming his paternity." He handed Betts a card containing Latifah's contact information.

Both Bella and Betts sat in silence, their mouths open.

"Miles, why didn't you tell me or Betts about this earlier? I knew about the pregnancy, but I didn't know he had reached out to NeNe." She didn't hide the irritation in her voice as she let go of his hands.

"The details were still under negotiation at the time of his death, Bella. Pharaoh made me promise, when I initially signed him, to always maintain his privacy. He went as far as having me agree to a gag clause in his contract in which we would not discuss or comment on such things as paternity claims. I gave you his contract after you began working exclusively with him. I hoped you would have come across it, but I guess you didn't review all the clauses. Besides, it wasn't my story to tell. It was his choice to tell you."

She crossed her arms. "His contract was over twenty pages, reviewed by you and NeNe. Furthermore, he was already a signed artist." She rubbed her forehead. "Pharaoh wouldn't have shared something like this with me. We didn't end on a good note."

"I understand your position. I hope you understand mine." He grabbed her hand and tightened his grip as she looked up into his eyes.

"Can you share what provisions he made for the baby?"

"Pharaoh agreed to child-support payments, which will automatically be deducted from his royalty checks and from the substantial money that he left in accounts with AriMusic, for the baby boy Latifah is carrying. I thought you needed to know you had a grandson coming, since I'm no longer legally bound to stay silent."

"Thank you. I plan to reach out to this young woman." She looked at the card. "Latifah? Her name is Latifah?"

"Yes, Latifah Elliott. She is a singer at AriMusic. I think that's where they met."

"So, are the two of you staying in town? I heard an announcement about the upcoming tour early next year." Betts placed the card in the top pocket of her blouse.

"We haven't made plans to leave—" Bella began, and Miles finished her response.

"I'm hoping to convince Bella to go to Texas with me to look at a few ranches. Maybe we'll buy one close to her mother. Children need to know all their grandparents."

"Are you serious, Miles?" She perked up and flashed a bright smile. "I'm getting excited just thinking about getting away and spending time with Mom now that she plans to settle back in Texas. We've all been so busy. I miss her."

"Yes, grandmothers and grandchildren should know and love each other," Betts agreed.

"We need to get going. Thank you so much for your hospitality, Betts."

They all stood up, preparing to end their visit. Betts walked them to the door, where she said her goodbyes.

Once in the car, Bella told the driver to take the long way back home. She hit the partition button, creating a dark, cool space in the backseat, then the mood-light button. She chose songs from the love-songs playlist, and positioned herself in his lap. Facing him, she placed sweet kisses on his forehead, along his cheeks, and then thrust her tongue in his mouth. "Did I tell you how happy you make me and how much I love you?"

"Not in the last hour. Babe, you're way overdue." He sank

back into the chair and enjoyed the long ride home.

Chapter 57

B ella couldn't believe a week had passed since her in-laws had returned to New York. There had been a flurry of activity as she prepared for their trip to Texas. She hoped to finish a few projects before taking time off from the office. She missed Lecia and Cade, but enjoyed settling back into a routine in her home, where she was the woman of the house.

In her office, she powered down her computer, knowing it was futile to try to get anything accomplished with her mind unfocused. Miles had decided to stay home that day, so she thought it was a good time to go to his home office and see what he was doing. Unlike her, he usually didn't have trouble focusing on his work – sometimes to the exclusion of everything else around him. She hoped some of his hyper-alertness would rub off on her, since she didn't want to spend any time doing work in Texas that she could've completed at home, if only she could settle down.

She took the short walk down the hallway. As usual, he

was multitasking, talking through his headset, looking at a set of lyrics for music he was producing on one monitor, and looking at another set of computers for the sales projection for the upcoming tour. Sometimes looking at the activity always swirling around him made her tired.

As she stood in the doorway admiring her hunk of a man, he smiled and beckoned her to enter. She took a seat in the chair across from his desk. She noticed that lyrics in a folder entitled *Tut's Tribute* were open on the screen before he clicked off the headset and turned his attention to her.

"Taking a break from the action? I checked on you earlier and your head was buried in whatever was on your screen. I didn't want to interrupt you." He took a sip of his coffee.

"I wish I was getting as much done as you seem to be accomplishing, but I can't get my mind to focus on mundane things today. Maybe I'm just too excited about returning to Texas and seeing my mother again."

"That could be the case, or maybe you're just tired. A lot has been happening the last few weeks – it's been a little overwhelming for me, too. I want to finish a few things before we go, so I'm pushing through the fatigue. It may surprise you, but I plan to unwind a little and unplug from the office. I'm hoping you'll do the same thing."

She opened her mouth, shocked he wasn't planning to move the operation to Texas and pretend he was on vacation.

"You never cease to amaze me. I thought I was going to have to go ranch shopping by myself, or maybe me and Mom. So you're serious about a working vacation, where the work is locating a home in Texas?"

"Yes. It's what I promised you in North Carolina. I told you *we* – that means you and me – would find a place out there." He pointed at himself and then her. "If we find the right location, I'd like to invite my uncle Vincent out to Texas with us to look at the site and begin working on plans. You know that if he comes, NeNe will make her way out to Texas to spend time with her father. She's still a daddy's girl."

Bella got up to hug him and get closer to the computer screen. She accepted his invitation to sit in his lap. "Have you decided which songs you plan to include on the tribute album? I couldn't believe how many additional songs he had." Tears formed in her eyes. "Do you think somehow he knew he was going to die, and he gave the songs to you for safe-keeping? Did he say how he wanted you to use the songs?"

"He didn't say, but I'm sure he knew we were going to drop some of them. I don't think Tut had the ability to discern the future, but he and I spent a lot of time talking about our personal actions and their consequences. Maybe he understood there was some danger to returning to the places he once hung around before he became famous."

Bella scrolled through the list of songs and noticed that Tut had listed a songwriter Bella didn't know on the credit line of many of them. "Who's Marcus Hamilton? Did he help Tut write his new songs? I notice there's a different vibe to the lyrics on the songs where they collaborated."

"I had Darien do some research on him. Marcus Hamilton is a singer, songwriter, self- proclaimed slam poet, and rapper. He hasn't seen much success, but somehow Tut discovered him. They worked together on several of the tracks."

Darien came into the office to join them. "I'm not disturbing anything, am I? One of the housekeepers let me in and told me I could find the two of you back here."

"No, come in and have a seat."

"Hi, Darien." Bella climbed out of Miles's lap and pulled up another chair to join the conversation.

"Miles, I found some old videos of Marcus Hamilton. The man's flow is crazy." He joined his hands as if in prayer and smiled in excitement. "I think we should sign him. He hasn't been marketed right, but with your skills, Bella's marketing genius, and our music-engineering staff, I think we have another star in the making. You said you liked his lyrics. Pull up the link I sent you – signing him is a no-brainer."

Miles paused to pull up the video of Marcus. They all got quiet as the video started.

Bella looked at Miles as his body stilled and he stared at the video in a trance-like state. She had seen that look before.

He blinked and looked at Bella before speaking.

"Listen, Darien, this guy is good, but I don't want to start another project just yet. I'm still in my feelings about what happened to Tut." He briefly closed his eyes. "We have a tour planned for next year, and I want to finish the Tribute to Tut project before taking on something else. I don't want to speak for Bella, but she has her hands full promoting Pele and the collaboration with GDMob. We both need to take a little rest and some time to reset. You know Bella hasn't seen her mother in months."

She didn't realize they were both looking at her and waiting for her to say something.

She blinked in disbelief. *Did I just hear him put family first?*

"Yeah, we need some time off in Texas to relax and introduce the twins to their Texan roots. That's important to me right now – and we could benefit from getting out of town while things are still hot with Tut's murder case, especially with Dark's connection to it. He runs in dangerous circles, and I don't want any of his past dealings to somehow become a problem for Miles or AriMusic."

"Bella, don't worry about it. I have assurances that neither

Dark nor his people will be a problem for us, but I agree that we should get out of town and take a break."

Darien shook his head. "I understand you both need a break, but at least consider it, man – and you, too, Bella. I think signing this guy is the right thing for AriMusic. He's a diamond in the rough. He's got the 'it factor.' With a little work, it'll shine through."

"Let's talk about this again after we get back from Texas. I plan to deliver on my promise to Bella to buy a little homestead there."

"The two of you in the country? On a ranch? I'll believe it when I see it."

Bella jumped out of her chair, astonished. She beamed. Her smile so wide it pained her lips. As she did her happy dance, Miles and Darien laughed.

"I'll start working on the travel plans." Darien got up, still laughing, and departed.

"Did I tell you how much I love you?" She moved toward him, exaggerating the sway in her hips.

He extended his arms and squeezed her. "Yes, but I never tire of hearing it. Say it again."

"I love you, Miles Moore, keeper of my flame, love of my life, man of my wildest dreams."

"I love you more, Bella, my most cherished gift, my soulmate in this world and the next, the one for whom my heart beats."

They both loved playing the game of coming up with different ways to verbalize their love.

He sucked and bit her lips, then guided his tongue into her mouth, sliding in deeper as he caressed her tongue, leaving her breathless. Their hearts, now synced, thumped wildly in unison as she trembled in his arms with delight.

Pulling away, she inhaled his labored breath while they touched foreheads in silence. There was nothing left to say.

Epilogue

One year later...

Huffing as she gathered their things to disembark from the plane, Bella stuffed toys, sippy cups, and jackets into her bag, barely hiding her disappointment that the limo driver wasn't allowed to drive the car onto the tarmac.

"There's something going on with Homeland Security, Bella. I just got word we'll have to walk a short distance through the terminal to the limo, and there will probably be paparazzi waiting for us. We can let the nannies wheel the twins to the car while you and I walk together."

"I don't like those optics, Miles. We're hands-on parents. We usually transport them when they're with us."

"Bella, aren't you the one always complaining about the photographers' bright lights and how they disturb you and Ariana?"

"Yes, we're a lot alike in not wanting the attention, but we'll get through it. You take Ashe and I'll walk with Ariana.

Ms. Burnside and Carmen can gather the rest of their things and we'll have the second limo bring them to my mother's ranch."

"Okay, let's do this." He opened a compartment between their seats and pulled out four sets of dark glasses. "I purchased these for us after I heard the paparazzi got word of our trip to Texas. I knew we would run into them eventually." He handed adult and kid-sized sets of glasses to Bella while Ms. Burnside came up to the front of the plane where they were seated with the twins in tow.

Ashe broke free from her grasp and made a beeline for his father. He knew the routine – he and his dad exited first, followed by Ariana, who either walked behind them or was held in her mother's arms, her head resting on her mother's shoulders.

Miles took Ashe by the hand and led the way down the stairs and into the airport. They entered the terminal and passed through the secure area, but within yards of exiting the TSA area, they were greeted by at least four members of the paparazzi. Cloaked in his sunglasses, dark shirt, and pants, Miles stopped briefly to wave. He looked down at Ashe, who was covering his eyes, and bent down to place the shades over his son's eyes.

Now comfortably shaded from the bright lights, Ashe also smiled and waved at the paparazzi just like his father.

Bella placed Ariana on her feet to straighten her glasses, and instead of motioning to get picked up like usual, she toddled ahead to join her brother and her father. She wore a red, white, and blue cheerleader-style outfit with the word "Texas" embroidered across her small chest, and Ashe was clad in a red-and-white shirt with matching blue jeans. They both loved the cowboy boots Grandma Joan had sent for them.

Bella tilted her head, amazed Ariana had come out her shell, at least for today. Each of them smiled for the camera while Bella waved to those in the crowd cooing and smiling at her two adorable children. She joined Miles, who took each child by the hand, and she placed her hand on his elbow to take the short walk to the limo waiting outside to take all of them to Grandma Joan's house. There had been some delays, but construction on their sprawling new ranch was nearing completion.

"Thanks for bringing me back to Texas, Miles. Wherever we roam, Texas will always be my home."

"I'll do whatever it takes to make you happy forever." He wrapped his arms around her, and she laid her head on his shoulder, savoring her moment of pure bliss. As if things couldn't get any better, Bella saw her mother come out of the crowd. A bright smile spread across her face.

"Welcome home." Joan walked briskly toward them with a twinkle in her eyes and arms outstretched.

Thank you for reading *Face the Fire.*
If you enjoyed reading the book, please do us a favor and leave an honest review where you purchased it.

Sign up at **authormichelesims.com** for updates and giveaways. Your support is appreciated.

Acknowledgments

I would like to thank my husband Tony for your love and endless patience in completing this project. A special thanks to Dr. P. Hankins, Dr. S. Gibson, Ms. J. Melvin, Ms. Bonita Thornton, Auntie MidnightAce Scotty, and Mama Toni Bonita for your support of my writing career. To Ms. L. Smith, thank you for your invaluable insights on this project. To my sweet Lola, thank you for reminding me of the importance of cuddles and taking a break to enjoy my author journey. Thank you, The Book Khaleesi for guiding this project to completion.

My thanks also go out to you, my dear readers. Thank you for reading and sharing my stories. I hope you all enjoy this latest installment of the Moore Family Saga.

Michele Sims is the "author-ego" of Deanna McNeil and creator of the Moore Family Saga. She loves writing hot love stories and women's fiction with multigenerational characters. She is the recipient of the 2019 RSJ Debut Author Award, the 2018 RSJ Aspiring Author Award, and first runner up in the Introvert Press Poetry Contest for February 2018. She is a member of LRWA, in Charleston, SC.

She lives in South Carolina with her husband who has been her soulmate and greatest cheerleader. She is the proud mother of two adult sons and the auntie to many loved ones. When she's not writing, she's trying to remember the importance of exercise, travelling, listening to different genres of music, and observing the wonders of life on this marvelous planet. She has worked on several collaboration projects and plans to work with other authors in the future.

Visit her website:
https://authormichelesims.com

Email:
michelesims2122@gmail.com

Made in the USA
Coppell, TX
29 December 2022

10066537R00197